WOMEN
IN WAR

WOMEN IN WAR

Edited by

Celia Lee and Paul Edward Strong

Foreword by

Gary Sheffield

Pen & Sword
MILITARY

Published in 2011, reprinted in 2012
And re-issued in this format in 2019 by
Pen & Sword Books Ltd,
47 Church Street, Barnsley, S. Yorkshire, S70 2AS

ISBN: 978 1 52676 661 8

CIP data records for this title are available from the British Library

For more information on our books, please visit
www.frontline-books.com, email info@frontline-books.com
or write to us at the above address.

Printed and bound by TJ International Ltd, Padstow, Cornwall

Pen & Sword Books Ltd incorporates the imprints of Pen & Sword
Archaeology, Atlas, Aviation, Battleground, Discovery,
Family History, History, Maritime, Military, Naval, Politics,
Social History, Transport, True Crime, Claymore Press,
Frontline Books, Praetorian Press,
Seaforth Publishing and White Owl

For a complete list of Pen and Sword titles please contact
PEN & SWORD LTD
47 Church Street, Barnsley, South Yorkshire, S70 2AS, England
E-mail: enquiries@pen-and-sword.co.uk

Or

PEN AND SWORD BOOKS
1950 Lawrence Rd, Havertown, PA 19083, USA
E-mail: Uspen-and-sword@casematepublishers.com

Contents

List of Contributors

Dr George Bailey OBE MBA MA graduated in ecology from the University of Edinburgh, and then researched animal energetics at the University of Exeter. Having lectured in environmental management for seventeen years, he was elected to the former Greater London Council, where he served for nine years. He gained an MBA, specialising in international business policy, which he then taught for sixteen years. Studying part-time at the War Studies Department of King's College London, he focused on the First World War, about which he has written extensively. He is an Honorary Professor from involvement with various British and European Universities. He was honoured in 1994 for political services in London and the Southeast.

Leicester Chilton graduated with a teachers certificate from Christchurch Teacher's Training College. He was the Principal of Christchurch East School (now retired), which provided a varied range of educational services. He is an historian, and has published books on historical and other topics: *Thine is the Kingdom* is a science fantasy novel about alien influence on human history; *Out of Asia: A Study of Polynesian Migration in the Pacific*. He has written several papers on the human condition including, 'Human Evolution'; 'Spiritual and Religious Beliefs'; 'Human Impact on the Environment'; and 'Influences on Human Behaviour'.

Mark Connelly is professor of modern British history at the University of Kent, where he runs the War Studies degree course. His publications include: *We Can Take It: Britain and the Memory of the Second World War*; *Steady the Buffs: A Regiment, a Region and the Great War* and *Reaching for the Stars: A New History of Bomber Command in World War Two*.

Imogen Corrigan served for twenty years in the British Army in the Women's Royal Army Corps (WRAC), and the Adjutant General's Corps. Having served in the UK, Germany, and Hong Kong, she retired in the rank of Major at the end of 1994. A lifelong interest in medieval art/architecture and the people who created it has led to a 1st class honours degree in Anglo-Saxon and medieval history, at the University of Kent, 2004. She is currently undertaking a PhD at the University of Birmingham on 'The Function and Development of the Foilate Head in English Medieval Churches'. She works as a freelance lecturer in Anglo-Saxon and medieval history, and also runs lecture/study tours. She is currently writing a book: *The Race for the Sky: The Building of the English Cathedrals*.

Ms Grace Filby, graduated BA (Hons), Cert.Ed., in biology, psychology and education, Keele University (1974). She is author of *The Health Value of Bacteriophages*, co-author of the scientific review, *Bacteriophage Therapy for the Treatment of Infections* and editor of *Discovering Reigate Priory*. She contributed to the revised *Equal Treatment Bench Book*. Her key public talks have included 'Dignity at Work' and 'Churchill's Secret Reigate'. She is a Fellow of the Royal Society of Arts, a Churchill Fellow and a Millennium Fellow.

Mrs Christine Halsall graduated BA Humanities, Open University (1979). She is the biographer for the Medmenham Collection, and has given talks on the role of women in photographic intelligence in the Second World War. She is currently writing a book, 'Women of Intelligence: Medmenham 1941–1945'. She is a member of the British Commission for Military History, and a Friend of the Imperial War Museum.

Dr T. A. Heathcote, graduated TD, BA (Hons) in South Asian history (1959), PhD on British Policy in Baluchistan (1969), School of Oriental Studies, University of London. He is author of: *The Indian Army, 1822–1922*; *The Afghan Wars, 1839–1919*; *The Military in British India, 1600–1947*; *The British Field Marshals, 1736–1997*; *The British Admirals of the Fleet, 1734–1995*; *Vicksburg, the Gibraltar of the Mississippi, 1862–63*; *Nelson's Trafalgar Captains and their Battles*; *Mutiny and Insurgency in India, 1857–58*; *Wellington's Peninsular War Generals and their Battles*. Currently, he is working on *Baluchistan in the Great Game: The Western Defence of British India*. He is a Fellow, Royal Historical Society; Member of the British Commission for Military History; Curator, Royal Military Academy Sandhurst Collection (Assistant Keeper First Class, latterly also Principal Curatorial Officer Ministry of Defence), 1970–1997.

Mrs Elspeth Johnstone, graduated with an MA in British First World War Studies, University of Birmingham (2009). She is a member of the Western Front Association and has written several articles for the London Branch magazine *Firestep*. She has also contributed to Mike Hanlon's *Great War Society* website. She is Secretary of the Douglas Haig Fellowship, and a member of the Society for Army Historical Research, and the British Commission for Military History.

Dr Halik Kochanski read modern history at Balliol College, Oxford, and obtained a PhD from King's College, London. She has taught at King's College, London, and at University College, London, and is now an independent historian. She has presented a number of papers at military history conferences. Her publications include several articles and *Sir Garnet Wolseley: Victorian Hero* (1999). She is currently writing a book, *Poland and the Poles in the Second World War*. She is a Fellow of the Royal Historical Society, a member of the Army Records Society, the Society for Army Historical Research, the British Commission for Military History and the Institute for Historical Research.

Celia Lee graduated BA (Hons) Humanities, Open University, 1980, having specialised in English and history. She is an Honorary Research Fellow of the Centre for First World War Studies, University of Birmingham. She is the author of *Jean, Lady Hamilton (1861–1941): A Soldier's Wife*; *Winston and Jack: The Churchill Brothers*, and *The Churchills: A Family Portrait*. Currently, she is writing a study of the public work of HRH The Duke of Kent, *A Life of Service*. The subjects of her public talks include the Churchill family, and Jean, Lady Hamilton.

John Lee is an Honorary Research Associate of the Centre for First World War Studies, University of Birmingham, and a member of the British Commission for Military History. He is the author of *A Soldier's Life: General Sir Ian Hamilton 1854–1947*, *The Warlords: Hindenburg and Ludendorff* and *Gas Attacks: Ypres 1915*. He gives public talks and lectures on these subjects.

Georgina Natzio is a Defence Writer and is a freelance essayist of many years' experience. She specialises in aspects of military science and military sociology. She has joined discussions broadcasts by the BBC. Essays published include 'The Future of Women in the Armed Forces'; 'British Army Servicemen and Women 1939-45, their Selection, Care and Management'; 'On the Military Significance of Being Female, Infantrywomen – an Ethical Dilemma?' She is a member of the Royal United Services Institute for Defence and Security, the Society for Army History Research, the European Research Group on Military and Society and the British Commission for Military History.

Dr Juliette Pattinson, PhD Lancaster University (2003), is a lecturer in modern history at the University of Strathclyde. She is an Associate Lecturer with the Open University and a member of the Women's History Network and the Social History Society. Her book *Behind Enemy Lines: Gender, Passing and* *the Second World War* is based on her interviews with secret war veterans. She has also published articles on women and violence, gendered captivity and oral history methodology, as well as an edited collection: *War in a Twilight World: On Partisan and Anti-Partisan Warfare in Eastern Europe.* She is currently writing a book on the First Aid Nursing Yeomanry.

Tatiana Roshupkina, BA (Hons.) English and German, Novosibirsk Pedagogical University, Siberia, Russia (1978–1982), MA in bilingual translation, Westminster University, London (2000–2002), was formerly a lecturer at the Siberian State University of Telecommunications and Informatics, and a translator for the Department of Applied Electrodynamics. One of her specialist fields is translation into Russian of scientific articles published in English in magazines in the UK and Japan, and the translation of material for theatre dramas. Currently, she works in London for an investment bank in the translation/presentation centre. She is writing a book on *The Russian Embassy in London.* She is an Associate Member of the Institute of Translation and Interpreting, a member of the Churchill Centre UK and the Biographers' Club.

Mike Ryan is Managing Director of the advanced Defence and Aerospace concept development Avpro. He frequently appears on TV as a defence analyst, commenting on military and political matters. He is a prolific author, having published: *Warplane of the Future; X-Planes; Chariots of the Damned; Secret Operations of the SAS; The Encyclopedia of Special Forces; The Operators; Baghdad or Bust; Special Operations in Iraq; The Hurt Locker; The Army Cadet Force 150th Anniversary;* and the *Devil's Playground.*

Paul Edward Strong is a government researcher and historian whose work has focused on the evolution of command systems throughout history. He has made a special study of the coordination of the offensives of 1918. He has also lectured on the history of fortifications, the role of women in twentieth-century warfare and on the role of governance in defeating an insurgency. He is currently writing a study of warfare, governance and the role of leadership. He is the author, with Sanders Marble, of *Artillery in the Great War.*

Jonathan Walker is the author of *The Blood Tub; Aden Insurgency; Poland Alone.* He has also edited a new edition of Rowland Fielding's *War Letters to a Wife,* and contributed to the recent volume, *Counterinsurgency in Modern Warfare.* Furthering his research into female roles in war and society, his next book is *Passion and Power,* a study of three mistresses in the Great War.

Foreword

Over the millennia of human conflict, women have too often featured as the passive victims of male violence. Given our nature as human beings, who survive as a species by shared social behaviour, this has properly and increasingly been a moral dilemma. Should the bearers and carers of children, of humankind's future, not be protected in some way from the vicissitudes of war? The previous record does not encourage optimism on this score. In spite of the concept of chivalry in the Middle Ages medieval warfare was not noted for its leniency towards women and children. The fate of populations of besieged cities that fall to storm are a sorry reminder of the depths to which men may sink. However, the nineteenth century saw real efforts to control excesses in war and impose relatively civilised rules on its conduct. Protection was offered to civilians in general, and to women and children in particular.

But, since the days of the French Revolution and the subsequent Napoleonic Wars, the scale of warfare has increased exponentially. The practice of conscripting a large proportion of the available (young) manhood into the armed services has placed a huge strain on national economies. It was inevitable that women would step forward to share the burden placed on society by war. It would not be long before the military began to make use of their services.

Active involvement in war by women is not new. Mothers will, of course, go to extraordinary lengths to defend their young, and history is replete with examples of women taking up arms to fight for their survival. The early legends of the formidable Amazons, or the Scythian princesses and their skills at horse archery, show that women were capable of fighting and of impressing men with their ability. The armies of both sides in the American Civil War contained several hundred women serving in the ranks as private soldiers; the British army had its Hannah Snell and Mrs Christian Davies serving in the ranks in the eighteenth century.

Very important was the sheer power of endurance, the element of normality, imparted by the presence of women amongst service men at the fighting fronts, and their abiding strength in keeping the home front functioning, both in the factories and the homes. From the First World War (1914–1918) onwards there has been an increasing mobilisation of women into the armed services, originally as support staff (clerical and transport, besides the more traditional nursing services) but with the addition of defensive combat roles (particularly in the anti-aircraft units).

These essays, arising from the work of a group of members within the British Commission for Military History interested in the question of women in war, addresses many of these themes across some one hundred and fifty years of conflict, but with special attention paid to aspects of the Second World War that have not received the attention they deserve.

That women could still be victims of war is obvious. In Chapter 1, T. A. (Tony) Heathcote shows how the presence of European women and children in India, liable to the most terrible massacre in a proto-national and racial uprising, deflected military commanders from their normal task of seeking out and defeating the enemy army in the field. The safety of the civilians became an 'incumberance' to Sir Colin Campbell. Though Chapters 5, 14 and 16 consider women as victims, the word 'passive' becomes somewhat redundant. George Bailey tells a story of the dogged persistence of his mother to escape with her family from invading German armies in 1940; Tatiana Roshupkina tells of the unimaginable suffering of women caught up in the siege of Leningrad (1941–1944) and the contribution they made to the defence of the city; Halik Kochanski relates the sorry tale of the women of Poland, victims of two ancestral enemies, and of resilience in the face of mass deportation and service in a foreign army.

The role of women as a 'normalising' influence in time of war is treated in several chapters. It is the main thrust of Elspeth Johnstone's essay (Chapter 3) on the First World War in which she clearly spells out the contribution of women and their organisations in maintaining the morale of the British armies in France and Flanders. One Base Commandant reflected: 'One woman at a YMCA hut is more valuable to me than truckloads of parsons and chaplains!' Mark Connelly (Chapter 4) pays tribute to the women whose patience and stoicism did so much to keep the British Home Front solid during the Second World War (1939–1945). His essay is at the cutting edge of the debate about whether war is an engine for social change or whether the state subtly used women in the labour force without materially changing their social status. He includes a discussion of popular culture and of sexual mores, the latter a topic also covered in other essays. Jonathan Walker (Chapter 11) covers the story of women recruited, via the First Aid Nursing Yeomanry, for the very specific role of making life bearable for agents about to be parachuted into Poland to work for the Special Operations Executive.

It is in the chapters on the Second World War that we see the extraordinary degree to which women were recruited into the British armed services in particular and the huge contribution they made in a number of specialist roles to which they seem to have been especially suited. In Chapter 6 Imogen Corrigan, herself the third generation of women in her family to serve in the

British Army, has conducted a unique and thorough study of the 93rd Search-light Regiment, Royal Artillery, which became the first all-female combat unit in the army, and she reminds us that the female Auxiliary Territorial Service engaged in seventy-seven specialist trades in the army alone. Georgina Natzio's Chapter 7 takes up these themes in her essay on homeland defence and the ethics of war, discussing the issues of women moving from a supportive to a combat role. Celia Lee's work on the Women's Royal Naval Service (Chapter 8) embraces a service where the recruiting slogan was 'Free a Man for the Fleet', illustrating precisely the motives behind much of the recruitment of women. But what began as fairly traditional work – nursing, cooking, domestic cleaning – soon expanded to cryptography, motor transport, wireless operation and gunnery training. Mike Ryan reminds us (Chapter 9) of the work of the Air Transport Auxiliary and the role of women pilots in delivering no less than 308,567 aircraft, of 147 different types, to where they were needed. Christine Halsall (Chapter 12) introduces us to the vital work of the photographic interpreters, whose impact on military planning and operations has still yet to be fully appreciated. This was a truly integrated service, with no 'glass ceiling' for its women operatives. As one of them said: 'You had to get it right; lives depended on what you did'. In Chapter 13, John Lee pays tribute to the astonishing work, only now becoming well known, of the code-breakers at Bletchley Park, the famous 'Station X'. His argument is that the work of a handful of geniuses at devising the methods of breaking fiendishly complicated enemy codes would have been pointless without the thousands of women, working 'twenty-four/seven' as we say today, in demanding, repetitive tasks to capture and translate enemy messages.

Juliette Pattinson's work on women secret agents (Chapter 10) tells of some extremely brave women whose sense of duty, often remembering a fallen loved one, sent them back into enemy-occupied France. 'You didn't think about being a woman at the time' is how one operative remembered the work. Their Gestapo captors certainly accorded them 'equal' treatment. The fact that four of these chapters (10, 11, 12 and 13) deal with women in the secret world of intelligence and espionage is itself interesting.

It should come as no surprise that the most destructive and bloody war in history, the titanic struggle between Nazi Germany and the Soviet Union from 1941 to 1945, should have seen women drawn into direct combat roles on an unprecedented level. The role of women in the siege of Leningrad and in occupied Poland is mentioned above. Paul Strong (Chapter 15) delivers a survey of the role of women on the Eastern Front, with particular reference to Finland, the Soviet Union and Germany, with asides on Romania and Poland. He raises the whole question of attitude to women and warfare by these states.

A small country threatened by a larger one (Finland and the USSR) found itself obliged to put a larger proportion of its women into the armed forces than any other state. Nazi Germany was ideologically opposed to the enlistment of women, or indeed their mobilisation in any aspect of war work, though some 450,000 would eventually serve as auxiliaries. The Soviet Union was renowned for its women fighters – as snipers, tank drivers, fearless pilots – but the million women in uniform were usually in the more traditional nursing and support roles.

A number of the chapters are all the more poignant for being based on family memoirs and the ardent desire to see loved ones remembered for posterity. Chapters 5, 9, 14, 16 and 18 are all in this category. Indeed the final chapter arose from stories told during the research for this book and reminds us that these are the memories of real people living real lives in extraordinary times.

Two of the chapters offer some real hope for the future. Leicester Chilton (Chapter 2) takes us into a non-European culture where women could be expected to fight for their kin, but the true compassion shown by Heni Te Kiri Karamu to a fallen enemy is an example of humanity that resounds through the ages. Grace Filby (Chapter 17) introduces us to a group of Georgian women scientists whose research into medicine, while having immediate military significance, offers us an example of international cooperation that is a happy note on which to end this survey.

The great people's wars of the twentieth century have shown that those countries that did not mobilise their female populations adequately were at best at a disadvantage, at worst doomed to fail. All combatant nations recognised the importance of women in their war effort; finding a role that equated with their own ideology was the key to success or failure. The United Kingdom certainly knew how to mobilise the whole of society for war. In its use of women it came to recognise that they had formidable natural talents; these were utilised without 'rocking the boat' culturally. Women excelled in a number of specialist roles, which could include armed combat. This book should inform the debate about the propriety of involving women in war, an activity that runs counter to much traditional thinking about the role of the female. It is a question very much in the forefront of thinking today as women are forming an ever larger proportion of modern armed forces.

This book is a blend of scholarly studies and personal experience and reminiscence by an impressive group of writers, both established academics and some less well-known names. It is an important contribution to a subject that deserves wider exposure.

Gary Sheffield
Professor of War Studies, University of Birmingham

Editors' Note

Celia Lee had an idea to set up a Women in War study group. Whilst attending a Conference of the British Commission for Military History (BCMH), at Lady Margaret Hall, Oxford, she had the good fortune to be seated at lunch next to Paul Edward Strong. They struck up a conversation, and Celia mentioned the idea to Paul, who was enthusiastic about it right away. Paul had studied the role of women in twentieth-century warfare. Several years later, when they had got the study group off the ground, seventeen of its members collectively wrote a book of essays on the subject.

Mr Michael Orr (Mike), who was then Secretary General of the BCMH, invited Celia and Paul to present a Women in War workshop at a BCMH weekend conference at the Centre for First World War Studies, University of Birmingham. It was the first time in the forty years of the existence of the BCMH that a women's workshop had been included. Mike, a brilliant organiser, ensured that the women's workshop slotted comfortably into the conference.

The conference and workshop took place in July 2009, and was chaired by Celia Lee and Paul Edward Strong, who together gave a short opening address. Between twenty-five and thirty people attended, including the BCMH President, the late Professor Richard Holmes, and members of the BCMH Committee.

Second World War Veteran, Mrs Thelma Stollar, *née* Fry, who was born in 1923, and was now in her late eighties, opened the workshop. From memory, Thelma gave a rousing, direct address to the audience about her wartime experience in the Women's Royal Naval Service (WRNS), and history was in the making. Thelma, a WREN radar mechanic (1943–1946), was trained in London and initially joined the Fleet Air Arm Station where she learnt about radar. She was then transferred to the Royal Navy at Portsmouth, Hampshire. She reported to Stone Frigate HMS *Collingwood*, which was to become the radar tramway for the navy.

Three well-researched papers were presented in the workshop on 'New Thinking on World War II (1939–45)', which was the main theme of the conference. Mrs Georgina Natzio, defence writer, and daughter of the distinguished military historian and army officer, Reginald George Bidwell (Shelford), was introduced to the audience by her husband, Conrad. Georgina gave an excellent paper on 'The Re-Establishment of the Women's Services during 1938–39'. The husband and wife team, Major Christopher and Mrs Christine Halsall, were introduced by Dr John Peaty, and gave a joint paper, accompanied with many wonderful archival slides, on the highly secret work carried out by women in photographic intelligence and interpretation at RAF Medmenham, Danesfield House, Bucks, 'Photographic Intelligence and the Role of Women'. Paul Edward Strong was introduced by John Lee, and gave a paper, also with some stunning slides, on 'Women in Military Service on the Eastern Front'.

Lively discussions took place on each of the subjects, and the workshop was deemed to have been a success. The Women in War group had come into its own, and this book, *Women in War: From Home Front to Front Line* is the next stage of its development. Professor William Philpott, the present Secretary General of the BCMH, who holds a personal chair in the History of Warfare in the Department of War Studies at King's College, University of London, is gratified that the support given by the BCMH to this initiative has resulted in this book. The editors and many of the contributors to this original and important collection of essays are members of the BCMH, sustaining the Commission's objectives and methods, while developing new insights into a neglected aspect of the history of war.

The editors would like to thank literary agent Mr Andrew Lownie for recommending Pen & Sword as a publisher.

Celia Lee and Paul Edward Strong
10 October 2011

> *Dedicated to all those women who*
> *gave their lives in the cause of war.*

Introduction

Paul Edward Strong and Celia Lee

Go forth into Ireland, and make a law in it that women be not in any manner killed by men, through slaughter or any other death, either by poison, or in water, or in fire, or by any other beast, or in a pit, or by dogs, but that they shall die in their lawful bed ... he who from this day forward shall put a woman to death and does not do penance according to the Law, shall not only perish in eternity, and be cursed for God and Adamnain, but all shall be cursed that have heard it and do not curse him, and do not chastise him according to the judgement of this Law.

(Cain Adamnain, AD 697[1])

The Cain Adamnain (laws of St Adomnan) is one of the first texts legally limiting the role of women in warfare in the West. The protective intent is very similar to those promulgated by the Pax Dei (Peace of God) Movement in the ninth century but there is a significant difference in the more detailed provisions; there is a section that deals with the role of women in combat. The text specifically notes that 'the work which the best women had to do was to go to battle and battlefield, encounter and camping, fighting and hosting, wounding and slaying' and describes in detail a battlefield atrocity, committed by a woman and witnessed by St Adomnan's mother.

Given that the subject was considered worthy of legislation in the seventh century, it is unsurprising that the inclusion of women in close combat in modern warfare is still hugely controversial. Women have always operated on the periphery of battle and where they have become directly involved in the fighting it is because the style of combat or the technology enabled more gracile individuals than close-quarter melee has usually required to take part. A notable example is the presence of young noble women operating as light horse archers in Scythian armies, recorded by ancient historians and proven by recent archaeology; these formidable women are often considered to be the most likely models for the dreaded amazons of Greek myth.

It is important to note that modern technical advances that enable women to carry deadly weapons do not solve the broader cultural issues that complicate the debate. In the past, women warriors either served disguised as men or in distinctive units with culturally circumscribed regulations designed to enable them to fight alongside their menfolk without disrupting the coherence or capability of the armies they served in; modern weapons do not enable such distinctions. In more recent conflicts, the same technical advances that have made it easier for women to carry modern firearms have also been utilised to send children into combat, thus widening the conflict until every individual capable of picking up a gun, whatever their age or sex, is both a potential killer and a potential target.

Why some feel that women should take an active part in close combat is an intriguing question. Some commentators even appear to assume that the inclusion of women in front-line units is far more important than the combat effectiveness of the unit they join. Part of the reason for this intensity of feeling is that from ancient times the full right of citizenship has often been perceived to be linked to service on the battlefield. As recently as the First World War, Australia and Canada saw sacrifice at Gallipoli and Vimy Ridge as their coming of age as nations and the role of women as nurses and in the factories made a huge contribution to the campaign to widen suffrage after the war – that thousands of women risked death or injury in the service of their country probably proved far more effective in convincing both Parliament and the country of the merits of female suffrage than the more famous pre-war political campaigns. This aspect of earning rights through the shedding of blood was fully understood and recognised by politicians of the time. General Jan Smuts openly refused to allow South African native units to serve in the East African campaign, even though he valued the service of the King's African Rifles battalions drawn from elsewhere in Britain's African Empire. The simple reason was that South Africa's tribes might expect a political dividend beyond the meagre pay expected by the hundreds of thousands that toiled (and often died) as porters and servants.[2]

The second reason is less well understood by those operating outside of the military community and is probably the most interesting factor currently being ignored by both sides in the otherwise wide-ranging debate. Combat service is seen as an indispensable stage in the training of senior commanders and it is almost inconceivable that an important strategic headquarters or a field command would be assigned to a woman while no female officer is permitted to command soldiers in close combat. Arguably, history strongly suggests that a number of remarkable women have been highly capable strategists and that there are several notable examples of women successfully acting as battlefield commanders.[3] With the exception of the unofficial requirement of commanding combat troops at a junior level, a precondition only enforced in the modern era, there is no evidence that a talented woman could not thrive when facing the complex challenges of a higher command role. One might even suggest that, as the process of decision-making becomes an increasingly complex mix, the time has come to review the way that higher command roles are assigned.

While the direct utilisation of women in the conventional infantry role may be limited by the requirement for both strength and physical endurance in combat and the realities of maintaining the esoteric bond between soldiers operating in a bitterly contested environment,[4] there is no reason why they should not serve in other capacities. A few of the examples in this volume deal with women in the line of fire but it is notable that the combat engagements where women appear to have excelled are specialist assignments – often in small teams and not in the combat infantry role that so mesmerises the political debate.

The intention of this volume is to illuminate the debate by exploring a wide range of examples of experience of women in conflict and to enable a degree of comparison. Inevitably many of the selected essays deal with the Second World War but we have included a selection of other examples so that the role of women in combat can be fully explored. Women have served in a bewildering array of roles and those nations that recognised the value of mobilising their population had a priceless strategic and economic advantage over those with a more limited vision of what women could contribute.

In Chapter 1 Dr Tony Heathcote introduces a key factor in the traditional view of the role of women in 'Sir Colin Campbell's Incumbrances: Women as a Factor in British Command Decisions during the Indian Mutiny 1857'. The Indian Mutiny began as a rising by discontented soldiery, but within days turned into a bloody civil war challenging British mastery of northern India. The campaign was fought with all the horrors of a servile war or slave insurrection, as the insurgents targeted all Westerners, Anglo-Indians and Indian Christians. They sought not merely regime change but sought to violently expel the British from India. The protection of dependants often inhibited British military decisions from the beginning of hostilities. Only when Lucknow was relieved, and what their Commander-in-Chief called his 'incumbrances' sent to safety, could he correct this distortion in his strategy. Women in this context were seen as something that should not be associated with warfare and reducing the risk of their involvement was a key objective.

Few warrior women left detailed records of their experiences and in Chapter 2 Leicester Chilton provides us with a stalwart Maori example from the nineteenth century, 'Heni Te Kiri Karamu: The Heroine of the Gate Pa'. New Zealand in the early nineteenth century was characterised by unrest and conflict as two diverse cultures struggled to share occupation of the same territories. Heni Te Kiri Karamu was briefly involved in the fighting and later in helping some of the injured participants from both sides.

In Chapter 3 Elspeth Johnstone considers how, by creating a 'Home from Home on the Western Front, 1914–1918', women made a huge contribution to the morale of the men of the British Expeditionary Force. Besides their traditional role as nurses, a huge array of women worked through voluntary and charitable organisations, and church-based groups, to provide an air of normality behind the lines for the millions of soldiers serving in France and Belgium. It was not long before women in uniform were taking over rear area duties and freeing men for the front.

Professor Mark Connelly in 'Working, Queueing and Worrying: British Women and the Home Front, 1939–1945', examines the Home Front. The Second World War is a key area of debate for historians of women in Britain. The war used to be presented as the moment when British women emerged 'from the dolls' house' into a wider world of opportunities, social, cultural and economic. However, in more recent years this perspective has been re-examined and it has been argued that, whatever advances British women made were in fact temporary, and a return to 1930s normality was demanded by British society in 1945. This chapter explores the role of British women on the home front, and how they contributed to victory in a plethora of ways. The chapter emphasises that heroism was often seen 'in the minor key', as the sheer ability to continue as normal was a vital part of Britain's progression to victory. British women not only worked in the war factories, on the land and in the forests, but also continued to be wives, mothers and primary carers. British women were multi-tasking as never before and it took some time for the British state to understand the complexity of this situation and to intervene in a helpful, constructive manner.

In 'Flight through the Retreating Allied Armies: Non-Combatants and the Blitzkreig of 1940', Dr George Bailey OBE introduces us to the plight of the refugee, linking us to the experience of those who were caught up in a conflict that could be both bewildering and terrifying as the Blitzkrieg rolled through the Low Countries and France. Tatiana's escape from Antwerp via Bordeaux and the last ship out of France well after the capitulation involved her getting her barely sighted and injured mother by foot and by train via Dunkirk to the UK through both retreating British units and German raids.

Major Imogen Corrigan, in Chapter 6, 'The 93rd Searchlight Regiment, Royal Artillery', introduces the role of the ATS in the First and Second World Wars. The recruitment of women was unpopular in both wars and Imogen examines the opposition to the ATS units and their eventual success, with particular reference to this, the first all-female military unit on active service in British military history.

Chapter 7, by Georgina Natzio, 'Homeland Defence: British Gunners, Women and Ethics during the Second World War', looks at the ethical aspects of the involvement of women in the conflict. The British and Germans were unsure of how closely involved women should be in the process of killing enemy combatants and their role in homeland defence stimulated bitter debate.

Celia Lee's chapter, 'Princess Marina the Duchess of Kent as Commandant of the WRNS during the Second World War', concerns the role of Princess Marina as she travelled all over the country, carrying out inspections of the women in the WRNS and keeping up morale in what was often mundane and tiresome work. She was one of the first members of the royal family to make a live broadcast during wartime, appealing for women and young girls to join the WRNS. The chapter also explains who the WRNS were and the contribution they made to winning the war.

In Chapter 9, 'Hurricanes and Handbags: Women RAF Ferry Pilots during the Second World War', Mike Ryan deals with the role of the Air Transport Auxiliary and their tireless work as maintenance crews and as ferry pilots. The statistics on the numbers of aircraft flown and the flight hours logged by the ATA are impressive, as Mike notes in his essay: 'ATA pilots flew more different types of aircraft than most operational pilots'. The ATA played a vital role in supporting the war in the air and the women who served in the organisation made a vital contribution.

Chapter 10, by Dr Juliette Pattinson, 'British Secret Agents during the Second World War', examines the extraordinary wartime experiences of the remarkable group of ordinary young women who were recruited by SOE. Using published autobiographies, official documents and interviews with surviving female agents to chronicle their wartime experiences, it examines why they were considered suitable recruits, the training they undertook, their operational missions and, for some, their experiences during captivity.

In 'Sue Ryder and the FANYs of SOE', Jonathon Walker reviews the experiences of Sue Ryder, from her recruitment into the First Aid Nursing Yeomanry to her work with the Polish Section of the Special Operations Executive. Sue was one of the agent handlers who chaperoned and counselled agents as they were prepared to be dropped into enemy-occupied Europe. Sue Ryder typified the breed of strong compassionate FANYs who fulfilled this role, and whose service extended overseas as the fortunes of the Allies improved in 1943.

Chapter 12 by Christine Halsall, 'Women with a Secret: Photographic Interpretation', looks at the remarkable work of the intelligence analysts at the

Allied Central Interpretation Unit who reviewed the hundreds of thousands of aerial photographs taken by the RAF. The unit, including the team that identified the V-weapon threat, made a vital contribution to the war effort, complementing the analysis done at Bletchley Park.

While the brilliant exploits of a handful of academics and intellectuals are justly celebrated for their work in cracking the fiendishly complex German Enigma code, their work would have come to naught without the thousands of women who processed the data at Station X. John Lee's Chapter 13, '"Station X": The Women at Bletchley Park', tells the amazing story of the Government Communications Headquarters at Bletchley Park, with a special emphasis on the essential role played by women of all three armed services and civilian workers from the Foreign Office.

Tatiana Roshupkina's 'Women in the Siege of Leningrad' takes us into the darkest days of the War in the East and the suffering of an entire population in one of the most brutal sieges of history. The city government mobilised the whole population and thousands of women struggled to assist in the defence of the city in the hope of keeping their families alive. Tatiana's mother witnessed the entire siege and its aftermath and her experiences show us the terrible price paid by the people of Leningrad.

Chapter 15, by Paul Edward Strong, '*Lotta Svärd*, *Nachthexen* and *Blitzmädel*: Women in Military Service on the Eastern Front', looks at the varied experience of women in the East. Paul examines the experience of women in both combat and combat support units on the Eastern Front in the Second World War, including sections on German intelligence officers, brutal *SS* guards, Russian snipers, Soviet tank commanders and the dreaded Night Witches.

Halik Kochanski's 'Women at War: Poland' tells the harrowing story of those families living in Eastern Poland where the German attack that opened the Second World War was almost the least of their troubles. Their homeland was invaded from the East by the Soviet Union, and they were uprooted, hounded by secret police and exiled deep within Stalin's empire. While some escaped to the West with General Anders's army, others were conscripted into the Polish units of the Red Army.

Grace Filby, in her Chapter 17, 'Women who Thawed the Cold War', looks at the role of women working as analysts and researchers at the Eliava Institute in Tbilisi, Georgia, during the Second World War and the Cold War. This chapter seeks to explore diseases and infections that have plagued society for many years, and have killed thousands of soldiers during wartime. Sir Winston Churchill and his family were no exceptions. The emphasis is on scientific research to produce antibiotics and other methods to prevent, curb and cure infection.

'War Veterans' is a series of four short accounts of service in the Second World War. Mrs Georgina Ivison, aged 101 years, and her daughters, Stella and Josie, related Georgina's life as an army schoolmistress, overseas in Egypt and South Africa. Nurse Theresa Jordan's story was told by her barrister husband, Dermot Hynes. Theresa was an Irish nurse, working at No. 10 Clearing Station, in North Africa and France, and was Mentioned in Despatches. Beryl, a 91-year-old lady, who had been in the Women's Royal Naval Service (WRNS), was one of four valets to the Duchess of Kent, Commandant of the WRNS, at her London base. Beryl later worked as a nursing assistant in a hospital set up in Billy Butlin's holiday camp in Wales. Mrs Mary (Minnie) Churchill, gave the address at the Air Transport Auxiliary Association's Annual Dinner, in 2002. Minnie's talk highlighted how women in the modern age have risen in status from the time when, during the war, official sources described them as having 'not the intelligence to scrub the floor of a hospital', to become fully fledged pilots.

Notes

1. Cain Adamnain, *An Old-Irish Treatise on the Law of Adamnan*, ed. and tr. Kuno Meyer, Oxford: Clarendon Press, 1905.
2. Edward Paice, *Tip and Run: The Untold Tragedy of the Great War in Africa*, London: Weidenfield & Nicolson, 2007, p. 296.
3. Countess Mathilda of Tuscany is the most impressive example. Boudicca is often cited as an example by those debating the talents of female commanders even though she proved to be an incompetent field commander in her only real battle. Intriguingly, the nation that has produced the most female field commanders in history is Iran.
4. Martin Van Creveld, *Men, Women and War: Do Women Belong in the Front Line?*, London: Cassell, 2001. This is the most lucid and effectively argued of the critical discourses on the role of women in combat, though it is worth pointing out that Van Creveld does occasionally ignore evidence that does not suit his assumptions!

THE NINETEENTH CENTURY

Chapter 1

Sir Colin Campbell's Incumbrances

Women as a Factor in British Command Decisions during the Indian Mutiny, 1857

T. A. Heathcote

In the late afternoon of Sunday, 10 May 1857, John Rotton, chaplain at Meerut, a major British station in northern India, heard one of his wife's servants urging her not to go to church. When he asked why, he was told that there would be fighting by the sepoys, the Indian regular soldiers who formed the vast majority of the East India Company's Armies. A prudent man, he placed his wife and children in the guard-room of the 60th Rifles, one of the regiments of the British Army then stationed in India, before driving himself to church.[1]

Among his congregation was Mrs Muter, wife of a captain in the 60th, waiting for the sound of the band as her husband's regiment came on church parade. When the regiment failed to appear, someone told her it had been called out to deal with a disturbance.[2] Most Army families knew the meanings of the various bugle calls and the words (or at least the politer versions) that the soldiers put to them. Chaplain Rotton and his flock might well have been expecting to hear the bugles of the 60th sounding 'Fall in A, fall in B, fall in ev'ry com-pan-ee', the words that the soldiers put to the 'Assembly'.[3] Instead, he heard the altogether more urgent 'General Alarm',[4] a thrice-repeated sequence of notes nowadays familiar mostly to cinema-goers with a taste for historical feature films, a call to which the soldiers, in their racist way, put the words 'There's a nigger on the wall, there's a nigger on the wall, there's a nigger on the wall'. As Mrs Muter and the rest of the congregation drove hurriedly home, they saw the entire horizon in flames. Sepoys from the three Indian regiments in the garrison, joined by civilian rioters and convicts released from the district gaol, turned on their British officers and every other European they came across. While senior officers struggled to find out what was happening, the families of the British units in the garrison fled to the artillery school, the only solid building in the camp. There, joined by the dependants of British officers from the mutinied Indian regiments, they all waited with increasing anxiety while the British troops marched about, quite literally in the dark, searching in vain for an opponent.[5] Finally the troops returned to protect their own families and, in the dawn, counted forty-one Europeans killed, including eight women and eight children.[6]

Thus began the Indian Mutiny, more accurately called the Revolt or Rising of 1857, during which the actions of the British military were distorted at both the strategic and local operational level by the need to protect vulnerable women and children. Massacres of non-combatants, such as occurred in 1857 at Meerut and elsewhere, were almost unprecedented in British Indian experience.[7] Even the Afghans, generally regarded as uncouth barbarians, had dealt chivalrously with the English ladies taken hostage during the Retreat from Kabul in the winter of 1841–2.[8] This was a period when Western social convention respected women, or at least ladies (the female members of the middle and upper classes), to a greater extent than at any other time in history.[9] That such respect did not extend to equal rights was immaterial to husbands, brothers and fathers who chose to perceive their wives, sisters and daughters as fragile angels to be protected at all costs from the hazards of war and the assaults of the enemy.[10] This protective attitude was intensified in colonial or frontier areas, where the scarcity of women of every class made them objects not only of social but economic importance. To soldiers of the British Army serving in the outposts of empire, the families of their officers and married comrades became substitutes for the families of their own that they had never had, or had left behind. As such, a regiment's 'married families' were the focus of men's natural protective instincts to which the circumstances of their service denied any other outlet. It was a matter of honour for a regiment to defend its own and, by extension, any other European women and children in its vicinity. Any attack on these, especially by individuals of darker pigmentation or alien religion, was a personal affront to the soldiers who should have protected them, keenly felt as an insult to their regiment, their race and their manhood.[11]

The importance of protecting its dependants was one of the major factors that led to the British force at Meerut remaining inside its lines instead of taking what would otherwise have been the correct military course, that of setting out immediately to pursue the mutineers. In consequence, mutineers reached the ancient Mughal capital, Delhi, a day's march away, where the local sepoy garrison joined them. Every *nasrani* (a Christian of any race) and Feringhi (from *farang*, a Frank or any kind of European)[12] found in the city was murdered regardless of age or gender. About fifty who survived the initial massacre took refuge with the titular King of Delhi, whom the insurgents restored as Mughal Emperor. A few days later, fearing for himself, he handed them over to be killed.[13] The military families, living outside the city, fled for their lives to the nearest British garrisons. It soon became clear that the British were facing not just another mutiny, but a full-scale insurrection, in which discontented soldiers were joined by disaffected civilians in fighting what became, in effect, a bloody civil war for the control of Northern India. As with any civil war, the insurgents represented a coalition of interests, but all wanted an end to British rule, a return to their own ways and, especially among Muslims, the protection of their own faith. Expressed in late twentieth-century terms, extremists sought regime change and resorted to ethnic cleansing, a genocide of British and other Westerners, Anglo-Indians and Indian Christians identified with them.

British commanders, caught off balance by the suddenness and spread of the outbreak, found themselves facing two problems. The first was that of mobilising their troops, located on the basis of peacetime requirements with none of the logistic support required for operations, and concentrating them to form a field army in the midst of a country that had suddenly turned from friendly to hostile. The second was that of protecting their women and children, normally left in safety when their regiments marched to war, but now in danger as once peaceful stations unexpectedly came under threat. In India as in Victorian society generally, most Western married women of childbearing age were either pregnant or accompanied by small children. Many older women, having spent their lives in a society with many servants and limited opportunities for exercise, were slow or overweight. Even the fittest were hampered by the fashionable clothing of the time, with tightly cut bodices and full, long skirts, quite unsuitable for the rigours of warfare or the hardships to which refugees are exposed in any age.[14] As soon as the risk to non-combatants became clear, government policy was to evacuate them to safer areas. In some places, however, the only short-term option was to stay put while the British element of each garrison took extra precautions.

One such episode was at Lahore, capital of the Punjab, where one British regiment and a British-manned troop of the Bengal Horse Artillery was faced with four sepoy regiments. It was decided to disarm the sepoys on 12 May, but to allay suspicion a Ball prearranged for the previous evening went ahead. Ladies who attended in spite of the tense atmosphere were puzzled by their escorts' insistence that, in the cool of the early dawn they must change out of their ball gowns into their riding habits and join those watching the parade. Only afterwards did they realise that it was to ensure that, if trouble occurred, they would be up on their horses and safe in the midst of European troops.[15]

The next day, when a mutiny seemed imminent, Lieutenant Arthur Lang of the Bengal Engineers complained that 'The Artillery ladies all fled in tears and fright and . . . won't come out of the Artillery hospital at any price.'[16]

Once the British secured their position in the Punjab, they turned to the recovery of Delhi, a city of vital importance as the focus of the insurgency. A field force was assembled and this, though weakened by the detachment of scarce British troops to escort women and children to safety in the hills, reached Delhi on 8 June 1857. With the Delhi force went a horde of the camp followers and their families without which no Indian army of the time could operate. With them, too, went several officers' ladies whose husbands had been assigned to the force after their regiments mutinied. Unwilling to be banished to the hills, and with nowhere else to go, they set up homes in bullock carts, the Indian equivalent of the covered wagons of the contemporary American West. When the force reached Delhi, its camp was joined by dozens of Anglo-Indian men and women who had escaped the massacre and been sheltered by local villagers. Traumatised by their experiences and with no means of providing for themselves, they proved a drain on the limited resources of the troops and were eventually evacuated to Meerut with a long convoy of sick and wounded. Despite spirited objections, the military authorities took this chance to order the officers' ladies back with them.

The only lady allowed to remain was the 28-year-old Harriet Tytler. She had escaped from Delhi with her two small children, but was so heavily pregnant with her third baby that she was unable to climb up onto the elephant supplied for her transport. She was later delivered of a son (baptised with the names Stanley Delhiforce) and survived all the hazards of life in a siege encampment to write her memoirs.[17] Having lost all her possessions in the escape from Delhi, she was left with nothing but what she stood up in and had to wear a sheet when her only dress was being washed. Her situation improved when her husband found a wooden hut to replace their bullock cart, and in August a relief committee belatedly sent clothes for the refugees. The packs, however, were soaked by the monsoon rains and Colonel Young, the Army's judge advocate general, wrote to his wife 'you never saw such an exhibition . . . every kind of female garment hung out to dry'.[18]

At Calcutta, capital of British India, it was at first supposed that Delhi would be the critical point and that the troops gathered there would soon recover it. British authority, however, was collapsing throughout Awadh, Central India and the North-Western Provinces, the territories north-west of the original British possessions in Bengal (not to be confused with the North-West Frontier Province later created from the trans-Indus districts of the Punjab). In some places the ethnic cleansing was confined only to men and, as had been the case at Delhi and Meerut, some sepoys helped their own officers and their families to escape. At Jhansi, however, fifty-six British and Anglo-Indians, including women and children, were put to death when they surrendered on 8 June. At Gwalior, on 14 June, about twenty British officers were killed by mutineers, but the ladies were allowed to go free. They headed for Agra, capital of the North-Western Provinces, which was one of the very few stations between the Punjab and Bengal with European troops. Along the way they were robbed of their jewellery and wedding rings (the latter usually hidden in the owner's hair) and inspected with a view to being sold as slaves, but all eventually reached safety. Elsewhere many were killed as they fled or while resisting attack.

At Kanpur (Cawnpore), 1,173 miles up the Ganges from Calcutta and about 300 south-east of Delhi, there was a substantial British and Anglo-Indian civil community, with a long-established military base held by an all-arms brigade of four sepoy regiments. The European troops consisted of some 400 regular soldiers and officers, with another hundred civilian volunteers. With them were 350 women and children, 210 of them belonging to the military. As tension grew, these numbers were increased by civilian fugitives from the city and surrounding districts. Fighting began on 5 June, when sepoys attacked the shallow British entrenchments. The British maintained a stout defence for twenty-one days, with fighting men and non-combatants alike suffering dreadful casualties from artillery and musketry, heat and disease. On 25 June, Nana Sahib, a Maratha prince who had assumed leadership of the Kanpur insurgency, offered them terms. If they surrendered their position, they would be given safe conduct by boat to Allahabad, 143 miles down the Ganges, and still in British hands. At a council of war, most of the junior officers argued for fighting on to the last man and the last round. The garrison commander, Major General Sir Hugh Wheeler, a 68-year-old veteran, was inclined to support them, despite having his wife and two daughters with him (his son and ADC had been killed earlier in the siege). The older officers advocated accepting the terms offered. Captain John Moore of the 32nd Foot, whose personal valour was beyond question, pointed out that the military position was untenable. According to the conventions of European warfare, there was no dishonour in surrendering to avoid useless bloodshed. The guns were finished; combat supplies of all kinds were running out; water, always vital but never more so than in the heat of the north Indian summer, was almost unobtainable; 250 people had died already and the defences were foul with the stench of unburied bodies.[19]

In the end, it was on the safety of their women and children that the decision of the British officers turned. They knew what had happened at Meerut and

Delhi, and what would happen if the insurgents got over their defence works, now crumbling under the monsoon rains. If there had been only soldiers present, they might well have defied Nana Sahib's summons and sold their lives dearly, with Kanpur going down in history as another Alamo.[20] But surrender offered a chance of survival for their women and children, so they came out on the promise of safe conduct. It was an irony of fate that Kanpur came to be remembered not as another Alamo but another Fort William Henry, where a British garrison in colonial New York surrendered on similar terms.[21] When the British reached the boats, firing broke out on all sides. Moore, the Hector of the defence, and Wheeler, a modern Priam, were killed at the boats with most of their command. About sixty men reached the bank and were slaughtered there. The surviving women and children, soaked and bedraggled, were led off into captivity like the women of Troy.

Once more, the fate of their women and children influenced British military decisions. Brigadier General Henry Havelock and the reinforcements approaching from Allahabad redoubled their efforts, pushing on through the monsoon, a season when movement was normally judged impossible. By 14 July, having covered 100 miles in eight days, they had fought their way to the outskirts of Kanpur, hungry, exhausted, dripping with cholera and dysentery, but buoyed up by the thought that on the next day they would rescue their kinswomen. The insurgents considered using these as hostages, but sepoys fleeing from Havelock reported that it was impossible to negotiate with the British, who were coming on like madmen, slaughtering every Indian male in their path, soldiers and civilians alike (this was, in fact, not very far from the truth). Accordingly, it was decided to kill all the captives so that the white soldiers would lose heart and turn back. This proved as disastrous a miscalculation as the decision of the British in the Kanpur garrison to surrender. On 17 July the bodies of seventy-five women and 124 children, some still alive, were thrown down a well beside their prison house.

The discovery of this atrocity drove the British into a pitiless rage. From the very beginning of the insurgency, inflamed by lurid and entirely inaccurate press reports of sexual crimes against European women, British soldiers had behaved as though they were the wrath of God. Now they turned from being avenging angels into avenging demons. Even moderate men such as Lieutenant Lang were affected. After taking part in the British recapture of Delhi on 21 September 1857, he reached the scene of the Kanpur massacre a month later. He wrote: 'I will never again, as I used to at Delhi, let off men whom I catch in houses or elsewhere ... I think now that I shall never stop, if I get a chance again.'[22] Viewing Wheeler's entrenchments, he who at Lahore had scoffed at the artillery ladies' tears and fright now wrote 'fancy poor delicate

Ladies and little children lying out, day and night, in that trench in June ...
I could vow my life to revenge, to take blood from that race every day, to tear
all pity from one's heart.'[23] During the rest of the British period in India, a
memorial over the well at Kanpur remained a place of British pilgrimage. At
the time, the cry 'Cawnpore' became a shout of race hate.

Some forty miles across the Ganges, the British at Lucknow, capital of the
recently annexed former kingdom of Awadh (Oudh), came under siege on
1 July. With a garrison of 1,600 fighting men, they were better placed than at
Kanpur, but their defences, enclosing thirty-seven acres centred on the
Residency, stretched for over a mile; their walls had been built for civil, not
military purposes; and there were 600 European women and children inside
them. After the fate of Kanpur, there was no question of surrender. True to
the frontier tradition of keeping the last bullets for the women, some families
arranged among themselves that if the insurgents crossed the walls, the husbands would shoot each other's wives rather than let them fall alive into enemy
hands. Others, including the senior British Army ladies present, decided that
they would await God's will and accepted official assurances that the time had
not come for such desperate plans. In the meanwhile, they helped their
soldiers' wives eke out the scanty rations, comforted the sick and wounded, and
cared for their own children as disease, hunger, and enemy action took their
toll. With their ladies' maids to help them, they did their best to maintain
morale by keeping up appearances and behaving as normally as possible.

More junior ladies, with servants no longer to hand, performed their own
domestic work, including the mending and washing of clothes, a hard task
given the amount of material involved. The Indian sun dried laundry quickly,
but its ultra-violet rays faded and rotted cotton fabric so that, as time went on,
one surgeon's wife was reduced to wearing a dress that had become almost
transparent. 'Luckily, crinolines are not necessaries', wrote the pregnant teen-
age wife of one junior cavalry officer.[24] Generous souls looked out spare clothes
for those who had arrived as refugees, and occasionally shared small luxuries,
such as tea, with their neighbours. Others, cooped up together and subject
to the miseries and privations of siege life, quarrelled and bickered among
themselves. Soap became a precious resource. Babies were born, but many died
along with their older siblings from malnutrition or infections. Rats and
bandicoots flourished and made the ladies shriek. Boils, resulting from poor
diet and lack of exercise, began to affect many. All were liable to be killed or
wounded if they left their shelters for fresh air. Cholera and other diseases took
a steady toll.[25]

Havelock's rush first to Kanpur and then on towards Lucknow strained his
logistic system to its breaking point. By the end of July he was still thirty miles

short of his intended destination. One-third of his artillery ammunition had been fired away, he had become isolated in hostile territory and had many sick and wounded who could neither be left nor evacuated without a strong escort that would fatally weaken his main force, by this time reduced to 1,300 effectives. Appreciating that to go on would risk the destruction of his own army (the only one the British had in the field) and, in consequence, of all those inside Lucknow, he fell back towards Kanpur, while his men, undefeated in combat, grumbled. By mid-September, more troops had gathered at Kanpur, under Havelock's old friend and senior officer, Major General Sir James Outram. On 25 September, 3,000-strong, they fought their way into the Residency. Mrs Harris, a chaplain's wife, wrote that she heard musketry fire, then cheering and the bagpipes of the 78th Highlanders. 'The state of joyful confusion and excitement is beyond all description. The big rough-bearded soldiers were seizing the little children out of our arms, kissing them with tears rolling down their cheeks and thanking God they had come in time to save them.'[26] She herself was seized and 'warmly embraced' by an old friend in the relieving force. Nevertheless, the intention of evacuating the garrison along with its non-combatants had to be abandoned when it was found that there was no transport to move them, and the insurgents closed in to continue the siege. Lucknow, in strict military terms, had not been relieved but only reinforced. In the haste to rescue its women and children, the only British field force in northern India had sacrificed its mobility by becoming part of a besieged garrison.

Command decisions now lay with the new Commander-in-Chief, India, General Sir Colin Campbell, at this time aged 65, and a veteran of many wars including, most recently, that in the Crimea. As an experienced and professional soldier, he knew that, from the purely military standpoint, his correct strategy would be to wait until the troopships already on their way from Europe delivered enough men for him to take the offensive in force. He nevertheless also knew that, from every other standpoint, the idea of deeming Lucknow expendable and abandoning those inside it to the same fate as those of Kanpur, was unthinkable. He was forced to continue with the existing strategy of sending troops up the Grand Trunk Road in penny packets as soon as each regiment disembarked. Campbell gathered his forces around Kanpur, and on 9 November, advanced towards Lucknow with 3,000 men. The next day, he sent to Outram:

> I am here with a weak force, deficient in all essentials, I have not ammunition for more than three days' firing; but I have come to hand out the wounded, women and children, and I have not means to

attempt anything more and I shall be thankful to effect this . . . Until the wounded and women are in my camp, the real business of the contest cannot go on, and all the efforts of the Government are paralysed.[27]

After heavy street fighting, the relief force reached the Residency on 17 November and arrangements were at once begun for its evacuation. The wounded and sick were sent off the next day. The families were given a day to pack, with instructions that hand baggage only would be allowed. Some of the ladies, faced by the loss of all their worldly possessions, begged Campbell to allow them a few extra boxes. When he would not be moved by their pleas, the more practical individuals sat up all night sewing valuables into their petticoats. Maria Germon, wife of an infantry captain, put on three pairs of stockings, three chemises, three pairs of drawers, one red flannel and three white petti-coats, four flannel waistcoats, a pink flannel dressing-gown skirt, a plaid jacket and a cloth dress and jacket, with a Kashmir shawl worn as a waist sash and containing various precious items. She then had to be helped onto her pony by her husband and a group of amused fellow-officers.[28] One officer of the relieving column, who had been sleeping on the ground for several nights, felt quite ashamed of his dirty appearance in the presence of ladies whom he had expected to come out looking miserable but who had put on their best bonnets and white gloves for the occasion.[29] William Russell, correspondent of *The Times*, later wrote that their gowns, though a year behind the fashions in Europe, did their owners credit, though he also reported suspicions that some had applied a little rouge.[30] If so, this is not to be wondered at in women who had been under siege for eighteen weeks. Two of the younger ladies visited the ruined Residency building and told Campbell, with gracious smiles, they would return shortly. 'No, ladies, no', he said, 'You'll be good enough to do nothing of the kind. You have been here quite long enough, I am sure, and I have had quite enough trouble in getting you out of it.'[31] There were those, however, who had more to contend with. Mrs Kate Bartrum, whose surgeon husband had been killed in the relief, feared that her bearers were taking her into insurgent lines, and made her escape on foot, carrying her infant son. Another young wife, who during the siege had suffered the death of her 2-year-old son weeks before her own 18th birthday, went into labour by the roadside. Travelling alone (her husband, like all the officers, was with his men), she was found by an officer of the 9th Lancers, who brought a military surgeon to deliver her of a baby daughter, Ada.[32]

In order to relieve Lucknow, Campbell had stripped his base at Kanpur of its defenders. He returned to find the base under attack and his stores in flames.

Taking personal command, he drove the attackers off but, with all his transportation crammed full of non-combatants, and 3,000 of his men committed to the protection of their ten-miles-long convoy, was unable to follow the retreating enemy. 'I am', he said in his despatches, 'obliged to submit to the hostile occupation of Cawnpoor, until the actual despatch of my incumbrances towards Allahabad has been effected.'[33] It was only when his transport and the escort returned from Allahabad, that Campbell was able to correct the distortion of British strategy caused by the need to protect their womenfolk. At last, the British could make war as they wished, not as they had to.

Notes

1. John Edward Wharton Rotton, *The Chaplain's Narrative of the Siege of Delhi, from the outbreak at Meerut to the capture of Delhi*, London: Smith, Elder & Co., 1858, pp. 3–5.
2. D. D. Muter, *My Recollections of the Sepoy Revolt 1857–58*, London: John Long Ltd, 1911.
3. A Bandmaster, *Trumpet and Bugle Sounds for the Army, with Words*, 9th edn, Aldershot: Gale & Polden, Ltd, [n.d.], pp. 27, 45.
4. Ibid., pp. 5, 14.
5. Lewis Butler, *Annals of the King's Royal Rifle Corps*, vol. III, London: John Murray, 1926, pp. 94–6 *et seq*.
6. Saul David, *The Indian Mutiny 1857*, London: Viking, 2002, p. 93.
7. The only comparable incident, though on a much smaller scale, had been the mutiny at Vellore (Vellur) in southern India in 1806.
8. T. A. Heathcote, *The Afghan Wars 1839–1919*, 2nd edn, Staplehurst: Spellmount, 2003, pp. 76–9.
9. The social distinction between 'ladies' (the female members of the families of commissioned officers and civilians of similar status) and 'women' (those in the families of ordinary soldiers and civilians) was strictly preserved in the language of official reports, reflecting the ordinary conventions of the time (see General Order of the Governor General of India in Council, 30 December 1857, cited in G. W. Forrest, *Selections from the Letters, Despatches and Other State Papers Preserved in the Military Department of the Government of India Relative to the Indian Mutiny*, vol. III, Calcutta: Military Dept Press, 1902. The memorial in Exeter Cathedral to the dead of the 32nd Foot at Kanpur and Lucknow includes four officers' ladies (named individually), and forty-three soldiers' wives. See G. C. Swiney, *Historical Records of the 32nd (Cornwall) Light Infantry*, London: Simpkin, Marshall, Hamilton, Kent & Co., 1893, frontispiece.
10. Such a perception clearly emerges in the final despatch of Brigadier John Eardley Wilmot Inglis, commanding the British garrison in Lucknow during the first part of the siege there. 'I cannot refrain from bringing to the attention of his lordship in council [i.e. the Governor General of India] the patient endurance and the Christian resignation which have been evinced by the women of this garrison. They have animated us all by their example. Many, alas, have been widowed and their children made fatherless in this cruel struggle ... and many ... have, after the example of Miss Nightingale, constituted themselves the tender and solicitous nurses of the wounded and dying soldiers in the hospital', 26 September 1857, Forrest, *Selections*, vol. II.

11. T. A. Heathcote, *Mutiny and Insurgency in India 1857–58: The British Army in a Bloody Civil War*, Barnsley: Pen & Sword, 2007, pp. 35–7, 213–24.
12. Lal Ram Narain, *The Student's Practical Dictionary of the Hindustani Language*, 2 vols, Allahabad, 1925.
13. S. N. Sen, *Eighteen Fifty Seven*, Delhi: Government of India Publications Division, 1957, pp. 71–6; William Dalrymple, *The Last Mughal, the Fall of a Dynasty, Delhi 1857*, London: Bloomsbury, 2006, ch. 5; David, *Indian Mutiny*, ch. 9.
14. James Laver and Amy de la Haye, *Costume and Fashion, a Concise History*, London: Thames & Hudson, 2002.
15. George McMunn, *The Indian Mutiny in Perspective*, London: G. Bell & Sons Ltd, 1931, p. 71.
16. David Blomfield, ed., *Lahore to Lucknow: The Indian Mutiny Journal of Arthur Moffat Lang*, London: Leo Cooper, 1992, p. 33.
17. Harriet C. Tytler, 'Through the Sepoy Mutiny and Siege of Delhi', *Chambers' Journal*, 21, London, 1896. Republ. as *An Englishwoman in India, the Memories of Harriet Tytler, 1828–58*, ed. A. Sattin and Philip Mason, Oxford: Oxford University Press, 1986.
18. Colonel to Mrs Keith Young, 6 August 1857, cited in Henry Norman and Mrs Keith Young, eds, *The Siege, Assault, and Capture of Delhi as Given in the Diaries and Correspondence of the Late Colonel Keith Young*, London: W. and R. Chambers, 1902, pp. 180–1.
19. Andrew Ward, *Our Bones are Scattered: The Cawnpore Massacres and the Indian Mutiny of 1857*, New York: Henry Holt & Co., 1996; Sen, *Eighteen Fifty Seven*, ch. 4; David, *Indian Mutiny*, chs. 13, 14; J. W. Fortescue, *A History of the British Army*, vol. XIII, London: Macmillan & Co., 1930, pp. 276–8.
20. Albert A. Nofi, *The Alamo and the Texas War for Independence, September 30, 1835 to April 21, 1836: Heroes, Myths and History*, 2nd edn, New York: Da Capo Press, 2001.
21. Daniel Marston, *The French-Indian Wars, 1754–1760*, Botley: Osprey Publishing, 2002.
22. Blomfield, *Lahore to Lucknow*, pp. 123–4.
23. Ibid.
24. K.S., 'The Diary of an Officer's wife Kept during the Siege of Lucknow', *The Graphic*, 15 June 1907, appendix in W. H. Fitchett, *The Tale of the Great Mutiny*, London: Smith, Elder & Co., 1908, p. 463.
25. Ibid., passim; K.B. [Kate Bartrum], *A Widow's Reminiscences of the Siege of Lucknow*, London, 1858, Mrs Maria Germon, *Journal of the Siege of Lucknow*, publ. privately, London, 1870; Hon. Lady Julia Inglis, *The Siege of Lucknow, a Diary* etc., London: James R. Osgood, Macilvanie & Co., 1892; Mrs J. A. Harris, *A Lady's Diary of the Siege of Lucknow*, London: John Murray, 1858.
26. Harris, *Lady's Diary*, pp. 119–20.
27. Forrest, *Selections*, vol. II.
28. Germon, *Journal*, pp. 120–1.
29. Captain Winter Goode, 64th Foot, letter in *The Times*, 15 January 1858, cited in R. Montgomerie Martin, *The Indian Empire*, etc., vol. II, *The mutiny of the Bengal Army*, London: London Printing and Publishing Co., 1858–61, pp. 470–1, footnote.
30. *The Times* report, 13 April 1858, Martin, *loc. cit.*
31. Ibid.
32. K.B., 'Diary', pp. 468–9.
33. Forrest, *Selections*, vol. II.

Select Bibliography

The Indian Mutiny had as profound an impact on the history of British rule in South Asia as did the American Civil War (fought only a few years later) on that of the United States. Indeed, in both cases the intensity of feeling generated by the conflict was, and sometimes still is, reflected in the various names given to these wars, and can be a cause of dispute, with Indian Mutiny being called the Sepoy War or the First War of Indian Independence, just as the Civil War can be the War between the States or the War of the Rebellion. Both wars have produced a vast literature, including political and military histories, biographies of leading figures, personal memories and diaries, regimental chronicles, studies of individual campaigns and battles, government reports, and narratives, aimed at all levels of readership. In both cases the sweep and drama of events, especially in episodes where women as well as soldiers were caught up in the fighting, have formed the material for many works of historical fiction and feature films.

Contemporary histories, almost by definition, reflect the views of their time, but are often valuable as they can contain primary sources on a scale that many modern publishers consider uncommercial. Those, and more recent works, used as background sources for this chapter include:

Beveridge, Henry, *A Comprehensive History of India from the first landing of the English to the suppression of the Sepoy Revolt*, 3 vols, London: Blackie & Son, 1865.

David, Saul, *The Indian Mutiny 1857*, London: Viking, 2002.

Edwardes, Michael, *Red Year: The Indian Rebellion of 1857*, London: Hamish Hamilton, 1973.

Forrest, G. W., *A History of the Indian Mutiny Reviewed and Illustrated from Original Documents*, Edinburgh and London: William Blackwood & Sons, 1904.

Heathcote, T. A., *Mutiny and Insurgency in India 1857–58: The British Army in a Bloody Civil War*, Barnsley: Pen & Sword, 2007.

Kaye, J. M., *A History of the Sepoy War in India*, 4th edn, London: W. H. Allen & Co., 1877–8.

Martin, R. Montgomerie, *The Indian Empire, with a full account of the mutiny of the Bengal Army, the insurrection in Western India and an exposition of the alleged causes*, 3 vols, London: London Printing and Publishing Co., 1858–61.

Sen, Surendra Nath, *Eighteen Fifty Seven*, Delhi: Government of India Publications Division, 1957.

Smith, Vincent A., *The Oxford History of India*, 3rd edn, Oxford: Clarendon Press, 1958.

Chapter 2

Heni Te Kiri Karamu

The Heroine of the Gate Pa

Leicester Chilton

The New Zealand scene in the early nineteenth century into which Heni Te Kiri Karamu was thrust, was characterized by unrest and conflict as two diverse cultures struggled to share occupation of the same territories. For thirty years or so following the discovery and exploration of New Zealand by Captain James Cook in 1769, external contact with the country was limited to the commercial activity of British and American sealers and whalers. This contact became more regular from about 1800, when European seamen came into New Zealand harbours to take on supplies and carry out some trading in such items as timber and flax. Then by the mid-1830s, traders themselves were beginning to take permanent residences on the coasts.[1] Christian Missionaries also arrived when the Church Missionary Society established stations in the far north.[2]

But during these times the country had no law and order. Shantytowns sprang up inflated by brothels and grog shops; muskets appeared and rapidly became a valued item of trade for the Maoris; inter-tribal wars among Maoris led to wholesale massacre; and European diseases and depravity further decimated the native population. It was because of this wholesale lawlessness that both Maori and the 2,000-odd British settlers were moved to request British intervention.

Traditionally, Maori had always fought rival kin groups. Conflict increased as their numbers rose, natural resources were depleted and insults demanding a response multiplied. Firearms revolutionised warfare around the Pacific in the nineteenth century, but the first muskets peddled by European traders were unreliable and slow to reload. When Nga Puhi first used muskets in battle about 1807, they were overwhelmed by conventionally armed Ngāti Whātua, a New Zealand Māori tribe. Seeking revenge, the Nga Puhi chief Ruatara, who was based in the main trading area, the Bay of Islands, bought more of these costly weapons.[3] They grew potatoes, raised pigs and processed flax on a large scale to exchange for muskets. From 1815, Nga Puhi war parties armed with muskets wreaked havoc across the North Island. Their victims faced exile, death or slavery.

In August 1820, the Nga Puhi chief, Hongi Hika, arrived in London with the missionary Thomas Kendall. Hongi had heard there 'were a thousand guns at the Tower'. After meeting King George IV, Hongi was presented with a suit of armour described as a 'coat of mail', as well as other gifts. On the way home, Hongi traded most of his gifts in Sydney for 300 muskets. Fortunately for him, he kept the armour.[4] In 1821, it was hit twice by musket shots during battle with Ngati Paoa that took place beside the Tamaki River. His survival gained him a reputation for invulnerability that served him well in future battles. Hongi's importation of 300 muskets though brought a new escalation of conflict. Over the next few years, he led huge musket armies against tribes from Tamaki to Rotorua. Nga Puhi suffered heavy casualties, but their opponents were crushed despite retreating into fortified pa (strongholds).[5]

Tribes under attack soon bought guns and launched their own campaigns. In 1822, Ngāti Toa, another New Zealand tribe, led by Te Rauparaha, a Māori rangatira chief, fought their way down the North Island from Kawhai to Kapiti. When Waikato tribes got muskets, they attacked Taranaki tribes. These, in turn, migrated south to join Ngati Toa in a confederation rivalling Nga Puhi's. This force defeated an opposing alliance before attacking Ngai Tahu in the South Island.[6]

But once all tribes had muskets, there were no more easy victories. The new gunfighter pa (fortified strongholds) stood up to musket fire and was difficult to capture. By the 1830s, campaigns were too costly, and with European diseases also taking a heavy toll, warfare gave way to economic rivalry.

At first reluctant to take action to deal with these troubles, but finally persuaded by the missionaries in 1833, the British Government appointed an 'Official British Resident' by the name of James Busby,[7] with the aim of exercising some sort of law and order. But Busby's particular statute did not invest him with much authority and he therefore had little success in his mission. At the same time, there was a strong desire by Maori to gain the literary skills of the Europeans. Maori tribes encouraged missionaries to settle in their areas to help them acquire these skills.[8] This not only gave them increasing standing with other tribes, but it opened up further trade links with the Europeans.

Then in 1837, plans for systematic colonization by the New Zealand Company forced the British Government to take action. Captain William Hobson, who was nominated as British Consul, began to negotiate the annexation of New Zealand, which led to the joint signing of the Treaty of Waitangi by representatives of the British Government and Maori chiefs from a number of different tribes. Signed in 1840, the Treaty recognised the prior occupation by Maori people of New Zealand. It also enabled the peaceful acquisition of land for settlement purposes and ensured that immigrants could come and live here in peace. It allowed the Crown to set up a government to establish laws and in return the Crown were to guarantee and actively protect Maori tribal authority over their lands, fisheries, forests, villages, treasures, and culture, and extend to them the rights and status of British citizens.[9]

In the midst of these unsettled, times, little Heni (Jane), was born to a Maori mother and a European father, at Kaitaia in the far north of the country. This baby girl began a life that was to be buffeted by the battles of war. Heni's date of birth is uncertain, but she was probably born on 14 November 1840.[10] She was also known as Heni Pore, Jane Foley, and Jane Russell. The identity of Heni's father is not clear. She is said to have believed he was named Russell, and he is also named in an obituary as Richard Russell, a ship's chandler, from Sunderland, England. But Heni's death certificate records that her father was an Irish sea captain named Thomas William Kelly.[11]

From the commencement of organised colonization in the 1840s, many Maori tribes opposed the sale of land, which was urgently needed by the settlers, but to each tribe was its homeland. To increasing numbers of Maori, this sale of land to the European government amounted to selling their country – the scene of their tribal traditions and the ancient legends on which their youth had been nurtured. They were feeling dispossessed, and bitter wars were being fought against British troops in many tribal territories.

In this turbulent setting, the young Heni attended two mission schools, including a boarding school for Maori children, where she became fluent in Maori, English and French. Exhibiting a high level of skill, she was appointed as an assistant teacher at the school as well as acting as a governess.[12] Heni accompanied her parents when they went north again, and there she met and married Te Kiri Karamu of the Arawa tribe, and they moved to Katikati, where their three sons and two daughters were born. But after a quarrel in 1861, the strong-minded Heni left her husband who was working as a gum digger, and took her children back to live with her mother in the Waikato district,[13] where they were destined to get caught up in several skirmishes with government troops.

Heni and her family supported the 'King' movement and fought with a section of the Ngati Paoa tribe in the Hunua Range. Along with her mother and sister, Heni had her young children with her. By tradition, Maori women did not fight, but in desperate situations there were exceptions when capable women fought alongside their warrior men. Heni was just such a person. For the most part though, they were enthusiastic supporters of their warriors and were deeply involved in sustaining them. Heni's group suffered some severe defeats, notably when the red silk flag named *Aotearoa*, which had been made by Heni (and which is today held in the Auckland Museum), was captured by a large party of Forest Rangers who took them completely by surprise. Four dead Maoris were left on the ground, and three were seen being carried off; several more were wounded. The Rangers sustained no casualties.[14]

Heni left a record to the effect that shortly before this it had been decided that they should make for the Waikato, and travel south through the bush by way of Paparata. In their party was an old *tohunga*, a man named Timoti te Amapo, who was gifted with the power of *matakite* (second sight). As the result of some vision or foreboding – a warning from his personal god – Timoti had advised Heni's party not to follow the track which ran straight toward Paparata, but to disperse into small parties and make their way through the bush to the common meeting place, so as to throw the ensuing troops off their trail. A number of their people however, did not accept the seer's advice, and continued on the well-marked track, while the others with Timoti, split up into small sections and struck into the trackless parts of the forest for a rendezvous going southward. Heni said:

> The consequence was that we escaped, while those who disregarded the old seer's counsel fell in with the Forest Rangers and had several men killed and wounded. It was on a Saturday that we parted company; the fight took place the next day. Eventually, the survivors of this skirmish joined us in the forest near the headwaters of the Manga-tawhiri River.[15]

'One of the Maoris in the camp,' said Heni,

> was a man named Te Pae-tui. He was terribly wounded, shot through both hips. His elder brother, Te Tapuke, seeing him fall, ran back to his assistance and stood by him, reloading his double-barrel gun, determined to defend his brother to the death. Te Tapuke a few moments later received a bullet through the forehead and fell dead by his wounded brother. After the fight the Forest Rangers attended as well as they could to Te Pae-tui's injuries, laid him on some blankets found in the camp, and gave him food and drink. His wife came out from the bush, weeping over her husband, and they treated her kindly, but they could do nothing for her husband, and they left her there. She remained tending the mortally wounded man until he died several days later. She was all alone then

and could not shift him, so she dug a grave herself and buried him there in the forest.[16]

This smaller party regrouped again and began once more to make their way southwards until, finding themselves hemmed in by a cordon of military posts, they camped for some time in a deep, forested valley southeast of the Wairoa River, living mostly on wild honey and cold water as they could not light fires or shoot game for fear of alerting the British troops. But one night they were able to slip through the soldier's lines, moving so close to the sentries, they could hear them talking. They waded through a swamp, escaped by canoe, and eventually reached Matamata where they remained for the summer of 1863–64. During this time, the ever-resourceful Heni was able to translate captured British military documents for Wirimu Tamihana, their powerful leader, to use to their advantage.[17]

On 2 April 1864, after the fall of Orakau, Heni's group abandoned their pa and accompanied a force of Nga Te Rangi warriors to Tauranga to combat large numbers of British troops that had landed at this east coast port in order to prevent Maori forces from sending aid to their allies in the Waikato wars.

Henare Wirimu Tarata, one of the leaders of the Te Rangi force, had previously become an early convert to Christianity while under the influence of Henry Williams at the Bay of Islands mission station. His Christian training led him to draw up a 'Code of Conduct', which decreed that enemy troops who were wounded or captured should be treated with compassion based on the premise that 'If your enemy is hungry, feed him; if he is thirsty, give him drink'. He commended such action then wrote them into his 'Orders of the Day' as instructions to the Maori forces as they made their way to Tauranga to confront the British troops.[18]

Although the government claimed that its intention was to prevent local Maori from lending support to the Kingite forces in the Waikato, it was also keen to increase the amount of fertile land available for British settlement. Provoking a fight in the Tauranga district would provide a reason to confiscate productive land. The build-up of troops had continued with the arrival of the 68th Durham and the 43rd Monmouth Light Infantry. Troops from these regiments constructed redoubts, or fortified positions, which bore their names, in what is now downtown Tauranga City. Altogether there were some 2,000, armed soldiers with a strong artillery train consisting of eight mortars, two howitzers, two naval cannon, and five Armstrong guns.[19]

The Maori warriors prepared themselves for a fight. They expected the engagement to take place at Te Puna, where there was deep enough water for troops to be brought up by boat. Their preparations included building trenches and fortifications over a long stretch of forest edge from Te Puna to the Waimapu, where they dug in and awaited the attack.

But it did not come and, impatient that the soldiers had not taken up their challenge, the Maori decided to move closer to the enemy camp. In considerable haste, warriors, women and children alike, toiled mightily to construct further fortifications. They built the new pa on a narrow ridge between two rivers just outside land already purchased for missionary use. Meandering entrenchments that were little more than shallow ditches were dug and masked by frail stockades hurriedly built with posts and rails sledged by night from a nearby farm, completed with flimsy stakes, sticks, and scrub, and flower stalks of native flax. It looked formidable enough but, in truth, was fragile indeed. At the mid-point, a gate in the fence allowed a long-established Maori track from the north towards the Kaimai Ranges in the south to pass through. This pa was simply named *The Gate Pa* after which the battle itself was named. The women who had helped construct the fortification had been withdrawn before the attack began, but Heni stayed on as she was considered a woman warrior, and able to fight as well as the men, and did not want to leave her brother Neri, who was also in the force.[20]

The British forces were well prepared. Though the red clay of the stockades was still raw on the waterfront, bell tents whitened the peninsula, and tall-masted warships laying at anchor down the harbour, provided a striking backdrop as boats came into the beach with load after load of bearded soldiers in their blue serge field-dress. The artillery rumbled along as General Cameron's siege batteries, brought from the Waikato, were assembled to throw shot and shell into the Maori entrenchments.

The batteries opened fire first, the heaviest fire in the war, at ranges of from 800 to 650 yards. The bombardment was directed chiefly against the main palisade to make a breach for an assault party. The unsubstantial construction was soon smashed in many places by the shells, and some of it only hung together by its ties. The earth parapet was sent flying in showers of clouds and dust. Heni was nearly killed by the first shots of the bombardment but was saved by one of the men who saw the cannon fire and pulled her down into the trench.[21]

In spite of the heavy bombardment that had started in early morning, it was almost evening on that rainy autumn day when the signal to advance was given. At the double, the British stormers covered the last hundred yards to what appeared to be a weak point in the Maori fortifications. Into the breach they poured – fighting was at close quarters now. Rifle and bayonet met tomahawk, and navy cutlasses clashed on double barrel guns and old flintlock muskets. The Maori were masters of the fine art of parrying a sword slash; masters, too, of the deadly tomahawk-blade on a long handle which gave the warrior a glorious reach for a blow that split a skull in two, and hidden in the skilfully designed trenches, they caused heavy losses among the officers leading the troops. But the troops finally gained the centre of the pa, and the retreating Maori were forced back inside by a contingent of the 68th Durham Light Infantry, placed south of the pa to cut off the retreat. In the ensuing confusion, the leaderless British forces, perhaps assuming that reinforcements had arrived, panicked and fled, leaving the pa to the Maori and the dead and wounded British troops.[22]

After the debacle of that first attack, the British regrouped and attacked again the following day when they 'took' the pa, finding it empty. They then discovered the left hand trench, which had been cunningly disguised and contained a small band of Maori, the Koheriki, still prepared to fight. The soldiers of the 43rd Monmouth Light Infantry rushed in with the bayonet, led by Lieutenant Colonel Booth, but the defenders fought with the fury of utter desperation. The young Heni Te Kiri Karamu, warrior supreme, was with them, and when she had fired a shot out of her single-barrel gun, she jumped back into the shallow trench to reload.[23]

When the soldiers were beaten back, Heni and her brother, and the rest of them, rushed out to the front of the pa in pursuit, but were recalled by a shout from the Koheriki leader, and firing began again. Heni fired several more shots. By this time an almost choking pall of gunpowder smoke was over the pa, and a drizzly rain began to fall creating a darkness that seemed dusk, though it was only 4.30 or so in the afternoon.

Heni was in the firing trench when she heard an English voice behind her calling feebly, 'Water, give me water!'[24] She turned and saw a wounded officer lying there, and near him were some soldiers in like distress. She remembered that there was some water in the rear of the trench, where an earth oven had been made to cook the breakfast that the warriors never had the opportunity of eating, for a cannon shot had sent potatoes and all flying. In spite of the bullets flying thick and fast, Heni slung her gun over her shoulder by its strap, and jumped out of the trench. 'Where are you going?' called her brother. Heni replied, 'Wounded men are calling for water, I must obey the call.'[25] Not another word came from the brother. He stood with his gun-butt planted on the ground, his hands gripping the muzzle. With admiration he watched his sister intently while she ran to fetch the water.

Heni went a few yards into the rear of the trench. As the fence in front was almost demolished, she must have been fully exposed to the enemy's view, but she was not hit. There was an old iron nail-can full of water which had been brought through the swamp before the battle began. She had to spill about half of it before she could conveniently carry it. She took it in her arms to where the wounded officer was lying. He was Lieutenant Colonel Booth, and although Heni did not know who he was, she recognised his uniform. He was the nearest of the soldiers to her and was rolling from side to side in distress. She dropped down by his side and took his head on her knees. 'Here is water,' she said in English.[26]

Tipping the can, she poured some of the water into her cupped hand, which she held close to the officer's lips so he could drink. Eagerly he swallowed and swallowed again when she gave him more. After a third swallow he feebly said, 'God bless you!' and she gave him more.[27]

Then, leaving the Colonel, Heni went to the other wounded soldiers, lifted them up so they could drink, and gave them water one by one in the same way. She placed the nail can beside the officer so that it would not spill, and ran back to the trench, reloaded her gun, and stood ready with her comrades to meet the expected second assault, which never came.

That night, the Koheriki party abandoned the battered pa and took to the swamp, into which the British fired every now and again. Heni, before leaving, gave the soldiers some more water and again left the can with a little water in it by the officer's side. He was still alive when the British entered the pa next morning but later died in the military hospital.

The Nga-Te-Rangi had already evacuated their dugouts when the Koheriki left – they were still ready to fight but their ammunition was exhausted. Although they realised that they would be attacked in overwhelming force next day, they gallantly decided to stay on. All told, the defenders in this engagement had suffered about twenty-five fatalities. But a few weeks later, the British troops brutally avenged their repulse. They stormed the Maori entrenchments at Te Ranga, a short distance further inland, and killed 120 Maori warriors, most of them with the bayonet.

The chivalrous fighting of the Nga-Te-Rangi and their allies in the cannon-battered Gate Pa, has been the theme of praise ever since that red day on Tauranga's shore. The humane code of conduct drawn up beforehand by the chiefs and Henare Taratoa's injunction to his comrades to feed the hungry and give drink to the thirsting, have won enduring fame. But much that is quite inaccurate has been written of Taratoa's deeds at the Gate Pa. It was not he who was the hero of this episode of giving water to a dying officer. Heni Pore, as she became known in later years, was the one to whom credit is rightfully due.

There is some doubt as to whether she or any of her Koheriki comrades in the left wing of the pa knew anything of the code of fighting drawn up some time before the battle. The Koheriki only came in from the bush the evening before the fight began. Perhaps Heni, in succouring the wounded, simply obeyed her own womanly feelings of humanity. She is recorded to have fought gallantly on the Government side in the years following the Gate Pa episode, and if ever a fighter in the New Zealand wars deserved a decoration for bravery under fire, it was she. But the heroic Heni received neither medal nor Mention in Despatches.

If it could be said that Heni Te Kiri Karamu was the product of the influences in her life – family, tribal, warrior, missionary; it would be equally true to say that her own inspirational influence went beyond those with whom she came into contact, by reaching out to touch the heart of a young nation.

The chivalrous conduct of the Maori at the Gate Pa is commemorated by a brass plaque in the church there, and a stained glass window in the chapel at Lichfield Palace, the home of the Bishop of Lichfield, England.

Notes

1. *History of the Bay of Plenty: A European Outpost*, http://hubgages.com/hub/History-of-the-Bay-of-Plenty-A-European-Outpost.
2. Ibid.
3. The Musket Wars were a series of 500 or more battles fought between various iwi (tribal groups) of Māori between 1807 and 1842, in New Zealand. The word *iwi* means 'people' or 'folk'; in many contexts; it may mean tribe or clan or sometimes a confederation of tribes. Northern tribes such as the rivals Ngapuhi and Ngāti Whātua were the first to obtain firearms, and inflicted heavy casualties upon each other and on neighbouring tribes, some of whom had never seen muskets. The wars were characterised by their brutality and ruthlessness – with treachery, the burning of villages, killing of prisoners, torture, slavery and cannibalism being commonplace.
4. Wikipedia encyclopedia, Musket Wars.
5. Ibid. (In Māori society, a great pā represented the mana of a tribal group, as personified by a chief or rangatira and they were built in defensible locations to protect dwelling sites or gardens, almost always on prominent, raised ground which was then terraced.)
6. See Wikipedia Ngāti Toa.
7. James Busby (7 February 1801 to 15 July 1871); a British Resident, who travelled to New Zealand, involved in the drafting of the Declaration of the Independence of New Zealand, and the Treaty of Waitangi. He is widely regarded as the 'father' of the Australian wine industry, having taken the first collection of vine stock from Spain and France to Australia. As British Resident, he acted as New Zealand's first jurist, and the 'originator' of law in Aotearoa.
8. Wikipedia.org/wiki/Musket_Wars.
9. See http://www.motorhomegroup.co.nz./new-zealand.html.
10. Heni's mother, Maraea (also known as Pihohau or Pikokau) was born on Mokoia Island on Lake Rotorua, the daughter of a chief.
11. Stephen Oliver, 'Te Kiri Karamu, Heni: Biography', from the *Dictionary of New Zealand Biography: Te Ara – the Encyclopedia of New Zealand*, updated 1 September 2010. Alfred D. Foley, *Jane's Story: Biography of Heeni Te Kirikaramu-Pore (Jane Foley). Woman of*

Profound Purpose, Auckland: A. D. Foley, 2004; http://battles at the gate/home/the-story-of-heni te kiri karamu.

12. Foley, *Jane's Story*; http://battles at the gate/home/the-story-of-heni te kiri karamu.
13. Ibid.
14. www.justice.net.nz/calendar/hen te kiri karamu of gate pa.
15. Quoted in James Cowan, *The New Zealand Wars: A History of the Maori Campaigns and the Pioneering Period*, vol. I (1845–64), Wellington: R. E. Owen, 1955.
16. Ibid.
17. Oliver, 'Te Kiri Karamu'.
18. Pauline Jacobs, *Heni Te Kiri Karamu of Gate Pa*, 11 September 2009, http://htkyouthgroup.org/index.php?option=com .
19. Ibid. and Cowan, *New Zealand Wars*.
20. Ibid.
21. Ibid.
22. Ibid.
23. Ibid.
24. Ibid
25. Ibid
26. Ibid.
27. Ibid.

Select Bibliography

Cowan, James, 'Hero Stories of New Zealand', in *New Zealand in History: The New Zealand Wars*, Wellington: Harry H. Tombs, 1935.

King, Michael, *The Penguin History of New Zealand*, Harmondsworth: Penguin, 2003.

Oliver, Stephen, *A People's History: Illustrated Biographies from the Dictionary of New Zealand Biography*, Wellington: Bridget Williams Books and Department of Internal Affairs, New Zealand, 1992.

Paterson, John, an account in a closing sermon, 198th Diocesan Convention, 3 February 2001, at Christ Church, Savannah, GA.

THE FIRST WORLD WAR

Chapter 3

Home from Home on the Western Front, 1914–1918

Women's Contribution to Morale

Elspeth Johnstone

For many British women the outbreak of the First World War offered an opportunity to press home their demands for 'full citizenship'.[1] The women's suffrage movement had sown the seeds of desire for equality but it was the war that harvested and gave recognition to the talents and capabilities of British womanhood. The women of Britain were to become indispensable through their contribution to the nation's war effort not only on the home front but in the war zones of the British army; especially in France and Belgium, known as the Western Front. As the war dragged on, confounding the early optimism that it would be over by Christmas, 1914, more and more women offered their services. They came from all sections of society, from the highest in the land to the lowest. Class made no difference; they were united in their desire to help and support the soldier at the front. This collective endeavour, to bring the comforts of the home front to the Western Front, was to prove so important in sustaining the morale of the fighting man.

The work of Red Cross nurses and those attached to the Voluntary Aid Detachments, the units under the administration of the Red Cross, has been well documented and recorded by Lyn Macdonald in *The Roses of No Man's Land*[2] and in Vera Brittain's *Testament of Youth*,[3] but the work of enterprising, individual women or those attached to the major voluntary organisations on the Western Front has been given less attention. Throughout the war there were a growing number of women behind the front lines, not just nurses, who ministered to the needs of the troops.

A vanguard of women crossed to France at the beginning of the war to open canteens for troops at the base ports and railway stations. Initially, the War Office feared the possibility of scandal incurred by the proximity of these women to the men; Lord Kitchener, Secretary of State for War (1914–16), wanted them removed. But as the base areas were under the control of the French authorities there was nothing that the Inspector General of Communications in France could do to stop the proliferation of canteens run by women.[4] Lady Angela Forbes was the first woman to set up a voluntary canteen, at Boulogne Station in November 1914, and later a rest hut at Etaples. She was followed by Lady Mabelle Egerton, who set up a coffee shop at Rouen Station the following month.[5] Forbes and the 'very gallant gentlewomen' who worked for her cheerfully provided everything they could for the troops.[6] She was adored by the men, many of whom were young, scared and had never left home before. She made sure she stocked their favourite foods; plenty of tinned salmon and plenty of custard.[7] Her work for the soldiers was 'untiring' and 'unostentatious'.[8] A soldier wrote this tribute to her:

> A never fading recollection of Etaples will be that of the kindness and hospitality we received at the hands of Lady Angela Forbes … The warmest of welcomes and the best of cheer awaited every soldier who crossed its threshold. Nothing that thoughtfulness could suggest and liberality could provide was lacking. Tact and understanding sympathy characterised the administration of every department. We left behind us blessings and thanks we could not express in words.[9]

May Bradford, the wife of Sir John Rose Bradford, the Consulting Physician to the British Expeditionary Force (BEF), arrived in France at the end of 1914, to serve as an official letter-writer for sick or illiterate soldiers. Working in the hospitals at Boulogne and later at Etaples, her attention to the welfare of the patients and their families earned her the nickname of 'Tommy's Little Mother'.[10] May said:

> I always told them I was glad that I reminded them of anyone they loved. One poor fellow, terribly wounded, used to watch the door, and, as soon as he caught sight of me, he would call out 'How are you, Mother? I do love you.'[11]

It was care of this sort, and the fact that it was administered by a woman, that was so important to the morale and welfare of the soldier. Women were to become an integral part of a large welfare effort providing the care, food and comforts needed by the troops behind the frontlines. Their presence was a 'priceless' contribution.[12] Charles W. Bishop, writing about the YMCA, said: 'Men who fight and suffer physical and mental hardship must have exceptional counter attractions if they are to survive the struggle.'[13]

Nursing was the only occupation within the Army that was open to women before 1914, but the contribution made by women to the munitions industry on the home front eventually altered the army's attitude in favour of employing women in other areas.[14] The first small voluntary canteens and huts, run by individual women like Lady Angela Forbes, were eventually absorbed by the larger voluntary organisations acceptable to the military authorities or by Expeditionary Force Canteens (EFC), run by the Army Service Corps (ASC). Working in the huts and centres of the voluntary organisations, and eventually in the EFC on the Western Front in 1917, women were to become of 'special value' to the military authorities.[15] They provided the female company that was 'craved' by the soldiers in France.[16]

Amongst those organisations that were fully accepted at the outset of the war, outside the administrative control of the army, and before the arrival of the Women's Army Auxiliary Corps (WAACs), in 1917, were the women workers of the Young Men's Christian Association (YMCA), The Salvation Army and the Church Army. The YMCA and Church Army had employed women since 1914, both organisations having lost many of their male workers to enlistment.[17] The Salvation Army had believed in the importance of a woman's presence since it first operated in the Boer War,[18] and all three associations acknowledged that much of their work was 'done infinitely better by women';[19] they offered sympathy and took a personal interest in the lives of the men which 'counted so much' to the soldiers.[20] Missing the companionship of mothers, wives, sisters and girlfriends the men really appreciated being able to talk to the 'lady volunteers'.[21] As a Base Commandant remarked on the services of one woman at a YMCA hut, 'she is more value to me than truckloads of parsons and chaplains!'[22]

By engaging the assistance of these three main voluntary organisations the military authorities provided the predominantly citizen army with the reassuring presence of familiar and well-established welfare services from the home front.[23] These organisations worked among the more marginalised sections of British society and were the product of the evangelical and missionary movements of nineteenth-century Britain.[24] For this reason they became acceptable and recognisable agencies of support for the BEF, providing the troops with refreshments, conversation and spiritual support.[25] More importantly they were a link with civilian life. When soldiers tired of the French and Belgian estaminets, and wanted something British,[26] they knew there was a place to go where the female workers provided an atmosphere of domesticity.[27]

The response from the established voluntary services at the outbreak of war was complemented by the emergence of other charitable organisations on the home front. Towns and local communities engaged in fundraising and establishing Comforts Funds for their own regiments. Many individual and groups of women collected funds for the war effort; it was a critical contribution which boosted the resources of the army.[28] An enterprising Miss Hope Clarke collected over £60,000 to donate to the Red Cross and other agencies. She was also able to buy fifteen motor ambulances, five motor hospital launches and two motor dental surgery cars, all paid for by the sale of old silver thimbles through her Silver Thimble Fund. A Bovril Fund, set up by Miss Gladys Storey, sent Bovril to all theatres of war,[29] and to show that even animals should be involved in the war effort, a lady supporter of the YMCA collected £1,000 from pet owners. This paid for the 'Dogs and Cats Hut at Rouen'.[30]

When it was realised that the war would continue into 1915, every effort was made by the military authorities and civilians, at home and on the Western Front, to keep the BEF's morale high by providing all they could for the troops' first Christmas away from home. The provision of creature comforts was 'organised officially and semi-officially as siege warfare was entered on'.[31] The increase in the work of the ASC at the bases and on the lines of communication was matched by a growth in the national effort to supply the troops with comforts from home. The end of 1914 saw a massive surge in charitable contributions from private individuals, clubs, businesses and industry.[32]

Newspapers sent copies out free,[33] and Comforts Committees sent anything from socks, gloves and hats to cigarettes. Comforts worth £5 million were supplied in the first year of the war.[34] 'Anything that the Post Office or Shipping Agencies accepted was sent.'[35] The Royal Engineers Postal Services increased their staff from 900 to 1,500 to cope with the volume of post for Christmas, 1914. The response from organisations and individuals in providing for the men at the front increased the parcel post by 345 per cent.[36] The efficiency of the postal service generally ensured that letters and parcels arrived at the front two to four days after posting.[37] Every man serving received a Christmas card from King George V and Queen Mary, and a gift box from Princess Mary.[38] The *Daily News* supplied Christmas puddings for the troops through a subscription fund. Half a pound of pudding per man was distributed.[39] Puddings were privately supplied by Lady Rawlinson, wife of General Sir Henry Rawlinson, to every man within the IV Corps.[40] As one army captain put it:

> If the people who send all the parcels only saw what tremendous enjoyment we have derived from them they would not for a moment regret having sent them. I think this Christmas will act as a good bucking-up tonic to us all.[41]

The proceeds from this activity on the home front were boosted even further by the work of the YMCA, the Church Army and the Salvation Army; the three voluntary services that came to dominate welfare on the Western Front. All of these organisations had experience of working with the army,[42] and all three of them were supported in their work with money donated, yet again by the civilian population.

Princess Helena Victoria (1870–1948), daughter of Queen Victoria, was an ardent supporter of the YMCA. After a consultation with Sir Arthur Yapp,[43] Her Royal Highness Princess Helena Victoria of Schleswig-Holstein suggested to General Sir John Cowans, Quartermaster-General to the Forces, that refreshments and recreational facilities should be provided for soldiers by the YMCA at the bases in France. Cowans gave the YMCA permission to establish centres at Rouen and Le Havre in November 1914. Provided that the YMCA undertook the organisation and cost of supplies, Cowans undertook to organise the transport. It was an example of 'his readiness to utilise every civilian and un-official agency for the comfort of the soldier'.[44]

Sir George Williams (1821–1905), who was a draper by trade, founded the YMCA, and was the first President of its National Council in 1882. It opened 250 centres in England within ten days of the outbreak of war, and by the end of hostilities they had more than 10,000 centres in all the theatres of war.

The YMCA had worked in the Volunteer Camps in the 1890s, and had continued to provide for the Territorial Force for thirteen years before the outbreak of the war. Having been attached to the Territorial Force on exercise at their summer camps prior to the war, the YMCA were somewhat experienced in running recreational activities and canteens for troops.[45] They believed that their work with the troops 'had a steadying effect upon the men ... and probably no single factor had more to do with the high morale maintained by the troops'.[46]

It was a belief shared by the wives of the military commanders. These were influential women, many of whom gave their full support to the YMCA, and who were possibly responsible for influencing their husbands' decision to use the services of the YMCA not just at the base ports but within army areas.[47] Lady Dorothy Haig, wife of General Sir Douglas Haig (Commander of the British Expeditionary Force (BEF) from 1915 to the end of the war), worked in a YMCA officers' hostel in London, and Lady Annie Plumer, General Sir Herbert Plumer's wife, was the lady superintendant of the YMCA's Aldwych Hut in London. Eleanor, Lady French, the wife of the Commander-in-Chief of the British Army, Sir John French, was a member of the YMCA Ladies' Auxiliary Committee for France, and Lady Henderson, wife of the Commander of the Royal Flying Corps, was one of the first volunteer workers in France. Princess Helena Victoria, apart from convincing General Sir John Cowans to use the services of the YMCA, was the President of the Ladies'

Committee for France and helped in recruiting women for overseas work.[48] In addition, she gained the permission of Lord Kitchener to arrange musical and theatrical entertainment for the troops. She engaged Lena Ashwell, a well-known actress and theatre manager, to organise concert parties for the men on the Western Front. Ashwell recruited twenty-five troupes of performers who were capable of giving 14,000 concerts a year.[49] Her first concert was given at Harfleur in February 1915, in a newly built cinema hut. One of the performers at this opening concert party was the young Ivor Novello, the composer of a new song, 'Keep the Home Fires Burning ('Till the Boys Come Home)'. The refrain was later to be heard being sung from every corner of the camp. Lena Ashwell later said: 'There were never such audiences in the world before . . . so keen, so appreciative, so grateful.'[50]

Over time more YMCA centres were opened at other coastal base camps, on the lines of communication and in all army areas.[51] By the beginning of 1918, there were 499 women working for the YMCA. They represented 40 per cent of a workforce which totalled 1,236.[52] They became the predominant voluntary organisation on the Western Front and their emblem, the Red Triangle, was claimed to be more familiar to the troops than the Red Cross.[53]

The Church Army had, by request of the War Office, assisted chaplains at the front during the Boer War in South Africa (1899–1902). Their first venture on the Western Front, September 1914, was opening a hospital for the French at Caen, under the administration of Lady Bagot.[54] By March 1915, they had opened centres at bases in France and most troop areas.[55] Huts, mostly staffed by women, were generally placed where they could be used by the troops on the move in and out of the line, providing tea and food.[56] Centres were provided for troops working on the lines of communication at railway stations and on barges for the water transport workers.[57] The Right Reverend Bishop Gwynne, Deputy Chaplain General to the BEF, said that the Church Army had really looked after the physical and social needs of the BEF and were 'an enormous help in keeping up the spirit and morale' of the troops.[58] The Church Army were also to work within Army areas, and their huts and tents were used constantly by army chaplains for Sunday Parades, Communion and Evening Prayer.[59] By the end of the war the Church Army employed 2,000 workers in its 800 huts in France.[60]

The Salvation Army's association with servicemen had started during the Boer War under the leadership of Adjutant Mary Murray,[61] who was the daughter of Major General Sir John Murray, and her work was supported by Sir Redvers Buller and Lord Roberts. She was the pioneer of work with troops and her understanding of a soldier's needs made the Salvation Army's contribution to welfare acceptable to the military authorities.[62] Her headquarters north of Boulogne at Wimereux were administered by Adjutant Mary Booth, the granddaughter of the founder General William Booth.[63] It was one of the first voluntary organisations to break down anti-feminist prejudices. It was part of its creed that: 'the [Salvation] Army refuses to make any difference between men and women as to rank, authority and duties, but opens the highest positions to women as well as to men'.[64]

By the end of the war, thirty-eight huts and centres were established in army camps along the channel coast.[65] The Mary Booth Hut at Etaples was one of the busiest, where up to 2,000 eggs a day were cooked on one stove. It was run by a woman known only as Mrs H–, and addressed by the troops as 'Ma', who was capable, according to one soldier, of cooking 200 eggs in twenty-one minutes. More than anything, 'Ma' was able to provide a home environment where men returning from the trenches, often 'dirty, verminous and footsore', were able to get clean, dry clothes and a hot meal.[66] It was the proud boast of these Salvation Army workers that they provided 'good, plain, wholesome refreshment' with a 'cheery, home-like style',[67] and that they were there to support the 'boys' by giving them something comparable to the atmosphere at home.[68]

The women of the Salvation Army were also involved in hospital visiting, providing comforts such as fruit and peppermints for the patients and writing letters to anxious relatives.[69] They also visited and placed flowers on the graves of loved ones from grieving families at home.[70] When Mary Murray returned to England she was made the secretary of the Naval and Military League, as she believed in the Salvation Army's responsibility to servicemen 'in peace as in war'.[71]

Until the YMCA and Church Army moved into Army areas in the summer of 1915, the extra food items that these organisations provided were only available in the rear areas. The soldier in the front line was reliant on the efficiency of his officers and quartermaster for his daily ration and for any little extras or luxuries he depended on his food parcel from home. Percy Jones, 1st Battalion Queen's Westminster Rifles, lamented the absence of YMCA canteens within reach of the trenches during the first winter of the war. For soldiers who had been used to the presence of the YMCA huts during the period of training at home, the arrival of a food parcel from female relatives meant a great deal. After receiving a Christmas food parcel from home Jones wrote:

> I don't think you people at home realise what a big part parcels play in our lives out here ... knowing someone at home has taken the trouble to go out and buy or make English things, pack them up

carefully with English paper or string on an English table, and then send them over the sea until they turn up in the trenches . . . I think my ideal hell would be the Front without parcels.[72]

This contact with the women of the family on the home front through the delivery of mail, comforts and food parcels was an important boost to morale.[73]

The food provided by the army for many working class citizen soldiers was better and more nutritious than food at home.[74] Lower class men and men from the slums of Britain thrived on the diet and put on weight.[75] In comparison to the 2lbs of bacon purchased weekly by a family of eight, a soldier was issued with 1lb 12oz. He was given an average of 7lbs of meat (frozen or preserved) a week compared to the 4lbs of meat and 2lbs of fish purchased by the family. For a middle-class soldier used to a better diet it could be a hardship, but extra luxuries were provided by senior officers, and these raised the spirits of the troops. Contrary to the stereotypical view of senior officers as uncaring individuals, most put the welfare of their men first. In later years, Alice Remington, one of Lady Angela Forbes's first women workers at Etaples regarded the film *Oh! What a Lovely War* as a ridiculously 'stupid picture'. It completely misrepresented the senior officers; 'they were not like that at all'.[76]

Many senior officers went to great lengths to provide extras for their men. The quartermaster's branch of the 17th Division set up a fish, eggs, and vegetable market and a soda-water factory at Arras. To bring the home front directly to the Western Front the Division was also provided with 'a fish and chips and amusement fair that could be moved as frequently as a travelling circus'.[77] The 51st Division ran retail and wholesale canteens, wet canteens and hot soup kitchens. Major F. W. Bewsher wrote: 'In fact, there was practically nothing which civilisation supplies which "Q" did not produce . . .'[78]

The 9th (Scottish) Division had two canteen caravans, 'Rob Roy' and 'Wee Macgregor', which were sent to the division out of funds raised at home by supporters of the regimental comforts fund. They followed the division up and down the line from 1915 to the end of the war, dispensing hot coffee, biscuits and cigarettes.[79] The task of looking after the 'citizen' soldier by his superior officers was enhanced by the work of the voluntary services who not only cared for the British 'Tommy' but also the Dominion and, later, American troops. The YMCAs of these countries worked in close cooperation with the British organisation.[80]

The Salvation Army also received the help of its overseas branches. Commissioner James Hay, head of the Australian Salvation Army, was able to contribute £10,000 to the Emergency War Fund through his War Work Department.[81] The Canadians sent five Salvation Army chaplains to the front who helped to operate the canteens and huts and distribute comforts sent from home. The first American Salvationists arrived on 21 August 1917, and with permission from General J. Pershing, Commander-in-Chief of the American Expeditionary Force, set up in the training area of the 1st Division to raise the morale of the troops.[82] The women of this first contingent were called the 'Doughnut Girls'. Short of supplies but wanting to give the soldiers some home cooking, the women could only muster the ingredients for making doughnuts. Louise Holbrook worked with her husband on the front lines with the United States 28th Infantry. Under the fire of German guns she was partially buried when handing out coffee and doughnuts to the troops. She returned to work three weeks later, and was known 'by thousands for boosting morale in the sight of battle on the front lines'.[83]

In light of the benefit that the presence of these women had on the well-being and morale of the troops on the Western Front the Army was slow to utilise this added source of support, even though the work of women attached to the large voluntary associations had been sanctioned from the early months of the war. The Women's Legion was established by Lady Londonderry (1878–1959) in 1915 with the support of General Sir John Cowans, Quartermaster-General to the Forces. By February 1916, the contribution of the Women's Legion,[84] as cooks and waitresses to the army at home, was proving acceptable to the Army Council as a useful addition to the workforce of the army. Following a proposal by Brigadier General Auckland Geddes that a uniformed Women's Corps should be formed to work in the back areas of the Western Front, the Women's Army Auxiliary Corps was formed.[85] In January 1917, they were authorised to serve abroad to ease the manpower shortage and release men, working on the lines of communication, for frontline service. On the Western Front they took over many positions previously held by men, as clerks, drivers, and cooks.[86]

The first draft of WAACs, one officer and fourteen other ranks, was sent to the EFC officers' club at Abbeville. The second was sent to the EFC Rest House at Boulogne. From February 1917 onwards they were to be found in many of the canteens, cooking and serving, and driving motor transport for the EFC.[87] These canteens had been established on the lines of communication in February 1915 'to assist and ameliorate the condition of the soldiers on active service'.[88] Before this the military authorities had made no plans to supplement the basic diet of the troops with canteens in the field, and local tradesmen in France and Flanders were charging extortionate prices in shops and estaminets for small luxuries.[89] By December 1918, there were 295 canteens with approximately 700 WAACs augmenting the male personnel of the EFC.[90] With the arrival of the WAACs there was a marked difference in troop discipline and morale.[91] In recognition of their calm and efficient service in kitchens, clerking or working as gardeners in the war cemeteries, they were awarded the patronage of Queen Mary in April 1918.[92] The Corps also took the title of Queen Mary's Army Auxiliary Corps (QMAAC) when, that month, the Queen became the Commandant-in-Chief of the Corps.

The combination of care provided by the army, the voluntary services and the growing contribution made by women to the well-being of the soldier, brought aspects from home that transformed the Western Front into a micro-cosm of British and colonial society. Jaqueline de Vries wrote: 'Britain relied on its civilians as much as its soldiers to win the first "total war" in history.'[93]

Had the care and encouragement of the citizen army been absent in 1918, the collective effort of the BEF, Dominion and American forces would have been jeopardized. In the last hundred days of the war they were capable of pushing the demoralised German army into retreat and winning the war. These were not the actions of demoralised troops. It was the growth of the civil–military partnership and its attention to the welfare and morale of the fighting man, in providing the most important components of daily life, food and care, which made a significant contribution to their victory.

By the end of the war the army was predominantly composed of volunteers and conscripts, 'civilians in uniform', who had retained their individualism.[94] They were the product of civil life, not military tradition, and were less mal-leable as a result. They required a different form of encouragement to provide them with a unity of purpose and a determination to succeed. John Baynes pointed out that their welfare was the key to success: 'An effort such as was sustained over the four years of the First World War would not have been possible had the administrative requirements for maintaining morale not been adequately met.'[95]

Predominantly working class, they were 'imbued with a resilient optimism, built to resist and endure'.[96] Sustaining these qualities in the alienating con-ditions of trench warfare required a combination of military organisational expertise and an understanding of the benefits of civilian voluntary help. General Head Quarters made an enormous contribution to the welfare and morale of its citizen army through the complex logistical organisation of sup-plies,[97] but, without the additional care offered by the voluntary services, and the inclusion of women in this work, the morale of the citizen army would surely have faltered as it did with the allied French army in 1917. The com-bined skills of the civil–military partnership ensured that the spirit of the army was maintained and kept intact by replicating the civilian life of the soldier.[98]

The voluntary services of the YMCA, Church Army and Salvation Army, part of a long tradition of voluntary support for the army, brought a dimension of care not experienced before. The High Command's employment of the voluntary services where they were most needed showed an understanding of the special needs of the civilian army. Wherever the troops went, either in or out of the line, the support of one or more of these services was at hand to give physical and psychological support. Having these services near, in support of the fighting man, strengthened his resolve. They were a constant reminder of all things that were good from home. 'A cup of tea and a bun',[99] coming out of battle or before going in, provided a simple reassurance that someone cared for them. These services helped at all times to improve morale:[100] 'it is impossible not to be struck by the anxiety that is everywhere shown that nothing should be left undone that makes for the greater comfort and happiness and well-being of our soldiers'.[101]

It was not just a military engagement, divorced from everyday life; it was a conflict that brought the whole of society into the war. The proximity of the fighting on the Western Front turned the conflict into a people's war in which everyone contributed to the welfare of their men; their husbands, fathers, sons and brothers, fighting so close to the home front. Even from a great distance, the Dominion and American troops were given the support of comforts funds from home, and of their own voluntary services. The backing and 'solidarity of the home front' was a major contribution in sustaining morale on the Western Front.[102]

The work of women throughout the war on the Western Front and the continued support of those at home was a determining factor in the successful outcome of the war. Women were at the centre of providing for the fighting man and creating a link with home, which helped motivate and sustain the resolve of the army.

Notes

1. David Mitchell, *Women on the Warpath*, London: Jonathan Cape, 1966, p. xv.
2. Lyn Macdonald, *Roses of No Man's Land*, Harmondsworth: Penguin, 1993.
3. Vera Brittain, *Testament of Youth*, London: Victor Gollancz, 1993.
4. Charles Messenger, *Call-to-Arms: The British Army 1914–1918*, London: Cassell Military Paperbacks, 2006, p. 244.
5. Ibid.
6. Harold Harvey, *A Soldier's Sketches under Fire*, London: Biblio Bazaar, 2008.
7. Imperial War Museum (IWM), Sound Archive (SA), No. 511, Alice Christobel Remington.
8. Harvey, *Soldier's Sketches*. Words used in the dedication of his book to Lady Angela Forbes.
9. Ibid. Harvey of the Royal Fusiliers, was invalided out of the army, May 1915.
10. Mitchell, *Warpath*, pp. 204–5.
11. Ibid., p. 206

12. IWM, Department of Books (DB), 3884, George A. Birmingham (pseudonym for J. O. Hannay), *A Padre in France*, London: Hodder & Stoughton, n.d., p. 123.

13. IWM, DB, 15035, Charles W. Bishop, *The Canadian YMCA in the Great War*, Canada: National Council of Young Men's Christian Associations of Canada, 1924, p. 89.

14. Ian Beckett, 'A Nation in Arms', in Ian F. W. Beckett and Keith Simpson, eds., *A Nation in Arms: A Social Study of the British Army in the First World War*, Manchester: Manchester University Press, 1985, pp. 14, 15.

15. IWM, DB, 5082, J. C. V. D. Durell, *Whizzbangs and Woodbines: Tales of Work and Play on the Western Front*, London: Hodder & Stoughton, 1918, p. 36.

16. Ibid., p. 36

17. Sir Arthur K. Yapp, *The Romance of the Red Triangle*, London: Hodder & Stoughton, 1918, p. 64; and Edgar Rowan, *Wilson Carlile and the Church Army*, London: Church Army Bookroom, 1928, pp. 186, 187.

18. Salvation Army International Heritage Centre Archives (SAIHCA), Adjutant Mary Murray, *The Salvation Army at Work in the Boer War*, London: Salvation Army, International Headquarters, 1901, p. 109; and Arthur E. Copping, *Souls in Khaki*, London: Hodder & Stoughton, 1918, p. 4.

19. Yapp, *Red Triangle*, p. 64.

20. Sir Arthur Yapp, *The Times*, 19 May 1919, repr. in *The Times*, 'On This Day', 19 May 2005.

21. IWM, SA, No. 10168, Donald Price.

22. Yapp, *Red Triangle*, p. 67, quoting a remark made by an unnamed Base Commandant.

23. See Rowan, *Carlile*, William Booth at www.oxforddnb.com/view/article/31968 also, University of Birmingham Special Collections (UBSC), YMCA, E21 (vol. V, 1921), War Emergency Work of the Association, p. 10.

24. In conversation with Michael Snape, Dept. of Modern History, University of Birmingham, 21 September 2009.

25. The three organisations have been chosen as they were the most influential. There were others, for example, the Catholic Club, the Catholic Women's League (amalgamated in 1918), and the Scottish Churches Huts, www.1914-1918.net/ymca.htm.

26. IWM, SA, No. 544, Charles Robert Quinnell.

27. Michael Snape, *The Back Parts of War: The YMCA Memoirs and Letters of Barclay Baron, 1915–1919*, Woodbridge, Suffolk: Boydell Press for the Church of England Record Society, 2009, p. 17.

28. See Jaqueline de Vries, 'Women's Voluntary Organisations in World War I', in Women at Work Collection of the Imperial War Museum.

29. www.1911encyclopedia.org/Women's War - Work.

30. Yapp, *Red Triangle*, pp. 44–5.

31. Captain J. C. Dunn, *The War the Infantry Knew 1914–1918*, London: Abacus, 1999, p. 96.

32. De Vries, Women at Work Collection.

33. Dunn, *The War the Infantry Knew*, p. 96.

34. Messenger, *Call-to-Arms*, p. 469.

35. Dunn, *The War the Infantry Knew*, p. 96.

36. The Institution of Royal Engineers, 'The Work of the Royal Engineers in the European War, 1914–1919: Postal Section Part IV, Section 4, Army Postal Services, Royal Engineers Special Reserve (Postal Section)', *Royal Engineers Journal*, 30/3 (September 1919), p. 115. The increase in letters was 90 per cent.

37. John Terraine, ed., *General Jack's Diary: War on the Western Front 1914–1918*, London: Cassell & Co., 2000, p. 89.

38. The boxes contained tobacco and a pipe, Terraine, *General Jack*, p. 89, although according to Messenger, *Call-to-Arms*, p.469, they contained a packet of cigarettes, an ounce of pipe tobacco and a photograph of Princess Mary; non-smokers received a writing case.

39. The National Archives (TNA), WO 95/25, Adjutant General (AG), General Head-quarters, Diary, 1914–1918, 10 December 1914.

40. Malcolm Brown and Shirley Seaton, *Christmas Truce: The Western Front, December 1914*, London: Pan Books, 2001, p. 111.

41. Captain Bryden McKinnel, letter written from the front, Boxing Day, 1914, quoted in Lyn Macdonald, *1914–1918: Voices and Images of the Great War*, London: Penguin Books, 1991, p. 50.

42. SAIHCA, *All the World*, pp. 185, 187, 188.

43. Sir Arthur Yapp, 1869–1936, Secretary of the National Council of YMCAs. The Red Triangle, symbolising spirit, mind and body, was introduced by Yapp in 1914.

44. Major D. Chapman-Huston and Major Owen Rutter, *General Sir John Cowans GCB, GCMG: Quartermaster-General of the Great War*, vol. II, London: Hutchinson & Co., 1924, p. 105.

45. Snape, *Back Parts*, p. 18.

46. UBSC, YMCA archive, E21, *YMCA Yearbook*, 5 (1921), 'War Emergency Work of the Assoc.', p. 5.

47. Snape, *Back Parts*, pp. 47, 57; Haig and Plumer were the first to employ the YMCA in the First and Second Army areas in July and August 1915, respectively.

48. Snape, *Back Parts*, pp. 32, 47, 57.

49. www.1911encyclopedia.org/Women's War - Work.

50. Lena Ashwell, extract from 'Modern Troubadours'. in Joyce Marlow, ed., *The Virago Book of Women and the Great War*, London: Virago Press, 1999, pp. 118–19.

51. J. E. Edmonds, *Official History of the War, Military Operations France and Belgium 1916*, vol. 1, London: Macmillan & Co., 1932, n. 1, p. 139.

52. Snape, *Back Parts*, p. 32.

53. UBSC, YMCA archive, E21, 'War Emergency Work', p. 5.

54. IWM, DB, 1110, *The Church Army 'Blue Book': The Report of the work of The Church Army among the Criminal, Outcast, Careless and Distressed. During the Twenty-one months – 1st October, 1913, to 30th June, 1915; and of the Special War-Work of the Society during the first year of the Great War*, Oxford: Church Army Press, 1915, p. 15. The hospital was later closed, and still under the administration of Lady Bagot was moved to Dungavel, near Glasgow, to attend the sick and wounded of the Navy. Rowan, *Carlile*, p. 190.

55. Edmonds, *Official History, 1916*, vol. I, p. 141.

56. Rowan, *Carlisle*, pp. 186, 187.

57. Ibid., p. 186.

58. Ibid., pp. 188, 189.

59. *Church Army 'Blue Book'*, p. 19.

60. Edmonds, *Official History, 1916*, vol. I, p. 141.

61. Murray, *Boer War*, pp. vi., vii.

62. SAIHCA, 'Glory of Beginnings', p. 1, Salvation Army lecture leaflet, anonymous.

63. F.A. McKenzie, *Serving the King's Men: How the Salvation Army is Helping the Nation*, London: Hodder & Stoughton, 1918, p. 17.

64. Mitchell, *Warpath*, p. 14.
65. SAIHCA, *Under the Colours*, 22/11 (November 1918).
66. McKenzie, *King's Men*, pp. 34, 35.
67. SAIHCA, *All the World*, April 1915, p. 205.
68. IWM, SA, No. 655, Thomas Eustace Russell. Russell was a volunteer canteen assist. with the Salvation Army.
69. SAIHCA, 'Glory of Beginnings', pp. 9, 10.
70. McKenzie, *King's Men*, p. 20.
71. SAIHCA, *All the World*, April 1915, p. 361.
72. IWM, Dept of Documents (DD), Jones, P246, p. 170.
73. *Royal Engineers Journal*, 30/3 (September 1919), pp. 114–27.
74. Beckett and Simpson, *Nation in Arms*; Jay Winter, 'Army and Society: The Demographic Context', p. 196.
75. John Baynes, *Morale: A Study of Men and Courage*, London: Cassell & Co., 1967, pp. 155–6.
76. Remington, IWM, SA, No. 511.
77. Colonel W. N. Nicholson, *Behind the Lines*, London: Jonathan Cape, 1939, pp. 182, 250.
78. Major F. W. Bewsher, *The History of the Fifty First (Highland) Division 1914–1918*, Uckfield, East Sussex: Naval & Military Press, n.d., p. 269.
79. John Ewing, *The History of the Ninth (Scottish) Division 1914–1918*, London: John Murray, 1921, repr. by the Naval & Military Press, Appendix viii, p. 416.
80. Yapp, *Red Triangle*, pp. 30, 31, 41.
81. SAIHCA, Lieutenant Colonel Bond, *The Army that Went with the Boys: A Record of Salvation Army Work with the Australian Imperial Force*, Melbourne: National Headquarters, 1919, p. 7.
82. Evangeline Booth and Grace Livingston Hill, *The War Romance of the Salvation Army*, London: J. T. Lippincot & Co., 1919, pp. 23, 27.
83. *Doughnut Girls*, pp. 1, 3, ww1.salvationarmy.org.ukuki/www_uki_ihc.nsf.
84. Chapman-Huston and Rutter, *Cowans*, vol. II, p. 84.
85. Mitchell, *Warpath*, p. 222.
86. Beckett and Simpson, *Nation in Arms*, p. 15.
87. Captain E. Vredenburg, *West and East with the Expeditionary Force Canteens*, London: Raphael Tuck & Sons Ltd, 1919, pp. 34, 42.
88. TNA, WO 32/5087, 'Institutes for Troops quartered or employed on the Lines of Communication', 10 December 1914. For formation of the EFC, see Edmonds, *Official History, 1916*, vol. I, pp. 132–4, John Fortescue, *Canteens in the British Army*, Cambridge: Cambridge: University Press, 1928, pp. 46, 47, and Vredenburg, *West and East*, pp. 6–8.
89. Fortescue, *Canteens*, p. 45.
90. Edmonds, *Official History, 1916*, vol. I, p. 134.
91. Durell, *Whizzbangs*, p. 36.
92. Mitchell, *Warpath*, p. 227.
93. De Vries, Women at Work Collection.
94. IWM, DB, 91/11, J. G. Fuller, *Troop Morale and Popular Culture in the British and Dominion Armies 1914–1918*, Oxford: Clarendon Press, 1990, p. 33
95. Baynes, *Morale*, p. 101.

96. John Bourne, 'The British Working Man in Arms', in Hugh Cecil and Peter H. Liddle, eds., *Facing Armageddon: The First World War Experienced*, Barnsley: Pen & Sword Select, 2003, pp. 341, 350.
97. J. M. Bourne, *Britain and the Great War 1914–1918*, London: Edward Arnold, 1994, pp. 222, 223.
98. Bourne, 'Working Man in Arms', p. 349.
99. UBSC, YMCA, *Y.M.': The British Empire Y.M.C.A. Weekly*, 2/103 (December 1916), p. 1245, a popular refrain of the troops at the time, sung to the tune of 'Two Lovely Black Eyes'.
100. Bernard Livermore, *Long 'Un: A Damn Bad Soldier*, Bartley, West Yorkshire, 1974, p. 46, quoted in Richard Holmes, *Tommy: The British Soldier on the Western Front 1914–1918*, London: HarperCollins Publishing, 2004, p. 341.
101. Durell, *Whizzbangs*, p. 66.
102. Gary Sheffield, 'The Combat Soldier and his Officer' (lecture), Centre for First World War Studies, University of Birmingham, 24 January 2009.

Select Bibliography

Beckett, F. W., and Simpson, Keith, eds., *A Nation in Arms: A Social Study of the British Army in the First World War*, Manchester: Manchester University Press, 1985.

Chapman-Huston, D., and Rutter, Owen, *General Sir John Cowans GCB, GCMG: Quartermaster-General of the Great War*, vol. II, London: Hutchinson & Co., 1924.

Fortescue, John, *Canteens in the British Army*, Cambridge: Cambridge University Press, 1928.

Messenger, Charles, *Call-to-Arms: The British Army 1914–1918*, London: Cassell Military Paperbacks, 2006.

Mitchell, David, *Women on the Warpath*, London: Jonathan Cape, 1966.

Snape, Michael, *The Back Parts of War: The YMCA and the Letters of Barclay Baron, 1915–1919*, London: Boydell Press for the Church of England Record Society, 2009.

Vredenburg, E., *West and East with the British Expeditionary Force Canteens*, London: Raphael Tuck & Sons Ltd, 1919.

Yapp, Arthur K., *The Romance of the Red Triangle*, London: Hodder & Stoughton, 1918.

THE SECOND WORLD WAR

Chapter 4

Working, Queueing and Worrying
British Women and the Home Front, 1939–1945

Mark Connelly

The Second World War was the first in which British women had taken part as enfranchised citizens on a mass scale, and the twentieth century's crucial test of citizenship has been service to the state in time of war. Due to the demands of war, women moved into nearly all types of employment and uniformed service. Historians have debated for many years the long-term significance of this movement into previously male-dominated spheres. Professor Arthur Marwick, an exponent of the idea that war is an engine for social change, believed war work brought women out of their homes and into a wider world, which may have been temporary for some, but established a significant precedent meaning that the post-war world could never return to its 1939 standards.[1] A more subtle argument has been advanced by Penny Summerfield. She has shown that the Second World War forced the complementary forces of patriarchy and capitalism, prevalent in the powers of the state, to face up to the problem of labour supply which demanded female workers. She contends that in trying to achieve a solution suitable to both capitalism and patriarchy the State often severely constrained the role of women and did little to alter the unequal position of women within British society.[2] This chapter will explore some of the main themes in the lives of British women on the home front in the light of these historiographical ideas.

Facing a significant shortage of labour, Britain went further than any combatant nation in the Second World War by gradually conscripting and enlisting nearly all women. Women were enlisted through various acts: the National Service Act 1941, the Registration of Employment Order of the same year and the Employment of Women Order 1942. It created a situation whereby all women aged between 18 and 40 could be conscripted by the government. In turn, this had a significant effect on the type of women in employment; by 1943 47 per cent of the female industrial force was married, and one-third had children.[3] Absenteeism was high, which can only partly be explained by domestic duties and problems. There was the constant issue of prejudicial and intolerant attitudes from the male workforce, poor pay and lack of facilities. It became increasingly difficult to persuade women to serve their country by working in factories, most wanted non-industrial jobs. The problem was exacerbated by the Ministry of Labour's insensitive approach to female demands and needs, with the view expressed that women wanted to take simple options, even going as far as implying that many would rather be prostitutes for the sheer profit margins than patriotically support the nation.[4]

This situation created a desperate desire to produce a positive image of women in war. The Ministry of Information therefore enthusiastically supported the successful film production duo Frank Launder and Sidney Gilliat in their plans to make a film celebrating women in the factories. *Millions Like Us*, released in 1943, emphasised the importance of female labour to the war effort. Horrified by the thought of factory work, the young, naive heroine, Celia (Patricia Roc), is told by another woman, 'There's nothing to be afraid of in a factory. Mr Bevin needs another million women, and I don't think we should disappoint him at a time like this. The men at the front need tanks, guns and planes. You can help your country just as much in an overall as you can in a uniform these days.' Celia gradually gains confidence and begins to like her job making aircraft components. She finds that living in a government hostel is not so bad and makes friends with a variety of women from different backgrounds. But the film skilfully avoids the trap of patronising its audience by being too upbeat; the downside is also explored. The foreman tells them, 'Now you'd better understand there's not much glamour in a machine shop', and Celia's life is touched by tragedy as she marries a young air-gunner who is soon killed in action. Here was the gritty reality of war: a reality that was not denied by the government because it was impossible to avoid the fact of casualties, but the way this experience was interpreted could be shaped in particular ways. Thus the message of the film is that Celia's tragedy can only be palliated by the victory of the just.

Another powerful image of women's war work was produced by the artist Dame Laura Knight. In 1943, she was commissioned by the War Artists Advisory Committee to paint the heroine of the factories. Ruby Loftus was the first woman to be employed on the highly skilled work of screwing the breech ring of the Bofors gun. Considered to be the prerogative of a man with a nine-year apprenticeship behind him at the Royal Ordnance Factory, Loftus had gained the skill by the age of 21 after two years' training. Knight painted Loftus at her lathe and produced a masterpiece of heroic realism, which (unwittingly?) reflected the pro-Soviet celebration and idealisation of the working class so prevalent in British wartime culture. Hair tied up in a turban, clad in a blue overall, Loftus bends over her lathe with a look of concentration and experience. In the background other women are involved in similar tasks. Produced in postcard form, this very English Stakhanovite was distributed to factories across Britain.[5]

Evidence of a more mundane reality is certainly not hard to find. Men on the home front rarely readjusted their role to help accommodate women who had taken on war work. Most women continued to play domestic roles, caring for children and running the household. In wartime this often meant queuing for hours, mending clothes long after they would normally have been discarded and trying to ensure childcare during work hours. Even women without a job would have found their traditional role a lot harder to perform in the difficult circumstances imposed by war.

The demands of war industry which pulled in more and more female labour created a vast army of women factory workers often burdened by dull jobs and long hours. Cinema was the great escapist pastime for women beset by wartime responsibilities and burdens.[6] These women longed for colour, excitement and glamour in their precious leisure hours and one studio in particular, Gainsborough, gave it to them. Most critics loathed Gainsborough melodramas with their bodice-ripping, slashed-shirt romping. Slammed for their shoddy history and unashamed excesses, Gainsborough's films were, however, just what hundreds of thousands of British women wanted.

The Wicked Lady (1945), Gainsborough's most successful film, starred Margaret Lockwood and James Mason as a pair of outlaw-lovers. Set in a heavily stylised seventeenth century, *The Wicked Lady* shows the past to be a place of romance, intrigue, dashing men and sensual pleasure. Margaret Lockwood is attracted to robbery after becoming bored of her dull husband and life in the countryside. Revelling in the excitement of highway robbery, she ends up paying for her bad ways by dying alone and in agony. By contrast, the good girl whom she has wronged (Patricia Roc) gains the love of a decent and honourable man who will make her very happy. But the moral lesson of *The Wicked Lady* is actually far more ambiguous. Lockwood's character may get her comeuppance, but her life is so much more glamorous, sexy and rewarding than Roc's that the benefits of virtue appear stultifying. Sue Harper has shown how young women and adolescent girls in particular idolised Lockwood's image and aspired to copy it. She quotes a Birmingham survey in which 67 per cent of schoolgirls admitted imitating Lockwood, 'thus endorsing Ted Black's instinct that she had "something with which every girl in the suburbs could identify herself".[7]

As well as films that hinted at sexual intrigue, women liked romances. Some of the most financially successful films of the war years were the Hollywood-made British melodramas such as *Waterloo Bridge* (1940), *Mrs Miniver* (1942), *Random Harvest* (1942) and *The White Cliffs of Dover* (1944). All four films were produced by Sidney Franklin for MGM, and each of them 'centres on the pain and anxiety caused by wartime separation or loss, and each offers a strong, maternal and caring woman as a source of safety and serenity amid the heartaches of war'.[8]

It is a rural, idyllic, hierarchical village England that is celebrated and perpetuated in these MGM films. Ironically, the harmony of this strictly class based England, which was so popular at the British box office, was facing intense pressure due to the realities of war. *Random Harvest* is typical of this mini genre: men and women find love and contentment, often across class barriers, and, despite the odd fractious moment, British society retains its cohesion due to deeply entrenched values of respect, humility, duty and service. A box-office smash in Britain, *Random Harvest* was the most successful film of 1943, revealing a public eager to soak up tear-jerkers.

Mrs Miniver was the biggest financial success of them all. The film portrays the middle class Minivers as representative of the nation and its core values. Mrs Miniver is the ideal matriarch, caring for her little children during the horrors of an air-raid, worrying about her hot-headed son, Vin, a Royal Air Force (RAF) pilot, and gradually pacifying the rather cantankerous Lady Belton, who worries that her granddaughter is lowering herself by falling for Vin Miniver. *Mrs Miniver* was an extraordinary box office success in both the USA and Britain and topped the British box office charts in 1942. The British people, women in particular, clearly wanted melodrama in their drab, hard-pressed, wartime lives. This was melodrama of a particular nature as it combined elements of the wartime reality with fantasy and so provided 'realistic escapism'.

Female tastes in films were therefore a little ambiguous, 'decent' romance was enjoyed; but so was the presentation of more illicit relationships. To what extent was the content of cinematic interpretations a reflection of wartime realities? John Costello's work has shown how the conditions of war created a situation in which attitudes towards sex altered.[9] Male and female lives were uprooted and transplanted to new environments or routines and in doing so forced a re-evaluation of morals. For many out of sight meant out of mind, and infidelity lost its power to shame and rein in desires. Complex emotional forces were unleashed by the war: that of heightened emotion due to fear and feelings of instability due to the unpredictability of events. It provoked a 'do as you please for tomorrow you may die' attitude. At the same time, the war had its own monotonous all-pervasiveness that provoked a desire for emotional release and excitement.

Inevitably sexual morals became a matter of concern to many and those of servicewomen were thought to be the most lax. The issue was intimately connected with concerns over the drop in legitimate births, the concomitant rise in illegitimacy and the growing use of contraceptives. Between 1940 and 1945, there were 255,000 births, out of which around 102,000 were illegitimate, representing a huge increase on the pre-war illegitimacy rate.[10] But it was the increased numbers of venereal disease sufferers that caused most morbid interest and debate. Obsessed with efficiency, the army was convinced VD would undermine its abilities as a fighting force, and was the continuation of a debate given much time during the Great War. But unlike the Great War responses, the government broke all taboos about the subject and began a full campaign of public education. In the autumn of 1942, the Ministry of Health began to publicise the problem of sexually transmitted diseases and placed a series of adverts in the press giving information and advice. Lurid posters were produced warning men and women against careless attitudes towards sexual hygiene *and* moral probity.[11] Men appear to have lost their shame about this subject quite quickly and sought medical attention earlier, thus lowering male VD rates noticeably. However, women probably still felt shame at contracting the disease and female VD rates remained high.[12]

Angus Calder referred to mid-war Britain as 'the India-rubber island', which contorted itself to meet the demands of total war. By 1944, the 'rubber island' had made room for 1,421,000 allied, dominion and colonial troops. The arrival of such vast numbers from an equally wide variety of countries and backgrounds increased the opportunities for both platonic and physical relationships. Such relationships often caused deep resentment in British men, but became an important part of life on the Home Front.

Early in the war Polish pilots were often identified as the charming lotharios sweeping British women off their feet. But it was Americans who became the most exotic prize, much envied by their less well paid and clothed British comrades in arms. Often considered to be 'enjoying the life of Riley' by British servicemen fighting 'the real war', it wasn't long before the Americans gained the description most Britons still recognise, 'over-sexed, over-paid and over here'. The arrival of large numbers of GIs created a stir in communities across Britain for they brought with them items that were severely rationed. Americans had sweets, cigarettes, butter and a host of other commodities in profusion. When combined with uniforms that made them look like officers and accents heard only at the cinema, it was hardly surprising that many women in drab wartime Britain started relationships with American soldiers. At the end of the war around 80,000 GI brides left the UK for the USA.[13] Strenuous efforts were made during the war to maintain the image of Americans as decent allies who had no intention of 'stealing' British women. What went unnoticed is that many GIs were in fact sober, shy, lonely young men who led quiet lives while encamped in Britain. Pamela Winfield, who first met Americans as a 17 year old at a Wimbledon town hall dance, recalled that 'in fact we found out that the majority were small-town boys, straight out of high school, and church-going. The vision that they were all wild and woolly was not fair.'[14]

This aspect of life with GIs was reflected perfectly in the film *Daily Mail* readers voted their favourite of the war. *The Way to the Stars* (1945) was a story of Anglo-American cooperation tinted with a hint of romance. An excellently crafted film with a touching Terence Rattigan script, it tells the story of an RAF airfield taken over by the USAAF. The remaining RAF personnel gradually come to terms with the boisterous Americans and both mix in the bar of the local hotel. Johnny Hollis (Douglass Montgomery), an American pilot, strikes up a friendship with the hotel owner, Toddy (Rosamund John). Missing his wife and children, Johnny finds Toddy to be an understanding friend. She is a widowed mother, having lost her husband, an RAF pilot killed in a raid over Germany. Drawn closer together, the two teeter on the verge of a romance but decency and mutual respect prevail and the moment passes. At the end of the film, Johnny reveals the new union of the great English-speaking family by sacrificing himself. Returning from a mission in a crippled bomber still carrying part of its load, he refuses to save his own life by bailing out and allowing the bomber to crash somewhere near the village, possibly endangering the villagers. Instead he attempts to land the bomber at the airfield, knowing and accepting the vast risk involved. Johnny dies that others might live. During the war, therefore, officially approved views of American servicemen were positive ones. 'Americans in British wartime features are "over here",' as Sue Harper has noted, 'but they are neither overpaid nor oversexed.'[15]

Attitudes towards sex did change during the war. Sue Harper implies a degree of liberation, mentioning the increased use of cosmetics particularly as a reaction to dull, Utility brand clothing.[16] However, it was liberation of a limited sort. For Lucy Noakes, the stream of advice on how to look good in uniform, how to get the best out of cosmetics and maintain good looks is something that reinforced traditional gender roles.[17] It is also very clear that the blame for spreading VD was placed on women, with men's behaviour hardly ever mentioned. So-called 'good time girls' were thought to be even more responsible for the increased numbers of those suffering STDs than prostitutes, and girls of up to 23 years of age could be sent to Borstal for sexual laxity.[18]

Women were under constant exhortation to remain chaste and wait for their husband or fiancé to return from the war. Women's magazines warned against infidelity; Constance Holt, the wartime editor of *Woman's Own*, recalled its clear and uncompromising advice:

> 'You can't do this to your husband, or even your fiancé, while he is away fighting for his country. You must break it up or wait until after the war and resolve it. You must not see this man'. We'd go as far as that – that was the advice we gave them.[19]

As Lucy Noakes has argued, such attitudes revealed the buttressing of traditional gender roles rather than their realignment or redefinition. Two, opposed forces were therefore at work, one liberating and new, the other traditional. In the Second World War the state encouraged women to take on men's roles, but at the same time reassured men in uniform that their women were ready to play doting wives and mothers as soon as they returned. Balancing these two female roles and ensuring that women were ready to do both was a tricky proposition. Graham Dawson has developed a complementary position with regards to male behaviour, stating that the image of the soldier hero provides men with a constant model of masculinity, shaping their perceptions and actions, which remains impervious to – and a defence against – changes in the economy and its concomitant reordering of working lives and roles.[20] Thus, men and women were expected to fulfil their traditional gender roles in the Second World War. 'Women and men, while fulfilling their roles as useful wartime citizens, were expected to do so within existing constructions of femininity and masculinity.'[21] Performing men's jobs did not necessarily emancipate women because their essential relationship with, and relative position to, men did not change.

A good measure of how far values were *perceived* to have changed came in July 1945, when the Archbishop of Canterbury used a sermon to urge a rejection of 'wartime morality', which was warmly welcomed and supported by other ecclesiastics.[22] Far from facing a wave of protest from people happy in the land of lotus eating, the majority of British people probably agreed with this stance. A return to normality was wanted by all, but that was hardly possible. Britain was financially and economically ruined in 1945, rationing would have to continue and become even more stringent, demobilisation would take a long time, and the fruits of victory would not be tasted for many years. However, most women were prepared to give normality a try, starting with their exodus from the work place. The vast majority of women re-embraced their roles as wives and mothers with remarkably little fuss. And who can blame them? Overworked, underpaid, forced to labour in often appalling conditions, many women wanted the security and relief of their former roles.

The home – and all its myriad demands – still looked better than the workplace, especially if the main breadwinner was coming home and eager to reassert his position after so many years of disorientation.

Nothing represents this desire for a return to normality better than that most English of films, *Brief Encounter*, screened 1945, the same year as *The Wicked Lady*. Now seen as a quintessential reflection of British culture, it was far from an unqualified success on first release, with many finding the film either too painful in its treatment of adultery or lacking credibility in its retreat from it.[23] *Brief Encounter* is the story of a middle-class woman, played by Celia Johnson, who escapes from her humdrum life as wife and mother to find romance with a charming doctor, played by Trevor Howard, but overcome by a sense of guilt and remorse, she puts duty first and breaks off her affair regardless of the pain it causes. The film, written by Noel Coward and directed by David Lean, called British women back to their 1939 selves. It was a demand for the restoration of normality after the years of upheaval, but it was couched in terms of forgiveness and acceptance. *Brief Encounter* therefore represents the closing of a chapter in British women's history.

British women played a vital role in the Second World War and that included those not formally in the uniformed services. In a total war of *materialschlact* the ability to outproduce the enemy was vital and that meant victory on the factory front. British women responded to the call magnificently. It was by no means an easy transition for those unused to the conditions and culture of the factory, but it was achieved. Alongside these toils, women often continued their domestic lives unaltered, being mothers and primary carers. Husbands, brothers and fiancés were often absent, leaving women to carry the domestic load utterly alone. This created a mixed culture in which many women were given the chance to do things well outside their normal experiences while also maintaining their traditional roles. The stresses created by this particular existence were often alleviated by simple escapism such as that provided by the cinema, and occasionally by friendships, both physical and platonic, with men they might never have come into contact with had it not been for the war. In 1945, women were largely forced back to their pre-war roles and many would argue that this has obscured a popular understanding of the enormous contribution made by women on the home front.

Notes

1. See, for example, Arthur Marwick, *British Society since 1945*, London: Allen Lane, 1982, pp. 67–71.
2. Penny Summerfield, *Women Workers in the Second World War*, London: Routledge, 1984. See also Penny Summerfield, *Reconstructing Women's Wartime Lives: Discourse and Subjectivity in Oral Histories of the Second World War*, Manchester: Manchester University Press, 1998.

3. Sue Harper ,'The Representation of Women in British Feature Films, 1939–1945', in Philip M. Taylor, eds., *British Cinema and the Second World War*, London: Macmillan, 1988, pp. 168–202.

4. Harper, 'Representation', p. 172.

5. Caroline Fox, *Dame Laura Knight*, Oxford: Phaidon, 1988, p. 102.

6. For the role of cinema in wartime see James Chapman, *The British at War: Cinema, State and Propaganda, 1939–1945*, London: I. B. Tauris, 1998; Anthony Aldgate and Jeffrey Richards, *Britain Can Take it: British Cinema and the Second World War*, Oxford: Blackwell, 1986.

7. Harper, 'Representation', p 194. See also Sue Harper, *Picturing the Past, the Rise and Fall of the British Costume Film*, London: BFI, 1994.

8. H. M. Glancy, *When Hollywood Loved Britain: The Hollywood 'British' Films, 1939–1945*, Manchester: Manchester University Press, 1999, p. 90.

9. See John Costello, *Love, Sex and War: Changing Values 1939–1945*, London: Collins, 1985.

10. Angus Calder, *The People's War*, London: Jonathan Cape, 1969, p. 312.

11. See Antonia Lant, *Blackout: Reinventing Women for British Wartime Cinema*, Princeton: Princeton University Press, 1991, pp. 75–9, and H. L. Smith, *Britain and the Second World War: A Social History*, Manchester: Manchester University Press, 1986, pp. 32–6.

12. Lant, *Blackout*, p. 313.

13. Calder, *People's War*, p 312.

14. Quoted in Peter Lewis, *A People's War*, London: Methuen, 1986, pp. 207–8.

15. Harper, 'Representation', p. 183.

16. Ibid., p. 177.

17. Lucy Noakes, *War and the British: Gender, Memory and National Identity, 1939–1991*, London: I. B. Tauris, 1998, pp. 64–74.

18. Harper, 'Representation', p. 179.

19. Lewis, *A People's War*, p. 152.

20. Graham Dawson, *Soldier Heroes: British Adventure, Empire and the Imagining of Masculinities*, London: Routledge, 1994, pp. 282–92.

21. Noakes, *War and the British*, p. 51.

22. Harper, 'Representation', p. 177.

23. Richard Dyer, *Brief Encounter*, London: BFI, 1993, pp. 4–7.

Select Bibliography

Aldgate, Anthony, and Richards, Jeffrey, *Britain Can Take it: British cinema and the Second World War*, Oxford: Blackwell, 1989.

Addison, Paul, *The Road to 1945: British Politics and the Second World War*, London: Jonathan Cape, 1975.

Calder, Angus, *The People's War, Britain 1939–1945*, London: Jonathan Cape, 1969.

Calder, Angus, *The Myth of the Blitz*, London: Jonathan Cape, 1991.

Summerfield, Penny, *Women Workers in the Second World War: Production and Patriarchy in Conflict*, Beckenham: Croom Helm, 1984.

Chapter 5

Flight through the Retreating Allied Armies

Non-Combatants and the Blitzkreig of 1940

George Bailey

Dedicated to my mother,
Tatiana (Saczkowska) Bailey,
28 September 1917–14 June 2009

The Refugee Path to Antwerp

During the 1930s the German military strategists will have recognized that the Schlieffen Plan, the German General Staff's strategic plan for victory in a war where it might find itself fighting on two fronts, France to the west and Russia to the east, implemented in August of 1914, came close to the double envelopment of the French and British forces. But for their weakening of the right wing by sending two corps to East Prussia to help drive back the Tsarist armies and the inward wheel to shorten their line of advance they would not have faced the 'Miracle of the Marne', the First World War battle fought between 5 and 12 September 1914, resulting in an an Allied victory against the German Army. Thus in May 1940, the Germans implemented a similar plan, and once again, Belgium faced overwhelming odds as the Blitzkreig began.

In Antwerp, the knowledge of the defeat of Poland the previous autumn, meant the Saczkowski family were well aware of the threat. Nikolai Saczkowski had been the Engineer Captain (First Class) of the Russian mine-laying cruiser *Yenisei* (named after the Siberian river described by the Russian writer, Anton Chekhov as 'a mighty, raging Hercules, who does not know what to do with his power and youth'). The *Yenisei* carried out a successful volunteer mission to slip into the German port of Danzig in the Baltic in May of 1915, and thereby to delay the passage of the German capital ships in order to prevent their leaving port to contribute to the German combined sea and land offensive towards St Petersburg. On their way back to Kronstadt the *Yenisei* was spotted whilst hugging the shoreline off Estonia, and was torpedoed by U–26 on the 23 May. Nikolai was the only officer to survive, though badly wounded, together with eight ratings.

His daughter, Tatiana, was born on 24 September 1917, as a sister to Nikolai junior. She was born in Yekaterinoslav in the Ukraine, where Captain Saczkowski had been sent by the Admiralty to take charge of all the factories manufacturing armaments for the Russian Imperial Navy, he no longer being fit for active service. After the downfall of the Tsar, he fought with the White Army, and later with the Polish Army, in its successful campaign to gain Poland's independence from Russia. Meanwhile his family remained in Yekaterinoslav. The Red Army took control of the town. The signing of the armistice between the Bolshevik and Polish Governments provided Marya Saczkowska with the status of a Polish citizen, so she and their children managed to join him at Modlin, near Warsaw. Unfortunately, as a former officer in the Russian Navy, despite being appointed to be in charge of the repair of engines for the Polish fleet, at the Navy Factory in Modlin, he faced great jealousy and he resigned in 1922, to project manage the construction of two timber saw mills in Suojarvi near Wiborg, then part of Finland. Though his father Jozef was Polish, his mother Matilda was Swedish, and they owned an estate in Honkaniemi, formerly part of Finnish Karelia.

As the East no longer had anything to offer him he turned to the West. Leaving his family in Poland, he was able to move to Antwerp in 1923, where he became employed first by the Ford Motor Company, and then from 1926, by General Motors Continental. His wife Marya and their two children joined him, and the family settled into a professional lifestyle as Nikolai eventually rose to become the Assistant Manager of the design department at the car plant. His son Nikolai trained as an engineer, whilst Tatiana studied to become a portrait painter.[1] Their mother, when in Russia before the First World War, had resigned herself to becoming an 'old maid' in the family home at 76 Ligovsky Prospect, St Petersburg, until she was swept off her feet by the dynamic naval captain. After problems with getting married in the Russian Orthodox Church because Nikolai was a divorcee, Marya temporarily joined his Swedish Lutheran Church. After the marriage on 22 December 1913, she returned to the Orthodox Church. Their son was born on 27 March 1915, and their daughter eighteen months later. Having given birth to her children in her late thirties, by 1940, Marya was partially sighted, partially crippled and aged 61.

During his days on the *Yenisei*, Nikolai had become friendly with the British submariner, Max Horton, who with Commander Noel Lawrence was greatly feared by the German Baltic fleet. So when Poland fell in 1939, Nikolai decided to sail to England and see whether the by now Vice Admiral Sir Max Horton could find him a post on a British ship despite being his being aged 61. Also as Polish subjects Nikolai and his son were expected to fight for the Polish Government in Exile. With American companies pulling out of Europe and closing plants, he told General Motors Continental about his need to reach England. On 9 March 1940, the company generously paid him off with a year's salary in American dollars because of the 'present international situation'. His son, Nikolai junior, had reached England four months earlier on 8 November 1939, and enlisted in the Royal Air Force.

Told by the British Consulate on 10 May that he had permission to go to England but that the next ship would soon leave, Nikolai returned home to pack a suitcase. His wife, Marya, was out shopping and he was unable to bid her farewell, and he walked to the docks at the port of Antwerp with his young daughter Tatiana, now aged 22. Though he boarded on time, the ship could not sail for three days because the German *Luftwaffe* had begun bombing the port. In the rush, he gave Tatiana a substantial sum in American dollars, which were later to prove quite invaluable.

These events mirror the experiences of David and Edward (Ed) Miliband's father and grandfather, who also climbed into one of the last ships out of Belgium. They also left behind their womenfolk, their wife and their sister.[2]

Exodus towards England

When Marya returned to find Nikolai gone, Tatiana told her that Nikolai wished them to stay for the time being because the general expectation was that the French, Belgian, Dutch and British armies would drive back the invading German *Wehrmacht*. It was thought that a repeat of 1914, using Belgium as a way past the Maginot Line of eastern France, was unlikely. Unfortunately the *Wehrmacht* decided to bypass the fortresses and began to attack through the Ardennes forest. The situation rapidly deteriorated, and Tatiana decided that the news of the advancing Germans meant that flight was necessary. Already, some time before, she had hidden her full-size portraits under the linoleum of the floors of their home. She conferred with the mother of her boyfriend Charles Desguin,[3] who said Tatiana could move in with the Desguin family if Marya left for England. Marya bluntly told Tatiana that she would not go without her daughter.

Rapidly a party of family friends was coming together, Marya and Tatiana, Armand and Nancy Coppieters, and their lanky son, Emile. Nancy was English and Emile held a British passport. With the father of Charles Desguin (who was the son of a previous Mayor of Antwerp) to give them support, and who had left his children to look after their mother, they meant to escape eventually to England. Now that the port of Antwerp was closed, the decision was taken to head southwest towards the Channel coast in the hope of finding a boat that would take them across the English Channel. Thus whilst her father's ship lay anchored in the docks, waiting for the bombing to lessen, unbeknown to him the Saczkowska women gathered up a few possessions into suitcases, and left with their friends on 13 May, taking a train towards Ostend since that port had not yet been subjected to bombing.

The diary of the flight across Western Europe has been reconstructed from family papers and documents drawn up at that time, and carefully preserved within the family. It makes interesting reading:

> **Friday 10 May:** Nikolai boards the ship scheduled to sail to Britain.
>
> **Saturday 11 May:** Emile Coppieters visits Tatiana to say that his family is thinking of leaving for England as he wants to join the British Army.
>
> **Monday 13 May:** Nikolai's ship finally sails from Belgium.
>
> On 13 May, Marya and Tatiana Armand, Nancy and Emile Coppieters, and Mr Desguin, left from Antwerp Central station by train towards Brussels, around lunchtime. From there they entrained to Ostend, reaching the town in the evening, where the party takes rooms in a hotel on the seafront.
>
> **Tuesday 14 May:** Finding that there are no ships leaving for England the party receive advice to leave Belgium and go to Le Havre. They decide to cross into France, and catch a train to Le Havre from Boulogne. On arrival, they take a tram towards La Panne. From there they take another tram towards the frontier near Bray-Dunes, and take rooms in a hotel for the night. Along the way, Tatiana asks a British soldier why German planes are bombing the seashore and is told that the *Luftwaffe* are trying to destroy the British searchlights.
>
> **Wednesday 15 May:** Reaching the frontier at lunchtime, the queue of cars waiting to be allowed into France prevents walkers being processed. Tatiana is told that there is a camp set up for Polish people. When the party discuss this Mr Desguin advises that they should remain together and not become separated. That night the frontier is closed to all wishing to cross, but a farmer takes them in and lets them sleep on straw in a large chicken coop. Marya and Tatiana have blankets in their suitcases and so try to sleep fully clothed covered by

them. Emile then tells them there are rats but is told to go to sleep. However the snoring of the others crammed into the coop keeps some of them awake.

Thursday 16 May: The refugee party leaves the chicken coop certainly not expecting to have to return to it. That day is spent waiting in a queue, but again without their being allowed to cross the frontier. So they have to return to the coop, which is reached by a small lane close to the frontier, to spend a second night sharing with other people and the rats.

Friday 17 May: Getting up at about 5.00am, the party again finds itself waiting at the frontier. Suddenly the border guards no longer try to stop the refugees, the frontier is thrown open, and the party grabs its suitcases and surges through. Beyond the frontier all is quiet once the motorcars have driven away. There is nothing more to do but to begin walking towards Dunkirk to seek to find some transport.

Morale begins dropping as kilometre succeeds kilometre. Resting in a field, Tatiana shares out the little food she has been carrying, but they know they must go on. They enter Dunkirk at around midday and, despite the town appearing quiet with people walking all around, when Tatiana meets a British corporal, he indicates imminent danger by telling them to keep walking onwards, and he very kindly gives her some chocolate. They are in a state of great tension, fearing the on-slaught of parachutists, bombers and tanks because of the German planes flying forwards and backwards over the town. There is no sign of any French or Belgian warplanes. It was only a week before the military evacuation began and British troops have already begun retreating towards the town. A few days later, she will hear that Dunkirk was heavily bombed soon after they left.

Tatiana and Emile go in search of a taxi-driver happy to accept the fare in some of the American dollars Nikolai gave her before his ship sailed. The driver is unwilling to accept Belgian francs, but delighted at the prospect of the dollars even though it means taking six passengers. For the equivalent of 500 francs, he transports them the 40 km to Calais, where he changes some of the dollars into French francs.

In the late afternoon the party finds a bus travelling to Boulogne. Arriving at the railway station, Tatiana and Emile ask for free tickets as refugees. But when they admit to having francs they are made to pay for their fare to Le Havre.

Saturday 18 May: They awake to again find at the port that there are no boats leaving for England. Receiving advice from an official, they reluctantly decide that they must try to reach Paris from where they can travel to Bordeaux, the port most likely still to have ships crossing to England. Meanwhile, they have to remain overnight waiting for a train leaving for Paris. Marya and Tatiana rent a room in an area that was normally patronized by local prostitutes and their clients but it is a matter of 'any port in a storm'.

Sunday 19 May: The party arrive at the railway station and take a train to Amiens, where they intend catching another train for Paris. As they wait for the train for Paris an air raid warning is heard, together with the sound of German bombers. The railway staff tell them to leave their suitcases and go into the town to find a café and have something to eat since the station is likely to be the target. The bombs have already begun falling when they reach a café. Marya sits motionless on a seat, and the others remain quiet, not feeling like talking. Tatiana observes a British army sergeant chatting to a woman at the bar. She shows him her small wooden crucifix from her First Communion and talks about trying to get safely to England. He reassures her that they will get there safely. As the bombing becomes worse Tatiana slides under a large table to find she is sharing it with the sergeant. During a lull in the bombing the party decides to return to the station to collect their suitcases. Tatiana says goodbye to the sergeant and the woman. Outside she picks up a jagged fragment of the shrapnel lying on the ground and puts it into her handbag as a souvenir. This fragment would eventually reach England. Hearing the station has been badly damaged by the bombing there seems little point returning to attempt to find their suitcases. Though Marya and Tatiana are lightly shod they agree with the others to attempt to walk the 43 km southwest to Grandvilliers, in order to try at the station for a train to Paris.

As they walk on and on, Emile suggests that Marya and Tatiana should get rid of their Polish passports in case the party find themselves trapped and captured by German troops, and perhaps killed. But Tatiana refuses, saying that she and her mother have to reach England, and they will need their passports to prove who they are.

They pass British soldiers waiting in the roadside ditches ready to fire at the Germans with machine-guns. Large lorries pass them by, carrying retreating Belgian and Dutch troops. The soldiers inside are exhausted and as a portrait painter, to her trained eye, Tatiana later said that their faces had taken on a green tinge.

As night approaches a French woman offers shelter to the whole party in the kitchen of her small house. Not being used to the countryside of *France profonde*, Tatiana is horrified to find that the house has no bathroom or toilet. They are given straw to sleep on and blankets to cover them, and for toilet facilities they all have to use the adjacent open field.

Monday 20 May: In compensation for the primitive sleeping conditions is the welcome hot coffee the lady of the house serves them for breakfast. They set out again on their journey, and as they continue walking, they begin to see German planes hovering overhead, their silver shapes discernible, bombs glinting in the sun as they fall to earth. Tatiana persuades the party to leave the main road, which is full of refugees and civilian cars. Keeping to the country lanes and hiding when aircraft are heard to approach, they remain safe.

By now, Marya is in a bad way with badly swollen ankles, and says that she simply cannot walk any further. She tries to give Tatiana half of her money, and asks to be left to her fate by the side of the road. Tatiana refuses to do this and from then on, Marya is helped to keep walking. In the late afternoon the party struggles into Grandvilliers and there rests in a café.

Tatiana tells her mother to get a drink for herself, whilst she goes up to a man having a beer to ask him about trains leaving for Paris. He turns out to be the mayor of the town and offers his daughter's bicycle to Tatiana so that together they can cycle to the station outside the town.

On their way, they are passed by convoys of lorries carrying soldiers who are heading south. Despite the circumstances and much to Tatiana's amusement the soldiers wave at her, showing they still are men and find a pretty girl attractive. At the station, they find that a train is leaving for Paris at 7.00pm. Returning to the café, Tatiana tells her mother that she must stay with the party whatever happens. Walking to the station the party finds the platform is crowded. When the train pulls in, there is chaos as people try to get on. Marya is pushed onto the train by Tatiana, who in turn is pushed on by Emile and his parents. All of the party eventually are aboard, seats are found for Marya and Tatiana, Emile settling down on the floor. Finally the train leaves, but during its journey it halts many times so they spend the night on it. Tatiana later recounts the halts as being 'very unnerving'.

Tuesday 21 May: The train arrives in Paris in the morning, and the party seek out a hotel to stay in whilst deciding what to do next. Again the American dollars prove vital as spending money as French francs no longer are acceptable.

Wednesday 22 May: Marya and Tatiana go shopping for spare underwear, having had to leave the clothes in their suitcases left behind in the bombed Amiens station three days earlier.

Thursday 23 May: Emile, with his English passport, goes with Tatiana to the British Embassy to apply for visas. Emile has grown up with Tatiana, they have spent good times together as soulmates so he feels able to be blunt with her. He tells her that she must stay calm when they talk to the Embassy staff as 'the English are always calm'. This is not easy for Tatiana as she is very stressed from what has happened during the previous fortnight. The Embassy staff are unsure what to advise but agree that it is best to travel to Bordeaux and look for a ship leaving for England. They know that there are no more ships leaving from northwestern France. The party entrains for Bordeaux, having paid for their tickets with American dollars. The journey proves to be slow as the railways are obvious targets for the *Luftwaffe* bombing.

Friday 24 May: The train eventually reaches Bordeaux. Since there was no way of knowing how long they would have to wait in the city before undertaking the next leg of their journey, the party finds rooms to rent at 59 Rue Lamartinie.

Leaving Marya at their lodgings, Tatiana goes with Emile to the port to look for a ship bound for England. But as she does not hold a British passport the British Consulate sends her away, priority being reserved for British subjects. Emile, having been born in London, holds British nationality. Whilst at the port there they see people they recognise from Antwerp, including the manager of General Motors International. He tells them he is trying to get to Spain.

Every day, Marya, Tatiana and Emile go to the Consulate hoping for safe passage to England, but without success. Even Tatiana's explanation that her father and brother are now in England is not enough. After a fortnight, because he has a passport and does not need a visa, Emile is told he must not wait with the others any longer, and that any ship will take him across the English Channel. Leaving the rest of the party he embarks for England.

The dollars have so far been paying for everything, and Mr Desguin and the Coppieters feel they should contribute to expenses. They get chatting to a farmer who has a vineyard just outside the city, and he offers them work. Later, he also offers work to the Saczkowska women that proves an attractive necessity because the supply of dollars is nearly used up. Marya decides that she wants Tatiana to stay with her in the lodgings to be close to the Consulate whilst waiting for a response to letters she has sent to her husband, Nikolai, hoping to receive a reply that he has written to the Consulate instructing them to issue visas to his wife and daughter.

Political conditions become more threatening as they hear that the French Government is moving south towards Bordeaux, ahead of the German forces. Repeatedly they go back to the Consulate asking if Nikolai has written, but none of the staff seem to know what is happening.

Tuesday 12 June: Mr J. Lambert, the Acting British Vice-Consul,[4] sends a request to London, asking for Marya and Tatiana Saczkowska to be given visas. These do not turn up, despite Tatiana having made it clear that her father and brother were already working and living in England, Nikolai junior being employed in the RAF.

Monday 17 June: Marya and Tatiana are standing with their landlady at the Consulate, surrounded by Jewish people, also desperate to escape from France, and Tatiana pushes her mother forwards holding their existing Polish passports, to be told that the request has been refused. Mr Lambert believed he should not be stamping their passports, as according to British regulations they were aliens.

Tatiana, having reached breaking point, no longer having the psychological support of Emile, breaks down in tears in front of Mr Lambert. He takes pity on her. She wondered later if being a pretty, young woman made the difference. He stamps their passports with the visas, saying that they must get on the next ship, which is leaving in an hour. He asks Tatiana: 'If I am put in prison in England for disobeying my orders, will you come and visit me.' Fortunately that did not happen to him.

The landlady takes Marya back to the lodgings to collect enough bread, butter and ham for up to three days' travel. Meanwhile,

Tatiana stands in a queue with both passports waiting to be given the tickets needed to leave France. Overhead a violent electric storm is raging. Knowing her way around the port the landlady decides to return with Marya to collect Tatiana. The three walk along towards the berth, carrying the few possessions Marya and Tatiana have retained. Some dockhands call out insults, which the landlady returns in a similar manner. The ship turns out to be an English coaler, sailing back to Newcastle from the Mediterranean. Marya and Tatiana say goodbye, and ask the landlady to explain to the other three what has happened. With no cabin space left for passengers, the coaler being packed with refugees, Marya and Tatiana are taken down into the empty hold in which they are told they will have to travel despite the coal dust.

There they meet a young Canadian priest who has been evacuated. When sailors find a mattress to sit on they offer the priest room on it. However, he prefers to spend much of the time on deck. The coaler is later shown to be the last ship out of France as the new French Vichy Government complies with the demands of their German masters to close the port.

Marya and Tatiana eat some of the sandwiches, and then settle down to sleep on the mattress but are aware that the coaler is zig-zagging violently as it hugs the coastline. Being such a humble boat means it is fortunate for those on board as it is less likely to get bombed.

During the crossing the periscope of a submarine is seen on the surface, trailing it for several hours. No torpedoes are fired and the U-boat does not surface. They later hear that another ship also sailing from Bordeaux and carrying soldiers and refugees was torpedoed, with the only survivor being a 12-year-old boy, whose parents went down with the ship.

Tuesday 18 June: The ham sandwiches brought from Bordeaux are already rotting in the heat, so the sailors bring Mary and Tatiana some food and drink. Because the coaler is on its way to the north of England, and knowing that these passengers are travelling with valid visas, the captain decides to land them at the port of Falmouth.

Wednesday 19 June: Disembarking at Falmouth to be met by immigration officials, Marya and Tatiana are interned in a detention camp as possible Fifth Columnist traitors, and then interrogated. Near paranoia about spies and traitors was perhaps understandably running rife at this time. However, Marya's husband, who has been in England since 13 May, is contactable and he is able to confirm his former military status and to tell the British authorities that Marya and Tatania are genuine Polish refugees, recently living in Belgium. Nikolai also contacts Emile Coppieters, who travels from London and who chats with another man as they walk towards the reception centre. It turns out this man is the main interrogator at the reception camp. The information Emile gives while they are walking matches what the two women have already told the interrogator. It allows him to release Marya and Tatiana, and they are permitted to travel to London with Emile to be reunited with Nikolai. Tatiana's brother now known as 'Nick' is already an RAF flight mechanic maintaining bombers at Prees Heath airfield in Shropshire. Because of his engineering skills he is denied the opportunity to become a rear gunner in a bomber, being told his mechanical skills are more important for the war effort.

Those Left Trapped in Occupied Europe
Meanwhile, with Western Europe under German control, and no prospect of escaping, Armand and Nancy Coppieters, and Mr Desguin, decide reluctantly that there is nothing more to do other than to return to Antwerp, where they have their homes and Mr Desguin has his family. They leave for Antwerp, and there they remain – apart from Mr Desguin who is later arrested with his daughter by the Gestapo and executed.

For the Coppieters, among their later recollections is watching a German soldier guarding a Jewish woman holding her baby. When the baby does not stop crying the soldier tells the mother that she will not need her child where she is going, presumably meaning to a concentration camp. He then takes hold of the baby and swings it against a wall, thereby crushing its skull.

Another memory is of the residents of Antwerp waiting to be liberated, when the sound of tank tracks was heard. People went out onto their balconies to be ready to welcome the Allied troops. As the tanks came into sight, to their horror they saw that the tanks were German. The tanks swept people off their balconies with machine-gun fire.

Meanwhile, Emile Coppieters with his linguistic skills, was serving in the 11th Armoured Division of the British Army as an interpreter. On 15 April 1945, Emile was in the first unit to enter and liberate Bergen-Belsen, the Nazi concentration camp in Lower Saxony. That terrible experience haunted him; he died tragically of cancer soon after the end of the war, having been appointed to a job in the Belgian diplomatic service.

Aiding the War Effort

The family are together again, and later, in 1940, Nikolai began working as a draughtsman designer in the Engineering Department of BSA Guns Ltd, Air Ministry Factory 81, at Newcastle-under-Lyme, which put to good use his engineering expertise. Three years pass, with Marya and Tatiana working in the same factory as Nikolai, doing the kind of work British women had to undertake to aid the war effort. Now a skilled fitter, Tatiana, using needle files, fits breechblocks to exacting tolerances, until they are ready to be placed in machine-guns fitted to Spitfires.

During the late spring of 1943, Tatiana is taken to a tea dance by her brother's girlfriend and there she meets a dashing, young Royal Artillery Captain by the name of Jack Bailey. A few months later they are married. In December 1944, during the Battle of the Bulge in the Ardennes, their son George is born in Corbridge, Northumberland, close to the Otterburn Ranges, where his father is testing guns. He is named after the King, George VI.

Conclusion

This is a true story of a young woman achieving her objective by reuniting her mother with her father in England. With her determination, Tatiana saved her mother's life. She was not a trained warrior but a woman from a sheltered upbringing having to take decisions for others under the massive impact of the German conquest of Western Europe in 1940. She saw the enemy planes and experienced their total war. Bobbing and weaving through Dunkirk, coastal ports and officialdom, she managed to keep up her courage until her mission was accomplished. As the war progressed she became part of the legions of British women at war in occupations that were providing the logistical means for the Nazi forces to be contained, and eventually overcome. As a Pole and later a Britisher she did her duty.

Tatiana married Jack Bailey, and I am their son. My mother often talked to me about those days. Eventually, I insisted that she record her memoirs for posterity. In the autumn of 1972, we visited the Coppieters in Antwerp. A tape recording was made of the discussions between Tatiana and Nancy. Later, whilst recording the family history of the Saczkowskis and Marya's family, the Chestoffs, I was able to match the dates to the events experienced by my mother and Nancy during the war.

In 1973, my mother and I, using the tape-recorded testimony of her escape to England, linked it to family records and official documents. A diary was produced of the ordeal that Tatiana and her mother and their friends had endured. My mother died on 14 June 2009, and I decided to pay tribute to her by writing her story in this chapter.

Notes

1. Professional name as an artist, Tatiana Saczkowska-Bailey.
2. Edward (Ed) Miliband, MP, Leader of the British Labour Party, Conference Leader's Speech, 28 September 2010.
3. Charles Desguin was later caught for his Resistance efforts, survived working in the factories linked to the Ravensbruck concentration camp, but suffered thereafter from tuberculosis.
4. J. Lambert, British Consulate in Bordeaux, original letter of 12 June 1940 concerning visa requests, now in possession of the author George Bailey.

Select Bibliography

At her death, Mrs Tatiana Saczkowska-Bailey bequeathed to her son Dr George Bailey OBE, the official documents and family papers and the tape-recording from which this chapter has been written.

Bond, Brian, *France and Belgium 1939–40*, University of Delaware Press, 1979.
Spears, Edward, *Prelude to Dunkirk (Part 1 of Assignment to Catastrophe)*; *The Fall of France (Part 2 of Assignment to Catastrophe)*, London: Heinemann, 1954.

THE SECOND WORLD WAR:
THE BRITISH FIGHTING SERVICES

Chapter 6

'Put That Light Out!'

The 93rd Searchlight Regiment Royal Artillery

Imogen Corrigan

It is often assumed that the Auxiliary Territorial Service (ATS) must have been a product of need, arising from a country already at war. In fact it was formed almost exactly a year earlier on 9 September 1938. This was by no means the first time that women had been enlisted into the British army, the idea first being conceived by Sergeant Major Edward Baker in 1898. He had been wounded whilst serving in the Sudan, and the unkind have said that he must have been hallucinating when he came up with the idea that led to the formation of the First Aid Nursing Yeomanry (FANY) in 1907. Their remit was to be a 'body of horsewomen who undertook to ride onto the battlefield and carry the wounded back to medical help'.[1] Romantic though this sounds, it would actually be an astonishingly courageous thing for a woman to do, especially given the social constraints and expectations of womanhood of the day. One might have thought that the idea could not have prospered, never mind flourish, but by the end of the First World War, numerous women's organisations existed such as the Women's Emergency Corps, Women's Legion,[2] Women's Defence Relief Corps to name but a few. Many of these were eventually incorporated into the Women's Army Auxiliary Corps, the forerunner of the ATS.

As early as December 1916, a survey had been carried out into the number of men doing non-combatant work, and whether or not these jobs could be undertaken by women.[3] Initially, it was found that they were entirely suited to being employed as clerks, cooks, drivers and orderlies, but by the end of the Second World War, ATS personnel would be employed in seventy-seven different trades.[4] Interestingly, just over sixty years after the survey, things had not changed radically, in that in 1978 the role for the Women's Royal Army Corps was defined as being to provide 'replacements for officers and men in such employments as may be specified by the Army Board of the Defence Council from time to time'.[5] Although the formation and maintenance of women's military organisations was not as smoothly or as easily achieved as it might sound, nonetheless a firm basis was there for women to work alongside and as part of recognised military units in the future. This meant that as it became increasingly clear that the army's manpower resources needed boosting, possibly dramatically, the building blocks were in place on which the ATS could be formed. So in 1938, with rumours of war, the notion of women in the armed forces should not have startled the general population. It did, and one of the problems that the ATS members had to deal with all the time was the assumption that women in the army were no better than they ought to be; a belief still held by some during the author's time in the army.

Miss Patricia Clementi, then a convoy driver, remembered being turned away from billets in Fleet because the local police said that it was a respectable town.[6] Mrs Ann Dykes (who would become a sergeant) described her mother's disgust at her daughter joining the army, as she was fully aware of the feeling in the press.[7] As Mrs Jo Awberry, (an ATS clerk) pointed out, the ATS was the biggest of the women's services so statistically there would be more cases of – for example – pregnancies out of wedlock, and it tended to put women off joining.[8] Mrs Mary Andrews (née Brotherton) believed that the then Princess Elizabeth chose to go into the ATS rather than the WRNS to try to improve the public's attitude towards it.[9] The impression the author gained from interviewing over sixty-five ex-ATS ladies was that on the outbreak of war those women who volunteered (and their rank was volunteer, not private) were often genuinely patriotic and wanting to do their bit as much as the men were. They were also sometimes using the army to save making a decision about a future career or indeed seizing the chance to have some sort of career at all, or fleeing the tyranny of domestic service or an oppressive parent – or a combination of any two of those. Far from being of low virtue, most of them were astonishingly naive by today's standards.

Although the young women were keen to get into uniform that they saw mainly as being glamorous, many of them had never left home before and homesickness was rife. Mrs Joan Hynson (née Sales) told how they had to bundle up their civilian clothes and post them back to their parents, which brought home to them that they were most certainly in the army now.[10] She described the shock of being put in a barrack room with up to thirty other girls, and how they worried about minor things. One night, for example, she left her newly washed ATS knickers on a chair to dry by the fire and they got burnt; she was terribly worried about having caused damage to army kit. Eileen Nolan (who would become Brigadier and the Director of the Women's Royal Army Corps (WRAC) talked about the hurly-burly of never being alone for a minute when she first joined up, and how when they were recruits they were not allowed to put family photographs out in the barrack rooms.[11]

The diminutive Daisy Strivens (née Tranter) enlisted in November 1941, and was sent to Pontefract. She had thought it would all be a great adventure, but was horrified by the prison-like appearance of the building and the rows of double bunks that seemed to stretch forever. She was allocated one of the top ones but simply couldn't get onto it, being extremely small. When she tried to swap bunks, she was told that there was a war on: she knew this; she just wanted to go to bed. Her own background had been reasonably strict, with her parents imposing a curfew of 21.00 hours. At Pontefract she was told it was 22.00 hours and, misunderstanding the information, walked miserably about wasting time until she could go to her bed.[12]

When all of these young women were probably aged about 12, decisions were being made at Cabinet level that would affect the future of many of their colleagues. Germany was rearming, and on 31 July 1934, it was decided to improve the air-defence system.[13] It was realised that searchlights would be an essential part of night defence; not only could they aid night interception of enemy aircraft, but they could indicate where the coastline was for returning British planes. When the lights went into action during the war, it was noticeable that as soon as they were switched on, enemy aircraft which had been flying low looking for their targets, instantly rose to about 20,000–25,000 feet, rendering their target identification and navigation aids much less efficient.[14] On 31 January 1935, a plan was approved which would be expensive: nearly 100 Searchlight Companies were needed comprising 2,334 lights, 3,000 Lewis guns, 464 three-inch guns and 43,500 men.[15]

From this it should not be construed that women were immediately involved in manning searchlights. In fact this was not to happen until the approval of the Prime Minister Winston Churchill was gained in September 1941.[16] Men were increasingly needed for deployment elsewhere so the options were either to reduce the number of lights, a measure General Sir Frederick Pile (General Officer Commanding-in-Chief Anti-Aircraft Command 1939–45) considered irresponsible beyond belief, or to consider employing women already serving in the ATS. By using the ATS and Home Guard it was estimated that 71,000 regular gunners could be used on other duties. Inevitably there was anxiety about how the ATS girls would cope, often miles from anywhere on bleak sites with potentially dangerous work to do. In fact these fears proved groundless as General Pile noted: 'They showed themselves more effective, more horror-inspiring and more blood-thirsty with their pick-helves than many a male sentry with his gun, as several luckless gentlemen found to their cost.'[17]

It should be noted that General Pile became one of the women's greatest champions. He was a far-sighted man, many of whose ideas were what would now be seen as common sense. At the time, when he proposed that ATS working on gun sites should be issued with a more practical uniform and receive the equal rates of pay if they were doing the same job as a man, his ideas were described by Sir James Grigg (then Under-Secretary of State for War) as 'breath-taking and revolutionary'.[18] Undaunted, Pile asked a distinguished engineer, Miss Caroline Haslett, to give her opinion on women's ability to work on gun sites and its associated tasks. She spent many Sundays watching women working at jobs usually done by men, and was able to report that they could do anything except actually fire the guns, and that was not for reasons of physique, but because public opinion would not accept it.[19]

Bearing in mind the general image of women in the army, great care was taken in setting up what would become the 93rd Searchlight Regiment, Royal Artillery. Where men and women worked together elsewhere in the army, several interviewees mentioned that men would find themselves with the initials SFM (Suitable for Mixed) or more intriguingly NFM (Not For Mixed) on their documents. Where individual men were chosen to work with women, they were vetted and not accepted unless they were happily married and trustworthy. Pile wrote about his difficulty in dealing with the senior ladies of the ATS, who seemed to be applying outdated ideas to a modern problem. One lady said that, 'Women might smash valuable equipment in a fit of boredom.'[20] Another opined that, 'Care should be taken that restriction of privileges should involve punishment. For instance, stoppage of smoking should only be given to smokers, and extra knitting to a proficient knitter is no punishment.'

The first mixed battery was deployed in Richmond Park in 1941, and became the object of day-trippers gawping at the women working so equally alongside the men in a military context.[21] This indicates the obstacles Pile had to overcome, but also that he was steadily laying down the basis for an all-female operational unit to proceed. It also shows how outgoing, not to say brave, those women were who volunteered to break away from the more acceptable woman's work of perhaps clerk or cook.

Unbeknown to many, there had been a trial run in 1941 to see if women really were up to it. Mrs Greta Nimse (née Scott) gave this account:

> They wanted forty people and they knew that inevitably some would drop out. I do remember that they needed people who had a sense of humour, were fit and fond of the outdoor life. It was advertised like that. It appealed to me because I didn't want to work in an office all the time. So off we all went and met up at Newark ... I was a Private then (well, a Volunteer, as we were called). They took all the ranks off everyone so we were all Privates. Then they put us through all these tests to see what instrument we could work on. I had quite

good hearing so I was on a sound locator. It was a thing that was really a little piece of metal, which you stuck in your ear; not very sophisticated! You had to listen for 'planes and you had a sort of 'phone and when you heard a 'plane coming, you telephoned the people on the lights. We used to direct them towards where the sound was coming from ... There was someone on bearing and elevation, the generator and there was a wheel that turned the lights ... We had a male Sergeant Major who was mad keen on drill. He wanted to prove to the War Office that women could actually do the job, which was quite hard physically. He was determined first of all that we would march like men. I think all the men thought it was the pits to be with women – most of them perhaps were unfit in some way although we didn't know that at the time ... We'd done nothing like this before. We practised deploying under canvas, moving the lights, cooking, cleaning, cleaning lats [latrines] and striking camp in every way. At the end of what I believe was six weeks training – we knew the War Office top brass were coming down to watch – we had to do a route march of sixteen miles; quite a long way carrying our respirators and things like that. When we got back, the brass were going to be there, waiting on the parade ground so we had to come on looking marvellous. I remember we stopped out of sight and he said to us that he knew we were all absolutely exhausted, but that he wanted us to go on there like Guardsman. 'I want to see bags of swank.' He told us to walk on there and show off and it didn't matter what we felt like. Well, he got us on our feet and we went on and I really do think we *were* marvellous.[22]

From there, Greta and her colleagues were posted to be attached to a male, Searchlight Regiment, but it was not to last: in the autumn an order came through cancelling ATS searchlight attachments and sending all the women back to their previous employments. This was a bitter blow and a source of bewilderment to those women who had taken part in the Newark experiment. However the following year (1942), by which time Greta had been commissioned, the girls heard news of the 93rd Searchlight Regiment being formed. She wrote to her previous commanding officer asking if there might be a vacancy for her, and received a telegram by return, ordering her to report for duty. 'I never got to a station faster.' On arrival she found that she had joined the only all-female regiment ever to be on active service in the British army. This is something that has never been achieved since, and it is likely it never will be now that women are integrated into male units. The 93rd Searchlight

Regiment even had a complete innovation: a female adjutant. It did, in fact, have a male commanding officer and battery commanders but – remarkably for those days – every one of the other 800 members of the regiment was female.

Greta's story is exceptional; most women took a more mundane route to the 93rd Regiment. Some were approached by their employing or ATS officers and asked if they would like to retrain for another role, but mainly the individuals seem to have been alerted by notices on daily orders.

Mrs Joan Hill (née Hewitt) told how she was at the Guildford Training Centre when a notice went up. It mentioned the fact that searchlight sites were in lonely, rural places, a fact of which she was fully aware as her husband-to-be was already working in a male searchlight unit. In fact, Joan's ATS officer tried to dissuade her on the grounds that she didn't look strong enough.[23] Along with many other volunteers, she did her training at Kinmel Park, near Rhyl, one of the two training depots for searchlight duties, the other being near Taunton. Mrs Barbara White didn't enlist until 1944, by which time her potential could be spotted during her recruit training at Wigton. She was a reluctant soldier initially, and would have preferred the WRNS had she had a choice, but said she came to love working with searchlights because one was actively involved in the war.[24] Mrs Gwen Gray (née Cornish), on the other hand, specifically chose the ATS when she was called up in 1942, because she wanted to work on guns, although at that stage she had no idea what working with searchlights might entail.[25] In their trade training, they did all the things the army usually requires such as drill and physical training, but they also learned about electricity, electronics, mechanics, how to dismantle and reassemble parts, first aid, map reading, Morse code and, of course, the ongoing maintenance of the lights.

Every day, each light was checked and cleaned, and a dummy run was held at dusk to make sure that it was ready for the night's work. All the searchlight ATS women interviewed talked of the routine of filing the carbon sticks on which the light depended, and how carbons frequently had to be changed every night, one minute being allowed for this task. Mrs 'Johnnie' Eden (née Newman) described a cooling fan on top of the light 'and if that went wrong you had to climb up to it and sort it out. I was once on the end of an electric shock that knocked me over. You could get burnt if you tried to change the carbon over when it was still hot.' The brilliance of these lights whose beams could reach to 25,000 feet was immense and equivalent to 510 million candle-power.[26] Naturally, the girls were warned never to look into the light itself and rumours abounded that, if you walked in front of it, it would make you sterile.[27]

Extreme weariness was an ongoing problem. Not only were they sometimes called out as many as nine times a night,[28] but the day held duties as well. Sleep was often sporadic, and at night the girls frequently snatched the occasional half hour, wearing full battledress.[29] They had three minutes to move from their bunk to getting the beam in the air from the moment that the alarm was sounded. On those nights when enemy action was not expected, they might put up the lights to allow RAF pilots to practise evasion and working with them. They felt very much part of the overall effort even though it was often dangerous: enemy aircraft sometimes tried to disable the light by firing down its beam, putting those near it at considerable risk, especially the 'Number Five' who was the person who actually put up the beam. 'We used to pray for wet weather' when the lights couldn't be used, said Mrs Pat Dakin (née Milling).[30]

Although the role of the Searchlight Regiments was to help night interception of enemy aircraft, in the event they came to have another equally important role; that of homing. Bombers returning from raids over Germany frequently came back in a very poor state, many unable to return to their home base and even more often unable to communicate, and carrying wounded personnel on board. As these aircraft passed over the coastline of Britain, they showed the colours of the day. This was a simple system, which allowed them to be identified as friend or foe. The colours (a combination of two out of three for example: red, red, yellow or red, yellow, red) would be shown by flares dropped from the plane so that they could be admitted into airspace over England without challenge. If they were unable to show the colours, spotters looked for Morse signals instead. The colours of the day were delivered by dispatch rider to all searchlight and anti-aircraft units, marked 'Top Secret', and all interviewees said that it was a prime duty to learn the colours as soon as they had been issued. 'If anyone showed the wrong colours, we had to assume it was Gerry', said Mrs Dorothy Farr.[31] They also had to assume that enemy aircraft might be following in behind the distressed RAF ones.

The civilian population were often bemused to see searchlight beams apparently wandering about the sky for no apparent reason, and then all pointing in the same direction. Civilians were generally hostile to the idea of having searchlights near them anyway, correctly perceiving that they attracted enemy bombing activity. Living on a searchlight site was no sinecure. Only three of the detachment of eight girls manning each searchlight were needed for homing. All those interviewed gave graphic accounts.

'It would be "Take Post! Homing Beacon!" It was because a 'plane was coming back either crippled or there were dying on board, and you had to get them back to the nearest place that could actually take them.'[32] Co-ordinates for bearing and elevation would be received in the Operation Rooms of numerous searchlight sites. The lights would then be shone straight upwards, and then dipped three times to attract the pilot's attention. Then they would lower the beams so that they pointed in the direction he had to go to pick up his next marker. In this way, pilots could follow paths of light in to safety. 'You'd hear the 'plane go over and then dowse your light and, yes, you did feel very emotional about it.'[33] 'We must have homed loads and loads of them', said 'Johnnie' Eden.[34] 'Many a crew got home that way. One once called us lovely ladies – we had grease all over us and cold cream to protect our faces. It was just a job.'[35] Perhaps it was to Pat Dakin, but she was also keenly aware of the importance of their work.

In fact this was a significant contribution to the war effort as General Sir Frederick Pile frequently acknowledged after the war. During the year of 1942 alone, 45,000 homing beacons were called for and it is likely that many more aircraft were helped, but no record was kept.[36] In the three months from 1 March to 1 June 1943, 274 aircraft were saved (including a German Focke-Wulf 190, which managed to get homed to Manston where the pilot landed intact and surrendered). The numbers of lives saved by ATS, Home Guard and Regular searchlight operators must have been immense.

Despite opposition from civilians, the searchlight girls also found themselves helping in search and rescue operations (this never stopped the local civilians from coming up to the site during raids when they knew no one would be on guard and stealing the detachment's coal – the girls could see them do it in the light, but were too busy to prevent them[37]). At Isleworth, Margaret Rose used the lamp to illuminate bomb damage, which was common practice.[38] Greta Nimse recalled a flying bomb having hit a pub in Greenwich.

> We always had a small searchlight mounted on the back of a lorry and this could rush off as required ... The rescue work and cleaning up was finished and everyone sat about recovering. In the strange silence, we all heard a faint mewing from the ruins. Exhausted as they were, the men set about finding the cause. Our light was still brilliantly illuminating all the cables, wires, fire engines, lorries etc, when, tottering down a ladder came this tiny little kitten! ... We couldn't have been more pleased. Milk was found for the kitten and plentiful drinks of advocaat (of all things – hit by the bomb!) for all and sundry. The searchlight seemed out of focus and definitely wavering after that.[39]

The searchlights may not have been popular with the civilian population, but they became almost symbolic at the time; when the sirens went, the lights went up and so there was visible evidence that something was being done on the home front as well as overseas. Mrs Jill Childs (née Jessop) worked with Ack-Ack (Anti-Aircraft) and spoke of the times she had seen the lights for crippled planes coming home. Numerous interviewees mentioned this, often stopping to spare a thought for those on board and admitting to feeling emotional at the time, though often through the sheer fatigue of a shift just ending. So iconic were they that on VE Day two lights were placed behind St Paul's Cathedral to make the famous Victory V sign. Other London landmarks were illuminated that night; Gwen Gray helped man the one lighting Battersea Power Station. She said that it would have gone well, but somewhere else on the site someone was so pleased to be able to show a light at last that they lit a bonfire over the cable. This was the first time in three years that she had ever known a light to break down.[40]

General Sir Frederick Pile was loud in his praise of the 93rd Regiment and said of them:

> The girls lived like men, fought their lights like men and, alas, some of them died like men. Unarmed, they often showed great personal bravery. They earned decorations and they deserved more. As a partial solution to our manpower problems, they were grand. But, like all good things, they were in short supply.[41]

Many of the members of the Regiment were equally impressed by him, describing him as enlightened and forward-thinking. To students of the period it is remarkable that a regiment of women could be employed on operational and dangerous duties which has never been done since, as previously mentioned. They also did it without attracting mass attention from the public, which may be partly because they were deployed in small detachments over a large area, rather than in one depot. Unnoticed by the feminist movements, the ATS in general and 93rd Regiment in particular did more to carry their cause forward than any amount of protest later, although this did not concern the women at the time.

The end of searchlight work seemed to come quickly to the ATS involved. It was obvious to them that the lights became redundant as the war ended. But it was hard that, after their ground-breaking work over an extraordinary three years, in the end they were mainly posted back to one of the first four trades available to army women in the First World War: clerk, cook, driver or orderly. However, as Mrs Nan Ovenden (née Craig) so aptly put it: 'There was no counselling then – we had the Sergeant Major instead.'[42]

Notes

1. *The Auxiliary Territorial Service*, London: The War Office, 1949, p. 1.
2. Of which the writer's grandmother, Gladys Brotherton, née Spencer, was a member.
3. War Office, *Auxiliary Territorial Service*, p. 1.
4. Ibid., appendix VI (iii).
5. WRAC Corps memorandum 1978

6. Author interview, Clementi, February 1997. Miss Clementi had the last laugh as she was able to contact her parents who were friends with a general and two colonels who lived near Fleet and who invited the girls to stay with their families.
7. Author interview, Dykes, August 1996.
8. Author interview, Awberry, October 1996.
9. Author interview, Andrews, October 1996.
10. Author interview, Hynson, September 1996.
11. Author interview, Nolan, August 1996.
12. Author interview, Strivens, October 1996.
13. F. Pile, *Ack-Ack*, London: Harrap & Co., 1949, p. 58.
14. Ibid., p. 181.
15. Ibid., p. 60.
16. Ibid., p. 222.
17. Ibid., p. 226.
18. Ibid., p. 188.
19. Ibid., p. 186.
20. Ibid., p. 190. One has to wonder if this was more of a reflection on her than on women in general.
21. Ibid., p. 191.
22. Author interview, Nimse, February 1997.
23. Author interview, Hill, December 1996.
24. Author interview, White, November 1996.
25. Author interview, Gray, February 1997.
26. Author interview, Bell, January 1997.
27. Author interview, Eden, February 1997.
28. Author interview, Farr and Glascock, October 1996.
29. Author interview, Rose, February 1997.
30. Author interview, Dakin, November 1996.
31. Author interview, Farr and Glascock, October 1996.
32. Author interview, Bell, January 1997.
33. Author interview, Dakin, November 1996.
34. Author interview, Eden, February 1997.
35. Author interview, Dakin, November 1996.
36. Pile, *Ack-Ack*, p. 268.
37. Author interview, Bell, January 1997.
38. Author interview, Rose, February 1997.
39. Author interview, Nimse, February 1997.
40. Author interview, Gray, February 1997.
41. Pile, *Ack-Ack*, p. 228.
42. Author interview, Ovenden, December 1996.

Select Bibliography

Pile, Frederick, *Ack-Ack: Britain's Defence Against Air Attack during the Second World War*, London: Harrap & Co., 1949.
Terry, R., *Women in Khaki*, London: Columbus Books, 1988.
War Office, *The Auxiliary Territorial Service*, London: War Office, 1949.
Women's Royal Army Corps, *Corps Memorandum*, London: WRAC, 1978.

Chapter 7

Homeland Defence

British Gunners, Women and Ethics during the Second World War

Georgina Natzio

Introduction

On 28 July 1939, General Sir Frederick Pile took over as Commander-in-Chief, Anti-Aircraft (AA) Command to work under the leadership of Air Chief Marshal Sir Hugh Dowding, Commander-in-Chief, Fighter Command on the Air Defence of Great Britain (ADGB), working at Bentley Priory and its grounds, Stanmore, Middlesex. Here the two leaders were joined by the Commandant of the Observer Corps; liaison officers from Bomber and Coastal Commands; the Admiralty, the War Office and the Ministry of Home Security.[1] It might have been thought that they would be solely commanding men – not so. A future chronicler of AA Command's complex operation within Britain's AA defensive system between 1939–45, following the official post-war historians and others in between, would demonstrate this for a new generation.[2]

By the close of 1944, more women were serving in AA Command than men, not only by General Pile's intention, but also as a result of personnel cuts and abstractions from AA Command. In a typical mixed battery made up of 388 personnel, the ratio was 89 men to 299 women. This was an enormous socio-military change, even allowing for British women's war-work during the First World War, when members of the Women's Auxiliary Army Corps (WAACs), working in France in uniform numbered 9,000 by June 1917.[3] Renamed as Queen Mary's Army Auxiliary Corps in 1918, the organisation's overall establishment would rise to approximately 57,000 women, employed at home and abroad,[4] a large statistic by any measure. Even so, some twenty years on, General Pile would be hoping to employ well over 100,000 women across a wide spectrum of jobs, including operational if not combatant tasks, as substitutes for men.

But were there deeper elements to the working environment which enveloped the uniformed women employed in Britain's homeland defence organisation between 1939 and 1945, other than the most pressing matters, such as family dependency, and female–male relationships on and off the gun sites? Much of the lives and attitudes of the men and women serving in uniform during the 1940s has been extensively documented in official histories, in sociological studies of the 1940s, civilian workforce and its output, and in a copious, intrinsically valuable, supply of memoirs. Not forgetting the extensive analytical work carried out on AA Command's behalf by different sociological and medical disciplines during the war period itself.

Ethical matters concerning women's contribution to the national war effort, however, have not always been presented collectively as a subject in their own right, and what follows is an attempt to gather the concept together, albeit in somewhat condensed form, taking AA Command's involvement in the Air Defence of Great Britain, and that organisation's considerable manpower demands in particular, which could be said to have served as a template for the successful pioneering of female introduction to a male, military, host organisation.

Female experience in industrial employment during 1939–45 is briefly highlighted for comparison. The Air Defence of Great Britain, involving all three armed services, the Home Guard and the Royal Observer Corps, as it had become by 1943, was conducted on an industrial scale; Fighter Command and the ADGB organisation were to undergo a structural revision and a doctrinal change in approach during that year.[1] General Pile remained from 1939 as Commander-in-Chief until the work of AA Command and Britain's air defence requirements were clearly perceived to be ready for closing down by April 1945. He was unusual during the Second World War for his endurance and staying power, assisted by the fact that he and Winston Churchill, the Prime Minister himself, who had had military experience when young, shared a highly creative and questing outlook in the way they envisaged handling war-related, social or technical matters. As individuals, it is clear from Pile's memoir, *Ack-Ack*,[5] that they understood each other. It is a reminder of Churchill's capacity for insight that, even though Pile was not widely popular within his own military generation, Churchill had the wisdom not to dislodge him from his prime position. The General, a gifted leader, had indeed welded together a strong sense of identity and purpose among thousands in the employ of AA Command.

Returning to ADGB's headquarters at Bentley Priory, it was there in the Operations Room, from information gathered in from diverse sources by the neighbouring Filter Centre, that intruding enemy aircraft and their positions were counted, plotted and timed, and their headings and estimated times of arrival at likely targets calculated. Results were then disseminated back across country from the Centre to appropriate fighter-and-gun operations rooms, then forwarded to command posts and on to gun, searchlight and balloon sites, after which barrage balloons would be flown. If weather conditions were dark, or darkly overcast at nights, the massive searchlight beams would be trained upwards in the designated direction, and guns brought into action against the *Luftwaffe*'s aircraft, illuminated in the intense glare of the lights. Members of the Auxiliary Territorial Service (ATS) and the Women's Auxiliary Air Force (WAAF) working in substitution jobs were closely involved in fighter-support operations from Bentley Priory onwards, all the way through to the sites mentioned. Anti-aircraft gunfire had to be very carefully integrated with Royal Air Force (RAF) fighter sorties directed against intruding enemy aircraft. To avoid accidentally downing RAF fighters hastily scrambled into the skies above, suitable procedures and new communications' links had to be devised or reconfigured each time the Gun Defended Areas (GDAs) were redrawn to meet changing *Luftwaffe* attack-patterns. Improved early-warning, radio direction finding (radar), prediction, fire-control and gun-laying equipment slowly began to be delivered – not a moment too soon after the friendly-fire disaster of the Battle of Barking Creek, 6 September 1939, revealed weaknesses in the reporting system.[6] Looking back, at first the task must have seemed impossibly intricate. Later, with improved equipment settled in, ground/air defence organisation became much more efficient, flexible and mobile.

Manpower Pressures

Anti-aircraft employments involved thousands of male and female volunteers and conscripts throughout 1939–45, who lived in hutted or tented accommodation according to whether the guns were static or mobile. By May 1941, AA Command's strength had risen sharply to over 300,000 men.[7] But in spite of the Command's heavy demand, its manpower strength-levels fluctuated continuously for a number of reasons. Fighter Command's manpower requirements were also high, it will be remembered. Further, logistic support and engineering maintenance for the RAF's and the Army's fighting echelons abroad were also highly labour-intensive.

Heavily pressed by events to expand, Fighter and AA Commands, together with RAF Balloon Command, turned to women as substitutes for men – the policy became known as 'substitution' – across a wide range of jobs. From AA Command alone, periodically thousands of trained men were sent overseas. General Pile's massive personnel requirement, dictated by the large abstractions of personnel already in hand or undergoing training in the Command, was increased by anticipated deliveries of equipment. But AA Command's manpower and equipment requirements were seldom met in full, and frequently failed in their coordination. Pile's private war to raise more manpower, equipment and funds for accommodation and maintenance was fought with charm and aggression against War Office and Treasury bureaucrats, and he became deeply unpopular among them, through his unremitting and at times successful efforts.

On 8 October, 1941, it was learned that 50,000 men needed to operate the promised equipment would, in fact, be diverted to the Field Force.[8] The particular troop diversion of October 1941 left AA Command with a strength of only 280,000 men, and a proposed ceiling, never achieved, of 170,000 female Auxiliary Territorial Service (ATS).

By 30 September 1943, AA Command was employing 57,178 members of the ATS. Heavy anti-aircraft batteries soaked up 48,950 ATS in semi-operational or support jobs. Light anti-aircraft batteries needed 1,637 ATS, while 6,591 ATS were employed with the searchlight units, eventually producing the preponderantly female 93rd Searchlight Regiment.[9]

In addition to the introduction of ATS members to work alongside its remaining male ranks, not least the male gun-crews, women officers with science degrees were recruited, and along with other ATS ranks educated in maths and physics were absorbed into AA Command's substantial training and experimental organisations. These ATS members evaluated equipment; observed and recorded male trainees' firing accuracy; and some among them learned to become trainers themselves.

Throughout 1939–45, the Royal Navy, the Army, and the RAF competed for female substitutes, competing for them, too, within their own arms and also with industry and agriculture. On closer inspection, manpower shortage nationally, an enduring and complex problem, was full of strange anomalies.

The Ethical Environment

The idea of employing women in anti-aircraft jobs to solve expected manpower problems was around for several years before the outbreak of war, and was taken up and investigated in 1938, by General Pile. Ensuring the well-being of women as well as men under his command came naturally to him. He regarded it as vitally important, not only for national morale but particularly in support of the female auxiliaries' families, to assuage anxieties about their well-being. Renowned for his gifts in managing his subordinates, he took the care of all ranks working under his leadership very seriously. In spite of the fact that some modern interpreters may view this approach as a form of cynical support for troops, the purpose of which is solely to preserve numbers, Pile made it clear that for him such care had a humanitarian cast as well. He was, in consequence highly regarded by many in the Command. He was also thoughtful about public opinion – in that he also minded about AA Command's reputation.

Radical though he may have been in his own outlook as to the jobs the new women volunteer recruits could be trained to carry out, the public nevertheless remained extremely uneasy as to whether women as child-bearers should be permitted to take life. For this reason, officially, ATS were forbidden to actually fire the guns. Thus in concert with opinions voiced in the House of Commons, they were never actually designated 'combatant'. Shelford Bidwell and Roy Terry, both historians of the WRAC, however, found material, which suggests that on occasion they had. Bidwell, a former gunner officer, noted that the prohibition became more absurd when, with the advance of automation the guns were fired by remote control from the command post. Terry recorded Chief Controller Leslie Whateley, Director ATS from 1943–6, as confirming that some women in contravention of the prohibition had fired the guns themselves, though this had not happened very often.[10]

The prohibition from actual combat applied to the ATS working in Royal Artillery units. It was a luxury which clearly the Russians facing invasion and driving off the German army with all the means they could find at their disposal could not afford. The Germans, confident in their own military status, and an initial belief in their invincibility, on the other hand, were slow to bring women into their anti-aircraft batteries, though the speed of female introduction increased as their times grew harder. The British, on the other hand, never fully believed that an invasion by Germany once abandoned would be tried again, so there was no profound incentive to bring women officially into full combatant service.

ATS members were all volunteers, until female conscription was applied under the National Service Act in December 1941, which was regarded as ground-breaking. To assuage public concerns volunteering was nevertheless still relied on in recruiting ATS members for anti-aircraft work. A volunteer requirement for women was considered to be an essential part of their ethical employment when in combatant surroundings such as gun, searchlight or RAF balloon sites.

Following discussions within the War Cabinet, it was decided that certain areas where it was regarded as essential for all personnel to be armed for their protection were initially prohibited to women. For example, WAAF air mechanics were excluded from servicing aircraft on front-line air stations in campaign theatres overseas where there was a real risk of being overrun by the enemy who might, or might not, take prisoners. Another exclusion prevented ATS AA personnel from entering British coastal sites, especially vulnerable to enemy attack from the sea. This particular prohibition continued until serious threat of invasion of the British mainland had died down.

Some inland gun-sites situated around key cities such as Manchester, for instance, meant that female anti-aircraft crew-members were highly vulnerable to attack from enemy aircraft from the earliest years of the war. General knowledge of this fact had no effect on the public's paradoxical outlook as regards female protection. But reality made its own demands when later the first mixed anti-aircraft batteries, with the women all volunteering to remain with their units, went to the Continent in 1944, in the rear of pursuit of the remnants of the German Armed Forces, staying in the regions of Antwerp and Brussels to deal with V1 attacks. One or two ATS on this deployment have been shown in photographs to have been carrying personal weapons in spite of an official ban against the arming of Auxiliaries. This particular ban persisted long after the war had ended in 1945.

Whether servicewomen should carry personal weapons was, it will be remembered, only finally resolved during the 1980s. Considering the matter, it seems likely that some origins of the public disapproval held by some women as well as some men may be traced to chivalric and religious tenets. During 1939–45 perhaps the idea was a sharp and unwelcome reminder of the desperate state, even after the perilous early years had passed, that the nation found itself in. This attitude, as mentioned, was carried alongside the pro-hibition excluding ATS from firing the AA guns. It seems likely that both strands of opinion had to do with a fundamental anxiety about providing for the future.

Against the arming of women during the critical years of the 1940s, fears of personal inadequacy were also likely to have been present within some male reactions. Amidst so much uncertainty, reassurance regarding the mixed batteries was difficult to convey. Somehow, General Pile and his Command's Staff managed to put this over to gunners, ATS and parents alike. Men who found themselves unable to accept working with women were moved on, thousands of others were, or became, content.

Driven by such anxieties, job-evaluation and candidate-selection, for example, not only took a deeply scientific and humane turn for female benefit but also worked for servicemen's well-being, markedly improving efficiency and reducing loss of skills to ADGB through injury or exhaustion. For example, after experimentation during 1941, it was not until women took over balloon sites from men in the RAF that the danger of whiplash from escaped heavy restraining cables was properly recognized. Whiplash injuries appear to have been accepted among the male balloon crews as an occupational hazard, rather than an avoidable risk to be resolved, perhaps, by better drills. The women did sustain other injuries.[11] WAAF Balloon deployments were run down, however, during 1944, not only because mobile units with greater physical strength were required to be sent overseas with D-Day in prospect, but also because, in the words of Squadron Leader Beryl Escott, 'too many women were in hospital with ruptured stomachs'.[12] Balloon Command was finally disbanded in 1945, with a special word in public recognition in the form of praise from King George VI to its airwomen.

The Nation at War – Ethics in Conflict
On the morning of 3 September 1939, as Prime Minister Neville Chamberlain announced that Great Britain was at war with Germany, a British artillery officer lately returned from India, driving from London to Plymouth to take a mechanisation course during the final phase of the Royal Artillery's conversion from horse-drawn to motorised traction of guns, suddenly noticed a strange thing. It was about midday, and a steady stream of traffic was flowing *towards* rather than away from the capital – even then widely recognised as a principal bombing target.[13]

This observation of an apparently reckless public move towards London suggests an idea of national unity rising above virtually every other consideration in an effort to survive. It suggests also that such a public attitude was more than a figment of the Ministry of Information's imagination. After conversations with naval and military male and female veterans of that era, together with readings through War Cabinet, Admiralty, War Office and Air Ministry files in the National Archives, it seems to this writer that directly or indirectly, awareness of an ethic of national unity, sometimes popularly identified as national morale, underpinned the resolution of many organisational or ethical difficulties which occurred within the national workforce and especially the armed services during 1939–45.[14]

And yet, even as bombs rained down, buildings fell into rubble, and unbombed-out hospital clinics and wards began to fill, some dissent in Britain continued virtually for the duration of the war. Industrial troubles rumbled on into 1945.[15] Labour-direction and dilution of male workforces by women despite the familiarity of a female presence in industry during the First World War (1914–18), became a focus of some industrial unrest and persistent male resistance. Labour disputes unresolved during the inter-war years resurfaced during 1939–45. Wartime workplace regulations set against necessarily fluctuating production demands exacerbated problems, particularly for married women conscripted into the labour force. In certain fields, skilled and unskilled industrial manpower capacity was hugely diminished, spread as it was across

the entire military, agricultural and industrial spectrum. Without the introduction of women to the land, the industrial labour force or to the Home
Guard, however difficult it was for some men to accept, despite the fact that
many men had seen craftsmen or skilled colleagues and many others leaving the
factories for the armed forces, certain parts of industry and the country's
defences would have foundered or been even more seriously hampered than
they were.

From the foregoing, it is clear that a sense of the need for national unity
which brought with it a degree of public conformity quite simply coexisted
with dissent among parts of the country's civilian workforce. Members of the
ATS were inevitably drawn from this background. It took the wearing of
uniform on the streets and a belief in the justness of the British war effort to
bring home the realities of possible failure to individual local communities,
even though the extension of women's industrial employments meant that men
feared their traditional roles of hunter-gatherer and protector would be under-
mined, and their jobs taken by women after hostilities ended. Despite such
complications, it might still reasonably be suggested that overall the battle for
national unity was won – but by a whisker. And by rather more than a whisker
within the three armed forces themselves. With an apparently low 'kill' rate,
during the 'Blitz', in May 1941 – it was mid-May before War Office agreement
was obtained for formation and training of the mixed batteries – AA
Command's problems had clearly started.[16]

Did an extra sensitivity to manpower losses among Great War veteran
members of the War Cabinet of 1939–45 enhance a collectively negative
attitude towards the arming of women? Consulted, Shelford Bidwell, himself
trained by veterans of that war, thought this was indeed the case.[17] John
Keegan has noted in his studies of warfare through the ages, the phenomenon
of wife-stealing as a cause of conflict. Women have also been used as pawns and
captives between conquerors and conquered, and there is a real threat to the
future of a tribe through the taking of women as much as the savaging of male
prisoners by an enemy. Could it be that indications of possible annihilation
through the placing of women in combatant tasks, armed for self-defence, was
too much for the British public to bear in the midst of a struggle for national
survival?

It is perhaps important to remember that far more is known today about
women's involvement in warfare as combatants than would have been the
case for public knowledge during the 1940s. Taken together do the foregoing
suggestions present a possible explanation as to why, even during serious
expectation of invasion of the British Isles between 1940 and 1942, some men,
military or otherwise, were at the very least ambivalent towards, if not directly

opposed to female substitution for males in the armed forces and elsewhere throughout the national labour force? If this may be taken as an accurate description of how matters stood, perhaps it might also be reasonably observed that perceptions of what it would take to survive the war were in conflict at a profound level. Thanks to help from Great Britain's friends, however, these perceptual divergences were never put to the ultimate test.

In 1938, advising Pile, Caroline Haslett, an electrical engineer with ergonomic interests, having studied the required tasks concluded that, although women could carry out most of them, neither manhandling the vastly heavy guns into or out of action nor hefting shells would be suitable for female labour. Her view was that women should not fire the pieces according to Colin Dobinson in his account of AA Command, though Pile himself had no objection to this.[18] This was the physical argument, placed into the life-giving ethical context, both nagged at by anxiety regarding the future.

Pile, on the other hand, was culturally at the sharp end of another perception, and under enormous pressure to provide for survival, using whatever novel routes to success could be identified. Thus it was that when women became proficient in the technical aspects of anti-aircraft warfare in which they were allowed to take part, it was fairly recognised that all-female crews would have been well able to operate a light 40mm AA gun.[19]

A complicated national background and military atmosphere, therefore, prevailed for all women deployed within the home defence system. Parallel experiences to those of anti-aircraft ATS can be found in the archive of the 93rd Searchlight Regiment, RA, and in the annals of RAF Balloon Command. These valuable records demonstrate how well, if the psychology was carefully thought out and honestly acted upon, women integrated with men in military society and eventually ran units where females were numerically greater than males, releasing men for combatant service elsewhere.

General Pile and his Staff in AA Command largely conquered inter-sex rivalry and identity problems, by emphasising the high national and operational value of male–female partnership, and by removing any association of inadequacy from perceptions of the male effort. As it happened, total ATS battle casualties for 1939–45 were low, with 389 killed or wounded.[20] AA Command's leadership had, nevertheless, by 1944, successfully convinced members of its mixed units and their families that defence of the country took precedence over all else in the ethical league-table. In the wider sphere, however, public approval never found its way to awarding members of AA Command appropriate battle honours or the Command itself a special war-service medal. This still seems mean-spirited, as the men and women working out on the air defences armed or unarmed were vulnerable: some units coming under direct attack from enemy aircraft when they were not simply in the way of falling bombs. But perhaps a lack of public acknowledgement of faithful and long-standing service exerted by so many might be put down to the degree of safety and security engendered by the AA batteries which was eventually felt – in spite of the harsh criticism that was made of them when enemy aircraft got through. In that era of managed information perhaps it is also, with hindsight, too much to expect the public to piece together the effects of the materiel shortcomings and manpower difficulties the Command experienced.

Morale and Identity – Best Military Practice
Male trainers had been surprised by female abilities in respect of all the artillery tasks they were being asked to carry out. The women in turn were also highly pleased with the men's encouragement, so morale all round in the Command's training establishments, and eventually out on the gun-sites was good, once clothing and accommodation requirements were sorted out.

The female auxiliaries learned to identify closely with fellow-members of the Royal Artillery they worked with 24/7 – through dark nights in the country-side, or under heavy bombardment in city environs, joining from below in the RAF's aerial battles. Moments of real danger amid long, dull stretches bonded the AA men and women as they worked together in frequently horrible, trying or extremely boring circumstances. General Pile made it clear in his memoir, *Ack-Ack*, that selection of suitable individuals was a prime factor in his Command's success in creating efficient mixed-gender units. Considering the ferocity of *Luftwaffe* attacks, it is remarkable that more ATS were not killed at their posts. This alone might indicate the effectiveness of the heavy anti-aircraft guns' fire in driving enemy aircraft higher, and in the increasing efficiency of the early-warning, raid reporting and data delivery system. Auxiliaries in particular who worked alongside the men were keen and un-doubtedly deserved, as the gunners made clear in their official historical narrative, to join the Royal Regiment of Artillery as fully fledged gunners, and they coveted its uniform's distinguishing marks.

The Director, ATS, during the early 1940s, Chief Controller Jean Knox, later Lady Swaythling, was however very anxious that members of her service should be prepared to serve with any arm or branch, as that was how, she said, auxiliary substitution deployment throughout the army was expected to work. She reserved the right to transfer ATS members anywhere at any time. To Pile and his Staff at AA Command however this made nonsense of all their training of female substitutes and threatened efficient AA functioning as they parted with thousands of trained male gun-crews. Operationally, it was essential for hard-earned female skills not to be lost. Differing views over their separate obligations to the state, ironically combined with a shared feeling of responsibility to AA Command's ATS members' families, unfortunately set them at odds with each other. Inter-organisational tensions thus set up were only resolved on the assumption in 1943 of the ATS leadership by Leslie Whateley.

A duty of care, as we would call it, imbued in Pile's own perception of military duty, also formed the basis of Jean Knox's public promise to families to exercise care for the women and girls under her command. The concept was closely related to ATS recruiting in general and to the AA units in particular.[21] When Pile suggested absorbing trained ATS members into the Royal Artillery, unhappy about ATS living conditions in the AA units, even though Pile and his staff were working hard to resolve major problems, Jean Knox found that morally she was unable to negotiate with him.

While she was absolutely unwilling to give up either control over, or protection of, any members of her service, nevertheless Jean Knox's adherence to her public promise was eventually officially acknowledged as having been of serious importance. It was also later acknowledged that she had, in fact, with the help of her deputy and successor, transformed the ATS into a smart, athletic and efficient workforce. The ATS ultimately fielded an extraordinarily wide range of skills hitherto alien to women, save to certain of their predecessors who had served in uniform during 1917–18. Between them, Jean Knox together with Leslie Whateley, turned round public opinion of the ATS from poor-to-contemptuous, to one of broad goodwill.

A succession of enemy fighter incursions into British air-space, bombing raids and changes of pattern and weapons, dictated reaction to *Luftwaffe* attack. On several occasions this meant, as mentioned earlier, that the whole gun defence layout had to be redrawn across the country. Batteries had to up sticks and literally break down hutted and tented accommodation for rebuilding where possible in specially designated areas for men or women at new sites, and set off towing mobile guns, ferrying prediction and communications equipment, carrying as complete a range of supplies as could be begged or borrowed. Spares of every kind – electrical, mechanical; communications; food, fuel supplies, water-bowsers, sanitary equipment, bedding, building materials – had to be moved across country.

Thus it was that, against the background under discussion here, with the complex manpower levels and the management pressures described, resolution of Anti-Aircraft Command's various redeployments, and their associated logistic and supply problems, were to emerge as a *tour de force* of sustained military planning and execution, each time the air defence layouts were redesigned to resist enemy attack. ATS members and the male gunners who were almost completely integrated by 1945, as demobilisation loomed, were responsible for achieving that together.

Conclusion

The years between 1939 and 1945 were packed with contradictions – in ethics, in practicalities, within simple occurrences – for both men and women. ATS members of all ranks were not officially declared members of the Armed Forces of the Crown, or their service gazetted as the Women's Royal Army Corps, until the war had been over for four years – 1 February 1949 – the ATS having only hitherto been allowed partial military status.[22] Even after their acceptance as substitutes for men, by insisting on a prohibition against ATS carrying personal weapons, or being trained to use them, wartime public opinion remained out of step with military necessity and simple justice. Even servicemen found this prohibition difficult to accept. As has been noted, photographic evidence does exist showing that among the mixed anti-aircraft units whose female members had volunteered to move onto the Continent in 1944 this rule was disregarded.

RAF Balloon and Anti-Aircraft Command official records show that servicemen were convinced that uniformed women were not being brought in to remove or undermine ancient male responsibilities for defence and protection but to help take the strain. When they saw the bravery of the women under enemy aircraft attack, the men ceased feeling threatened and were glad to form effective mixed teams and working groups. Anti-Aircraft and RAF Balloon Commands had achieved something socially important, as well as remarkable: their Commanders-in-Chief and headquarters' Staffs had successfully introduced the idea of male–female working partnerships at every level of military functioning from the technical to the practical in war-conditions.

Would it ever occur to any modern women, however, that they might find themselves on duty in a command post wearing the wrong clothes? The large collection of women's wartime service memoirs resounds to the clangs of tin hats being jammed on over steel hair-curlers as alerted anti-aircraft ATS ran with their male gun-crews to command posts and gun sites. But the Second World War was total in every respect. R. N. Currey provided us some of the flavour of this reality when she wrote:

> This is a damned inhuman sort of war,
> I have been fighting in a dressing gown
> Most of the night; I cannot see the guns,
> The sweating gun-detachment of the 'planes.[23]

Notes

1. John Terraine, *The Right of the Line, the Royal Air Force in the European War, 1939–45*, London: Hodder & Stoughton, 1985, part III, ch. 17, 'The Dowding System', pp. 179–80. Ken Delve also gives a good description of how the defensive system gradually developed through trial and error in his volume, *Fighter Command, 1936–1968: An Operational and Historical Record*, ch. 1, 'Development Roles and History: Control and Reporting – and Integrated Defence', Barnsley: Pen & Sword Aviation, 2007, pp. 10–14, 73.

2. Colin Dobinson, *AA Command: Britain's Anti-Aircraft Defences of the Second World War*, London: Methuen, 2001, ch. 8, 'Great Experiments', pp. 312–13, *et seq.*

3. Shelford Bidwell, *The Women's Royal Army Corps*, Famous Regiments Series, London: Leo Cooper, 1977, pp. 17–18.

4. William Spencer, *Army Service Records of the First World War*, Public Record Office Readers' Guide, 19, 3rd edn, Richmond: Public Record Office (PRO), 2001, p. 30. The National Archives, a government dept, was formed in 2003, from the former PRO founded in 1838, and the Historic Manuscripts Commission, founded 1869.

5. Frederick Pile, *Ack-Ack, Britain's Defences Against Air Attack during the Second World War*, London: Harrap, 1949.

6. Delve, *Fighter Command*, p. 192. Dobinson, *AA Command*, pp. 169, 289–91.

7. Dobinson, *AA Command*, p. 169.

8. Ibid., pp. 334–5.

9. The Auxiliary Territorial Service, appendix 6, contd, (iii) Analysis of Strengths on 30th September, 1943 by Trades, Employments & by Arms, etc with which employed, TNA/WO 2776/6. N. W. Routledge, *AA Command History of the Royal Regiment of Artillery: Anti-Aircraft Artillery, 1914–1955*, London: RA Institution, 1994, p. 400.

10. Shelford Bidwell, *WRAC*, ch. 3, 'AA Command', p. 126. Roy Terry, *Women in Khaki: The Story of the British Woman Soldier*, London: Columbus Books, 1988, pp. 154–5.

11. Beryl E. Escott, *Women in Air Force Blue: The Story of Women in the Royal Air Force from 1918 to the Present Day*, Wellingborough: Patrick Stephens Ltd, 1989, pp. 160–4.

12. Ibid.

13. This was recounted by Brigadier Shelford Bidwell, during a series of conversations which took place with the author, during the 1980s.

14. G. D. H. Cole and Raymond Postgate provide some background to an idea of national unity during the Second World War in their classic social history of Britain's working people, *The Common People, 1746–1946*, London: University Paperbacks, Methuen, 4th edn, 1949 (repr. with corrections, 1956, 1961), pp. 661–8, 667–8. Richard Croucher, *Engineers at War, 1939–1945*, London: Merlin Press, 1982, pp. 256–7.

15. See part II, 'Reality – The Industrial Machine', ch. 8, 'New Technology and Old Failings: Aircraft 1939–44', in Corelli Barnett's analysis of Britain's industrial history of the period, *The Audit of War: The Illusion and Reality of Britain as a Great Nation*, London: Macmillan, 1986 (Papermac edn, 1987), pp. 154–7, and part IV, 'The Limits of the Possible', ch. 12, 'New Jerusalem or Economic Miracle?' for wartime manpower paradoxes, pp. 260–1.

16. Dobinson, *AA Command*, pp. 309–11.

17. Shelford Bidwell, conversational series with the author, during the 1980s.

18. Dobinson, *AA Command*, pp. 308–9.

19. Bidwell, *WRAC*, p. 126.

20. Ibid., p. 132.

21. The Lady Swaythling, CBE, as Chief Controller, Jean Knox, Director, ATS, Interview with the author, 28 September 1982, and subsequent correspondence to 1990.
22. J. M. Cowper, 'How the Auxiliary Territorial Service Became Neither Auxiliary Nor Territorial', *Army Quarterly* (January 1961), pp. 212–17.
23. R. N. Currey, from his poem *Unseen Fire*, originally published in *This Other Planet [and other poems]*, London: Routledge, 1945. The poet was a schoolmaster before war broke out, joining the Royal Artillery, and later serving in the Army Educational Corps.

Select Bibliography

Barber, Richard, *The Knight and Chivalry*, London: Sphere Books, 1974.

Collier, Basil, *The Defence of the United Kingdom*, London: HMSO, 1957.

Howard, Michael, *War in European History*, Oxford: Oxford Paperbacks, 1976.

Hughes, B. P., ed., *History of the Royal Regiment of Artillery: 1919–1939*, London and Oxford: Brasseys (UK) Ltd, 1992.

Keegan, John, *A History of Warfare*, London: Pimlico, 1994.

McLaine, Ian, *Ministry of Morale: Home Front Morale and the Ministry of Information in World War II*, London: George Allen & Unwin, 1979.

Natzio, Georgina, 'British Army Servicemen and Women, 1939–45: Selection, Care and Management', *Journal, Royal United Services Institute for Defence [and Security] Studies*, 138/1 (February 1993).

Noakes, Lucy, *Women in the British Army, War and the Gentle Sex, 1907–1948*, London: Routledge, 2006.

Pile, Frederick, *Ack-Ack: Britain's Defences Against Air Attack during the Second World War*, London: Harrap, 1949.

The National Archives: War Cabinet papers, War Office, Air Ministry files and AA Command Official Narrative, from the Second World War, 1939–45.

Wightman, Clare, *More than Munitions: Women, Work and the Engineering Industries, 1900–1950*, London: Longman, 1999.

Chapter 8

Princess Marina the Duchess of Kent as Commandant of the WRNS during the Second World War

Join the WRNS – and Free a Man for the Fleet

Celia Lee

The Women's Royal Naval Service (WRNS) had been in existence during the First World War (1914–18). They were popularly known as 'the Wrens', because of the closeness of the initials to the tiny bird of that name. The WRNS had been created to free up men for technical and combat roles from jobs that could be carried out by women.

With the threat of war from Mussolini and Hitler in the mid-1930s, government moves were under way from 1935 onwards to provide a women's reserve corps to take over certain of men's jobs in the event of war. The WRNS was recreated in 1938, and recruitment was to take place through the Ministry of Labour. In September, the Government published a handbook containing details of the Women's Royal Naval Service. It stated that 1,500 women would be required to substitute Naval and Royal Marine ranks and ratings (a rating being the navy's equivalent of a private soldier) in time of war or emergency. On 22 November the Government issued a paper on the formation and organisation of the WRNS. Proposals for the reformation of the First World War organisation were submitted by the Admiralty to the Treasury on 11 February 1939. Dame Elvira Laughton Mathews DBE (Vera), an ex-suffragette, who had been in charge of the Crystal Palace WRNS unit during the First World War, became the WRNS Director on 11 April 1939. Vera was responsible to the Admiralty for the recruitment, efficiency, the welfare and discipline of the organisation, and with a small staff, set about organising the WRNS anew.

The call up of unmarried women within the age limits of 18–45 began in July 1939. It would later be lowered to age 17, and would include married women without children up to age 50. Enrolment and registration began immediately for those resident in the areas of the major naval ports such as Portsmouth, Plymouth, Chatham and Rosyth. Port Superintendents were appointed to take charge of the recruitment, efficiency, discipline and well-being of the women serving in their areas. Many of those recruited had already served in the First World War, and now brought their daughters to work alongside them. Three categories of employment were established: (1) Office Duties, which involved secretarial, cypher, code, clerk, accountant, shorthand-typist, telephone operator, or signaller; (2) the Motor Transport branch for vehicle drivers; and (3) General Duties, which were mainly of a domestic nature, including cooks, stewardesses, waitresses, messengers and orderlies.

On 3 September 1939, the Conservative Prime Minister Neville Chamberlain announced on the wireless that the United Kingdom was at war with Germany.

Initially, the WRNS were mostly from the middle class, though recruitment would extend more to working-class women as the war intensified. In the early stages, working-class women were mainly recruited into the munitions factories or industry. Service pay in the WRNS was low, but for many they were better fed than in civilian life, and their board and lodgings and uniform was provided free of charge. A lady who served throughout most of the war working first as a waitress serving officers in London, and later as an assistant nurse in Wales, today aged 90, recalls that her pay was £2.10s (£2.50) a week.

There were recruiting officers who covered the Midlands and northern England, and who were in contact with the Ministry of Labour and women's organisations to recruit women and girls. A separate recruiting officer covered Scotland from the end of 1940 until 1942. In Northern Ireland in November 1939, a WRNS Officer was appointed to the staff of Flag Officer-in-Charge, and a number of WRNS were recruited to posts similar to those in the rest of the UK.

In the more demanding jobs women wanting to work as Wrens had to have qualifications and, in some cases, work experience. Some may have had past experience in the Services, or in the WRNS or Admiralty, or practical experience of boat work, or had a family member employed in the Royal Navy or Merchant Navy, past employment as a cook or in domestic service, or a good qualification in German. By the summer of 1942, despite there being a shortage of staff, recruitment remained voluntary. Women applying for a job were expected to already have the skills necessary to carry it out. Training was given only for wireless, telegraphy, special operators and coders. Vera Mathews was of the view that, given the right training, women were perfectly capable of undertaking most shore duties formerly carried out by men. As the war lengthened the numbers of women needed increased, and those eager to join, but who had no experience, were given training.

From 30 October 1939, WRNS officers undertook a two-week training course at the Royal Naval College, Greenwich, south east London. From November 1941, it was lengthened to three weeks. From January 1940, the Ratings were given a two-week course known as General Service Training. The courses were held at Central Training Depots and involved instruction on general and naval subjects, as well as medical examinations, interviews, enrolment and kitting. There was also squad drill and physical training. A lot of the Wrens' time was spent on domestic work such as scrubbing, cleaning and waitressing. From March 1941, a new scheme was introduced for new entrants, who were trained as Probationary Wrens, and whose future categories was decided by the Chief Officer whilst they were still in training.

As time passed the work became more varied and demanding. From 1941 onwards, Wrens undertook work as radio and air mechanics, maintenance, torpedo and boats' crews, and formed nearly 85 per cent of the naval staff at the now famous codebreaking centre, Bletchley Park, Buckinghamshire.[1] From April 1941, the WRNS became part of Naval Personnel Services, rather than Civil Establishments. Their sphere of work widened even further to radar detection finders, cinema operators, gunnery dome operators, submarine attack teacher operators, meteorologists, bomb range markers, vision testers, cine gun assessors and anti-aircraft target operators. The greatest number of Wrens to be concentrated on a single project would be employed on Operation Overlord, the Allied invasion of Normandy beaches in France, during June 1944. The build-up of forces in preparation for D-Day began in early 1943. The largest numbers of Wrens were employed in the Combined Operations bases and establishments. Portsmouth Command was accorded priority.

Wrens hardly ever served on naval ships but were employed at sea in other areas. They assisted with training exercises during the Battle of the Atlantic (1939–45).[2] A few served as stokers, coxswains and codebreakers in transAtlantic convoys. They were in evidence in some numbers by late 1940, in the capacity of trained boat's crews in the southern ports, delivering stores, despatches and signals, as well as taking commanding officers ashore for sailing orders. They carried out their work regardless of the weather conditions, especially during the Normandy invasions, when boats' crews went across to France to collect damaged boats to be towed back to southern England.

The Navy eventually conceded that WRNS cypher officers and coders could carry out these duties in troopships. Two cypher officers and three coders were assigned to each ship that required them.[3] There were basically two methods of preparing a message for transmission. One was 'Coding' in which words or phrases were represented by symbols that would be recognised and decoded by the receiver. The other was 'Encipherment', in which letters in a plain text message were represented by other letters or characters according to a scheme. For instance the operator would press the letter 'a' on an electronic typewriter-like machine but it would print the letter 'z', and so on. A more advanced form was 'Superencipherment', in which the message was first coded and then enciphered, making it doubly hard to break, particularly if an enemy got hold of it. 'Cryptology' was the two-part science of Cryptography, encoding; and Cryptanalysis, the breaking of codes.

Her Royal Highness The Princess Marina of Greece and Denmark was born to Princess Elena and Prince Nicholas of Greece, in Athens, on 13 December 1906.[4] On 29 November 1934, at Westminster Abbey, Princess Marina had married Prince George, 1st Duke of Kent,[5] and fourth son of King George V and Queen Mary. The wedding was the very essence of a fairy-tale romance. The young couple were photographed in the Throne Room at Buckingham Palace with the King and Queen and the young Princesses Elizabeth and Margaret, who were bridesmaids.[6] Marina's new title was 'The Duchess of Kent' but for ease of reference she will be referred to throughout by her first name. By 1940, the Kents had two children, a son Prince Edward, and a daughter Princess Alexandra.

From the outset, Marina was an inspirational figure; royal, tall, beautiful and hardworking, she was ideal for a leadership role. Marina received a letter from Winston Churchill, First Lord of the Admiralty, inviting her 'to accept an honorary appointment as Commandant of the Women's Royal Naval Service, of which the Queen is Commander-in-Chief'.[7] At the Admiralty, Whitehall, London, on 23 February 1940, Marina joined the Navy as Commandant of the Women's Royal Naval Service. In her inaugural speech, she emphasised that women working in the WRNS would free male naval officers for other duties. The advertising slogan was: 'Join the Wrens – and Free a Man for the Fleet.'[8]

Marina's role was to travel about the country, visiting the chief centres of the WRNS, and thereby bringing pride and conscientiousness to the young women who chose to serve their country well. Marina was highly dedicated and brought a personal touch to the job. She would walk down a line of girls and would stop to talk to each one in turn, showing a genuine interest in each. She wore the WRNS uniform when she was on duty, carrying out inspections, which meant the women could identify with her and feel she was one of them. The uniform was provided by the government, and was a navy jacket and skirt, white blouse, tie, twill hat, black woollen tights (though some wore silk stockings), black shoes, and coxswains wore trousers. The hat was changed in 1942 to a flat sailor type cap.

In early April 1940, Vera Matthews arranged Marina's first visit, to the WRNS Headquarters at Charing Cross, southeast London. Marina entered the Director's Room and saw the charts being maintained, and thence to the Medical Superintendent's Room, which accommodated staff and volunteers. Lady Carter (whose husband was Secretary to the Admiralty) was a member of staff and was described by Vera for Marina as a *'gros bonnet'*.[9] She was then shown into the Registry and Drafting Room, where she saw the details of recruiting and other administrative procedures.[10]

On 11 April, Marina visited the Training and Drafting depot, WRNS, Campden Hill Road, southeast London. There she saw the Signal School, Teleprinter Training, Officers' Wardroom, stores, galleys, and messes, sickbay, a rating's cabin, and the canteens. She went out, onto the Main Deck to see a physical training class in action, and then to the ratings' recreation room.

On 24 May, Marina carried out an inspection of WRNS detachments at Mount Wise Royal Naval Engineering College, Portsmouth. She saw the Wrens on parade, and then visited the barracks, kitchens, and accommodation, and witnessed the Wrens at work in the kitchens and mess.[11]

In the midst of these public engagements a Nurse Kay arrived as a new nursing auxiliary at University College Hospital in London. She was not a trained nurse but an assistant nurse. Her duties were on Ward 16, and involved putting on surgical dressings, making beds, washing patients, doing their hair, tidying their lockers and plumping up their pillows. She also fed the patients who could not feed themselves, and handed the trays of meals around. She assisted in the preparation of patients for their operations in the theatre, and the removal of tubes after the operation had been performed. Then one day Nurse Kay's cover was blown when a patient recognised her as Princess Marina.[12] Her interest in nursing showed that she was not afraid to get her hands dirty. Getting involved in this way provided Marina with a deeper understanding of the work carried out by women during the war, and the suffering of the war wounded. Prior to that Marina had also gained some experience having worked as a volunteer at Iver and Denham Cottage Hospital, Buckinghamshire, which was convenient to where she lived with her husband and children.

Throughout 1940, Marina's engagements were as widespread as Chatham, Greenwich, Dover, Bristol, Portsmouth, Grimsby, Humber, Yarmouth, Skegness, Harwich Portland, Liverpool, Newcastle and Hull, and Rosyth and Glasgow in Scotland.[13]

During tours of inspection of the WRNS's quarters, Marina was received warmly by the volunteers and was very popular. She insisted on actually seeing the girls' quarters, and was concerned to satisfy herself that they really were comfortable. She even went into the galleys, and talked to the cooks and support staff. Marina's personal interest reassured the young people and married women who had given up their comfortable home life that she genuinely cared about their welfare and was appreciative of the contribution they were making in war work for their country.

Reports of Marina's work show great attention to detail and a positive and genuine interest in the work and surroundings. By the autumn, Marina was packing in as many visits as could be squeezed into a day. One particular seven-page report in her file at the Royal Archives, Windsor Castle, is a historic document in itself.[14] It details her visit to Scotland, and provides an insight into how a WRNS establishment functioned and the work it carried out, as well as the intricacies involved in maintaining such a place. Considering it was undertaken whilst a major war was raging all around them, it bears credit to the Officers in charge, and to the Wrens, and to Marina, as their dedicated Commandant. Nearly seventy years after it was written the report provides the modern reader and the historian with an educational insight into how a Member of the royal family like Marina carried out her duties, and how the Wrens operated. Theirs was something of a private world inside the greater world, and each was dependant on the other. Team working was the essence of success.

The report begins with Marina's arrival at Rosyth Royal Naval Air Station, Donibristle, at 11.15am on Thursday 24 October. Marina was met by a senior officer, and set out immediately on a tour of inspection of the Wrens of HMS *Merlin*. She saw the Wrens inside (rather than outside) in one of the hangars 'owing to inclement weather'. She met a number of women who had served in various duties since 1939. Marina was then driven to the ship's galley, and on the way there 'she displayed much interest in the various types of aircraft on the field, and in the fact that Wrens were to be trained as parachute packers'. In the ship's galley kitchen Marina was shown the week's menus, and such features as cooking of soup by steam, and the large electric mincing machine with its many functions. Marina always took into consideration women who had served for a lengthy period of time, according them due respect for their services. She was shown the recently extended mess, which catered for the increase in numbers, followed by the WRNS officers' mess. A number of officers were presented to her, and then morning coffee was served. Afterwards she visited the sick bay, speaking with the nursing sister-in-charge, who showed her the surgery and a number of sick rooms for officers and ratings. Proceeding to the Wrens' quarters, she inspected each room in turn, and the kitchenette, and then walking in the gardens, she asked if the Wrens tended them themselves.

Inspections by the royal Commandant ensured that everything was up to standard and that the Wrens were properly accommodated. In the recently built YWCA[15] building she was shown various rooms, the kitchen and canteen. Marina talked to the women about their work, and took 'the greatest interest in the many activities' connected with the YWCA.

Having departed at 12.03, she set off straight away for her next appointment at the Commander-in-Chief's office. On arrival it was raining and the planned parade inspection had to be rescheduled for the afternoon. In the meantime, Marina was formally presented to a number of officers, which was a great honour for many women who, but for the war, would never have shaken hands with a member of the royal family. Marina also met the women who kept the card indices up to date, and saw the photographic records kept by the Wrens. Different coloured cards were used for the different categories of information. She was then shown the rest rooms that were used by both officers and ratings.

Some of the cypher officers were present, and Marina spoke to them about the important work they carried out, of decoding incoming messages, giving important instructions for the Navy relating to the war. Marina saw the coding office, where ten Wrens were employed under the direction of a Warrant Telegraphist, whose job it was to operate, maintain and repair the wireless communication outfits. They showed her the log, and she 'remarked upon the neatness and care' with which it was kept. In a separate cypher office, which was run entirely by WRNS officers, Marina was shown the 'trap latch through which signals are passed from other offices'.

Then came the Telephone Switchboard Operators' room, where the operators were 'so heavily engaged in the receiving and transmitting of Naval messages' they 'were unable to do more than acknowledge the kindly smile they received from Her Royal Highness'. Marina was then shown through the typing room, the telephone room and the signal distributing office.

The Teleprinting Room was next, and Marina was 'initiated ... into some of the mysteries of a Teleprinting Machine'. This machine is rather like a typewriter but when a key is depressed it activates a number of letters and is for making coded messages. Throughout the visit Marina chatted to the women in a relaxed manner, giving them a sense of self-worth and conveying to them the value of their contribution to the war effort. At 12.45 hours, the royal visitor left in company with the Commander-in-Chief to attend lunch at Admiralty House.

One would think that Marina had undertaken a good day's work, but she was only just beginning. At 15.01, Marina arrived at St Leonard's Drafting and Training Depot where a number of officers were presented to her. She set off on another round of inspections to the dining hall, the Stillroom and the

Galley. She saw trainees being instructed in the valeting of officers' uniforms. Inspecting the Kitting Room she saw a new recruit being kitted up for work. She saw the sick bay and inspected the dormitories. All along the way, Marina listened to individual stories. In the Recreation Room Wren D. Cole told her of how she had served as Supply Assistant in the WAAC[16] during the First World War from 1914 to 1918. She had served in France as well as the British Isles, and was accustomed to kitting up as many as 200 men a day. She had been awarded both the General Service and the Victory medals. Wren E. McDonald told Marina that she had cooked for the King and Queen, when they dined at Broadlands.[17]

Having left at 15.14, Marina went on to the WRNS quarters at Abbey Park House where, accompanied by the Superintendent, and Mary, Lady Herbert, her lady-in-waiting, she arrived at 15.22 for another tour. They entered by the circular hall, where they were greeted by a line-up of stewards, and then they proceeded up the stairs to the large dormitory. Marina expressed her admiration of the light and airy sleeping accommodation, and commented on something that we today would take for granted, running hot water. In the Second Officers' combined office/bedroom, Marina's sharp eye for detail took in the Adam fireplace.[18] Through the office/bedroom window over coffee, she had a view of the garden, taking stock of the 'beautiful view of the countryside', which stretched 'away to the Forth', and she 'greatly admired' the hills beyond. A bathroom might not sound very inspirational, but Marina asked to see one of the five in existence.

Downstairs again, Marina was shown into the Ratings Mess Room. Here she found several Wrens 'sitting knitting and chatting round the fire'. Shaking hands with some of the women, she talked to them about their duties, and remarked upon the 'importance' of their work. Knitting was a necessity rather than a pastime as the proceeds, woollen socks, gloves and such like, would be posted off to the troops. Marina was then shown into the Wardroom where she spoke to the officer-in-charge of the work in 'Quarters'.

On their way to the kitchen the Second Officer prepared her for the staff, telling her: 'the cooks' are 'very good and very Scottish'. Marina replied: 'Oh good! I like them that way!' She shook hands with the women working in the scullery. Having looked at the 'menu book', she laughed and joked about the 'thirty vegetable marrows festooned round the kitchen walls'.

The First Aid equipment was inspected, after which they walked out into the west-facing rose garden leading to an annexe. Marina used the time to ask the accompanying officers about themselves, and enquired after the 'happiness of all the Wrens in Quarters'. She asked about the recreational facilities, and was told that there was 'an Abbey Park Rifle Club'. The annexe was the recreation room, where she found some of the women playing billiards.

On her return journey, Marina was 'amused' to find Wrens perched somewhat precariously on the fire escape, cameras at the ready, taking photographs. She called out to them 'laughingly' to 'be careful and not break your necks'. She was told of an Abbey Park Cine Film which had been taken, and asked the photographer if she had 'got any good shots of the Inspection'.

It was noted that 'it was with regret that the Abbey Park Wrens said goodbye to their Commandant'. As the car pulled away, Marina 'smiled and waved through the back window'. This 'last personal touch was symbolic of the whole Inspection. By her ease of manner, personal interest and pervading sense of humour' Marina 'had won the hearts of all and her charming personality' had 'left a lasting impression' on all who met her.

Yet Marina's day of inspections was far from over. At 15.45 hours, she arrived at Rannoch Moor Officers' Quarters, where she was escorted to the lounge to meet a number of officers. Marina showed a great interest in everything and 'asked many questions regarding personnel and quarters'. The place was packed with officers and a number of them were formally presented. There was tea and then a group photograph was taken in the garden. At 16.25, Marina left 'amidst cheers from officers and staff'.

Marina next visited the Mechanical Transport Establishment, arriving at 16.30 hours. She was shown the gymnasium and swimming bath and inspected the ranks. Marina always engaged in conversation with those presented to her and would listen to their stories of how they had entered the Wrens, and where they had worked previously. Next came the recreation room, complete with a wireless, piano and gramophone, and then the dormitories. Marina admired the dressing tables, which were placed at the end of each bed.

Descending into the galley, she saw the hot plate, pastry ovens and steamers, and the toast being made in an electric toaster, a luxury in those days. She chatted with the cooks and the wine steward, asking them how long they had been in service. There was also a surgery, with a 'well-stocked cupboard', and a visiting nursing sister.

The two mess rooms were inspected and Marina 'admired the view of the Dockyard, the River Forth and the Forth Bridge'. Before departing, Marina returned to the offices and was received by the Commander-in-Chief. At 16.44 'the cars drove off to the sound of three cheers' from the Wrens, who lined the road either side.

Still Marina's day's work was not complete. She had one last call at Port Edgar. They crossed to South Queensferry by the ferry, and arrived at Butlaw

Camp at 17.15 hours. In the road there were crowds of people, waving and cheering, as the car sped along. A parade of over thirty officers and Wrens was waiting and which Marina duly inspected. She showed particular interest in those who were telephone operators, employed on work of a most confidential nature. She inspected the Naval Officers' Mess, which was soon to be staffed by Wrens, when accommodation for them was got ready. With 'a kindly smile to all' Marina 'left by car for Edinburgh'. She had been carrying out inspections for six hours with scarcely a break except for lunch and the occasional cup of tea or coffee along the way.

With the ever-growing urgency to recruit more women and girls, Marina gave a radio broadcast appeal on 20 January 1941, to boost the numbers. The text is most revealing, as it provides an insight into the skills and duties which were already required of the Wrens:

> The Navy has to be fed, and cooks and stewards are wanted, particularly in the big training establishments for the Navy and the Fleet Air Arm. Ledger clerks and book-keepers are also needed, as accounts have to be kept. Morse [code] has to be transcribed by wireless telegraphists. Messages have to be taken by telephone operators, signals teleprinted and records kept. Shorthand typists are also wanted.

Marina went on to reassure those who might be tempted to join, but who might not have any relevant experience, that training would be provided:

> Many WREN cooks are being trained at the Royal Naval cookery schools. If you like household duties, the WRENS can make you a first-class steward. It may mean a sacrifice to leave your home and possibly work which interests you, but you will have the feeling that your new work is essential to our war effort.

A note of heroism and encouragement to the women then entered Marina's broadcast:

> I should like to say a word of congratulation to the many thousands of WRENS who are already serving their country. We are very proud of the wonderful way in which you have carried on your work during air raids, and at times of tension. We admire your courage, and we know that danger is met unflinchingly because the future happiness of our families and homes depends on victory. If you join the WRNS you will know that you have done your share, and are worthy of your country.[19]

The broadcast ended with Marina giving the name and address of the Headquarters to write to. The speech was a tremendous success, and over 3,000 women and girls applied immediately to join the WRNS. In the beginning, there had been resistance and concern from men about women taking over their jobs, particularly in the technical fields. Partly due to the efficiency of the women, and partly to Marina's broadcast, this opposition gave way to praise for the work of the Wrens. Marina's speech had been reassuring and had helped to smooth the way for more women recruits.

Following the radio broadcast, between April and the end of 1941, Marina embarked on a tough schedule of inspections of the Wrens all over the country, and was not deterred in her duty by bad weather conditions. Sometime around the end of October, she conceived her third child. Pregnancy did not deter her from completing her year's work up until December. On 12 November, she inspected the WRNS work at HMS *Heron*, Yeovilton, Somerset, a Royal Naval Air Station.

On 4 July 1942, Marina gave birth to Prince Michael.[20] Six weeks later, joy turned to grief when, on Tuesday 25 August, Marina's beloved husband Prince George was killed in a plane crash whilst on active service. Marina, like so many other women was now a war widow, and was distraught and tearful for a time. But the war was only halfway through, and she eventually regained her courage and threw herself once again back into her work.

By the beginning of November that year, Marina had returned to duty. On 3 November she made an intensive afternoon visit to WRNS Central Training Depot, Mill Hill, London. On 12 November, she inspected WRNS transport on Horse Guards Parade, saw WRNS headquarters at Admiralty House, and squeezed in a fifteen-minute meeting with the Prime Minister at No. 10 Downing Street. Her visit on 3 December to Portsmouth reminds us of the importance of that base, and how important was the work of the WRNS. Nine officers and 232 Wrens were seen working at the submarine base, a further four officers and 316 Wrens at the motor torpedo boat base, six officers and 382 Wrens at the training base and the torpedo school.

The year of 1943 was exceptionally busy. On 11 January, Marina visited Head Quarters, Coastal Forces, to see 120 wireless telegraphists in training there. The next day, she was at Head Quarters Flag Officer, London, to see how the WRNS ran the Message Room. On 29 January, she saw Head Quarters Combined Operations, and on 5 February the Accountant Ratings Training Establishment. This school had been created on 1 November 1941, and to date had trained 1,658 men and 700 women as accountants. Its current class numbered 500 men and 150 women. There was a ten-week course for men, and a two to three weeks course for women. Marina visited a submarine base on 8 February, to see WRNS cypher officers and on 23 February, she went to the Cypher and Plotting Rooms, Chatham.

To illustrate how her administrative staff looked after her, a letter of 9 March about a forthcoming visit to a Minewatching Post, written by Sybil Sassoon, Chief Staff Officer to Director of WRNS, and sent from WRNS Head Quarters, Queen Ann's Mansions, London W1, noted: 'I understand that the worst possible day has been chosen as far as the tide is concerned, and the Duchess will have to scale heights hitherto only passable to mountain goats!' Another note made sure the Court Circular said she was visiting the WRNS, and not any other service.

By 15 March Marina was visiting to WRNS working at Royal Navy gunnery schools, and, on 25 March she made a major visit to Plymouth, where many hundreds of Wrens worked at the major base, including complete boat crews. On 20 April, she received requests to visit two Signals Schools and she promised to fit them both in on one day, and offered to fit in other visits at nearby locations. This visit, finally embracing six establishments, took place on 27 May, and involved seeing the highly secret and important work done by the Wrens employed there.

The notes provided for a visit to WRNS HQ, Queen Ann's Mansions, London, on 29 June, provide an insight into how these things were managed. It lists nineteen offices to be visited (the last one was for 'powder and general re-fit'!), and reminders to congratulate Miss Jocelyn Woollcombe,[21] Superintendent, on her promotion. There were lists of people Marina had met previously, and of recent awards holders, and those who would attend a lunch. There was a note that Instructor Rear Admiral Hall was the only schoolteacher ever to attain Admiral rank. Another said that the Financial Secretary, Mr Hall, used to be a miner and 'is very Left wing' and was, therefore, exceptionally thrilled at meeting the Duchess. One poignant message suggested 'a private reference to the Director's anxiety about her husband would not go amiss'. Individuals were described as: 'a shy and charming man', 'very charming', 'has only one arm', 'is new from West Africa', and 'an attractive young officer'.

On 6 October, Marina gave a speech at the National Portrait Gallery, London, to open a WRNS Exhibition:

> The first Arts and Crafts Exhibition by the Women's Royal Naval Service, held in one of London's famous galleries, is an outstanding event, and I am delighted, as Commandant, to see so many works exhibited. One would expect that in a service as large as ours there would be many artistically minded people, but it is encouraging to

(*op left*) *Eastward Ho! August 1857*. Woodcut in *The Illustrated London News* (1858), after an oil painting by H O'Neill, for the 1858 Royal Academy Exhibition. Friends and families go ashore from British troopship in India.

(*op right*) Memorial to the officers and men of the Cornwall Regiment Light Infantry who died in e Indian Massacre 1857. (*Mrs Mary Heathcote*)

mmander-in-Chief, India, General Sir Colin mpbell, aged 65.

Heni Te Kiri Karamu, Maori warrior, wearing a kahu huruhuru (Maori feather cloak), headdress of native huia feathers, and tiki (neck pendant), c.1920–33. (*Alexander Turnbull National Library, New Zealand*)

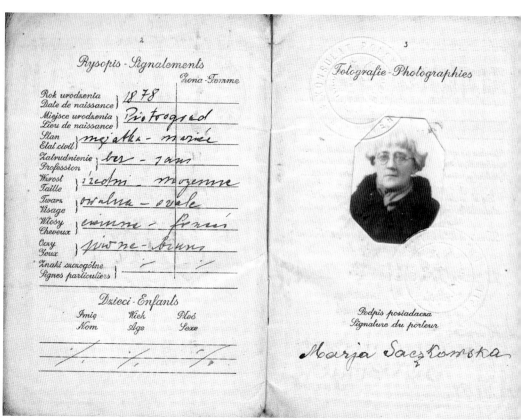

Rysopis · Signalements
Żona · Femme

Rok urodzenia / Date de naissance : 1878
Miejsce urodzenia / Lieu de naissance : Piotrogród
Stan / État civil : mężatka – mariée
Zatrudnienie / Profession : bez – sans
Wzrost / Taille : średni – moyenne
Twarz / Visage : owalna – ovale
Włosy / Cheveux : siwe – gris
Oczy / Yeux : siwe – bruns
Znaki szczególne / Signes particuliers :

Dzieci · Enfants

Imię / Nom	Wiek / Age	Płeć / Sexe

Fotografie · Photographies

Podpis posiadacza
Signature du porteur

Marja Saczkowska

Mrs Marya Saczkowska, photograph in her Polish passport issued in December 1939, just months before her flight to England.

Captain Nikolai Saczkowski, at the outbreak of the First World War, Petrograd; he escaped to England in September 1939.

Miss Tatiana Saczkowska (later Mrs Bailey), escaped to England in early 1940.

Driver Gladys May Brotherton (née Spencer), Women's Legion 1917.

Sergeant Gladys May Brotherton (née Spencer) ATS, and Lieutenant Mary Wandless Brotherton, her daughter, 17 May 1942.

An ATS girl with 'A' troo
484/139 (Mixed) Heavy
Anti-Aircraft Regiment,
Royal Artillery, at her
position in the control roc
at Haecht in Belgium,
10 January 1945.
(*Imperial War Museum*)

Private Joan Hill (née Hewitt).

Greta Nimse (née Scott), with General
Sir Frederick Pile and a civilian.

ATS women take a break at a 3.7 inch anti-aircraft gun site at Wormwood Scrubs in London, 22 October 1941.
(*Imperial War Museum*)

ATS girls operate a predictor at a 3.7 inch anti-aircraft battery, Dunfermline, Scotland, 6 January 1943.
(*Imperial War Museum*)

Red Cross nurses and patients in the Library of Blenheim Palace, converted into a hospital during the First World War. (*11th Duke of Marlborough*)

enheim Palace, hospital supply depot staff during the First World War. (*11th Duke of Marlborough*)

incess Marina the Duchess of Kent,
ommandant of the WRNS 1940.
RH The Duke of Kent)

Commodore Sir Gerard d'Erlanger.
(*Mrs Mary (Minnie) S. Churchill*)

Diana Barnato-Walker broke the sound barrier in an RAF Lightning 1963.

Amy Johnson, first woman to fly sol from London to Australia 1930.

Picture Post (16 September 1942), ATA Ferry Pilot: First Officer Maureen Dunlop.

Hazel Furney, WAAF, worked in photographic interpretation, RAF Medmenham 'L' Section, which kept a continuous watch on enemy aircraft production.

Polish FANYs at Latiano, summer 1944, Sue Ryder is fi.. on the right in the second row. (*Lady Niven*)

Flight Officer Constance Babbington Smith, photograp.. interpreter, RAF, during the Second World War, who discovered the V-1 rocket bei.. built from an aerial reconnaissance photograph taken over Peenemünde.

tion Officer (Photographic Intelligence),
rah Oliver (nee Churchill) RAF, Medmenham,
th colleagues during the Second World War.

Section Officer (Photographic Intelligence),
Sarah Oliver (nee Churchill), photographic
interpreter RAF Medmenham.

SARAH OLIVER
Daughter of Winston Churchill
Medmenham Photo Interpreter

Barbara Yardley with FANY friends (far left on the end), Second World War.

Shelagh Adams (second from left) with FANYs, Second World War.

HMS *Collingwood* radar maintenance and fitting staff, June 1945; WREN radar mechanic Thelma Fry (now Mrs Stollar) is in the fourth row on the right, second WRN from the end.

WRNS practising on a rifle range, December 1940.

Tatiana Sysoenkova (now Mrs Chernysheva) the little girl who slept in the window during the Siege of Leningrad 1941.

Nina Kochańska wearing the uniform of th 1st Polish Army on the Eastern Front, 1944

Hanna Reitsch revelling her role as Nazi German most celebrated aviatrix a visit to her home town of Hirschberg in 1941. Note the Iron Cross and Combined Pilot-Observe Badge.

udmila Pavlichenko, Heroine of the Soviet Union, in a well-known propaganda shot. It is doubtful if she would have considered blossom as suitable cover in the field! Almost certainly the most successful female sniper in history and arguably one of the tiny number of practitioners considered to have been true masters of the art.

Gräfin von Stauffenberg in front of a twin-engined Junkers Ju 88. Note the Iron Cross ribbon on the fashionable riding costume that she clearly used for flying on this occasion. The Ju 88 was meant to operate as a heavy dive bomber but Melitta's team soon realized that the aircraft was only capable of diving at an angle of 45 degrees.

ly 2007: Churchill Fellow Grace Filby (second from left) meets the staff at the Military Hospital in Georgia where phage therapy is routinely applied. One year on, this same hospital was a target in the Georgian-Russian War when a trauma surgeon was killed.

Members of No. 10 Casualty Clearing Station, Second World War, Sister Theresa Jordan is fourth from the left in the front row.

Nurse Theresa Jordan, Mentioned in Despatches, October 1945.

Mrs Georgina Ivison, army school mistress in Egypt and South Africa

By the KING'S Order the name of
Sister (Miss) T. Jordan,
Queen Alexandra's Imperial Military Nursing Service,
was published in the London Gazette on
18 October 1945,
as mentioned in a Despatch for distinguished service.
I am charged to record
His Majesty's high appreciation.

J. J. Lawson

Secretary of State for War

see how good is the talent. It shows also that, in spite of the strenuous lives which Wrens are leading, many of them devote their spare time to various forms of art and handicrafts, which are good for the mind, and allows them to relax for a short time from their daily tasks. I hope that this is the first of a series of exhibitions, and in declaring it open I would like to congratulate the organisers and contributors on their enterprise, which I trust will be seen by many people thereby helping the Royal Naval War Libraries.[22]

A visit to Wales rounded off this busy year.

By September 1944, the numbers of Wrens serving had reached 74,000 officers and ratings. Their work during wartime has been viewed as a huge contribution to the emancipation of women. For many it was the first responsible paid job in their lives, whether they were married or single. The year would see some visits to major bases, all of which clamoured for attention. Thus on 22 August, WRNS HQ wrote to Marina's office:

I am sorry to bother you when you are having what I hope is a very happy and healthful holiday, but I am being harried and harassed by Dover. It is a long time (four years) since the Duchess visited Dover, and they are anxious for her to grace with her presence their Annual Squad Drill Competition which they expect to hold early in October. I think it would be a good move if she could accept, and there is quite a lot to see there. I suggest one of two things: (a) that they decide to have the competition on either Wed Oct 4 or 11, and that HRH decides later on whether she will attend; or (b) that she should name a day convenient to herself during the first fortnight of October.

The letter has 'Yes, 11th October' written across the top.

Before Dover, a visit was fitted in to Royal Naval Air Station Arbroath on 14 September, and a further major Scottish visit was in the planning. We are reminded that not all 'sailors' are good sailors! Drawing attention to Dover's ideas for the visit, a letter concluded:

The programme, which you will receive in a day or two, will include a 'flip' in a motor launch round the Harbour, but that is, of course, subject to a glassy sea, as well as HRH's concurrence, as I believe she is no sailor. However, the Princess Royal made the trip the other day, and enjoyed it vastly.[23]

Headquarters were reassured that 'HRH' would take the trip, and say a few words about the Wrens working under fire at Dover.[24]

The visit was made on 11 October, and was a huge success. Marina gave the prizes at the WRNS Annual Squad drill, rifle shooting and handicrafts competitions, and made a speech:

> I would like to take this opportunity of telling all ranks of the Women's Royal Naval Service in the Dover Command how deeply I have admired their courage and devotion to duty during the last four years.
>
> From the critical summer of 1940, when I was last here, to the present day you have worked under fire by day and night, quietly and efficiently, with little rest.
>
> Together with the Royal Navy, you have carried out a magnificent job of great importance in the historic, defiant, and undefeated port of Dover.
>
> If the Women's Royal Naval Service carried Colours, Dover would be the first name of Battle Honours.
>
> I congratulate you on the work shown here today, and I am very proud of you all.[25]

The visits to Leith, Rosyth, and Donibristle required two days – 19 and 20 October – and was another packed and successful schedule, seeing the Wrens at all sorts of technical work.

In March 1945, Admiral Sir Martin E. Dunbar-Nasmith, VC, Flag Officer in Charge, London, requested a return visit to the Port of London Authority headquarters in April, which was happily complied with. The letter of appreciation speaks for all these visits:

> Dear Lord Herbert, I must send you a line to tell you how very much the Duchess of Kent's visit was appreciated by all in this Command.
> I am afraid we worked her very hard, but her interest and enthusiasm in all the departments visited was an inspiration to all the Wrens, both officers and ratings.
>
> M. Dunbar-Nasmith.[26]

The letter of reply was equally felicitous: 'HRH felt that the great heat must have proved rather a trial to those on parade, but hopes that they suffered no ill effects.'[27]

The requests kept coming and could not always be met. Thus a plea from Portsmouth to support their 'Navy Week' in May had to be refused because a visit was already planned to Eastern Command.

The war finally came to an end in August 1945, and one hundred Wrens had been killed on active service. There is a record at the Royal Archives that in the

1950s, in their eagerness, girls who wanted to join the WRNS wrote direct to Marina. Sometimes they aired their grievances when they did not get the kind of job they wanted. A girl who failed to reach the required standard for Stores Rating, i.e. a test in maths, spelling, and intelligence, might write and complain that she did not want to become a steward. Commandant Mary Lloyd would reply, saying Marina could not interfere.[28] Mary Lloyd also noted that it was a pity this type of girl would not enter the service as an officer's steward. She thought that 'in many girls' and 'in parents' minds there was still 'that stupid feeling of something derogatory about domestic work'.[29] No doubt their mothers remembered only too well their own days of drudgery in domestic service from which they were glad to escape into well paid jobs elsewhere.

Princess Marina's title was changed in 1951 to Chief Commandant of the WRNS, which she remained until her death in August 1968. In 1993, the WRNS were incorporated into the Royal Navy.

Notes

The author acknowledges the gracious permission of Her Majesty Queen Elizabeth II for allowing access to the papers of Her Royal Highness the Duchess of Kent, and other related letters and reports at the Royal Archives, Windsor Castle, and for allowing publication of extracts from the papers. The author wishes to thank the late Princess Marina's elder son, Prince Edward the Duke of Kent KG GCMG. The author also wishes to thank Miss Pamela Clark, Senior Archivist, the Royal Archives, Windsor Castle.

1. H. M. Fletcher, *The WRNS: A History of the Women's Royal Naval Service*, London: B. T. Batsford Ltd, 1989.
2. Ibid.
3. Ibid.
4. Formerly Grand Duchess Elena Vladimirovna of Russia. Neither Marina nor her parents were Greek.
5. The ancient title of Duke of Kent had fallen into abeyance and was revived for Marina's husband Prince George.
6. Sophia Watson, *Marina: The Story of a Princess*, London: Weidenfeld & Nicolson, 1994, chs. 4–5.
7. The Royal Archives, Windsor Castle (hereafter RA): Letter to Princess Marina from Winston Churchill, 23 February 1940; RA MDKDH/ARMFOR/WRNS.
8. Nurses did not join the WRNS, but were part of Queen Alexandra's Royal Naval Nursing Service. Medical and dental officers, however, who were commissioned directly into the Royal Navy, held Royal Naval rank and wore the WRNS uniform with the gold RN insignia.
9. A phrase used to describe Napoleon's Old Guard, meaning a highly experienced veteran.
10. RA MDKDH/MAIN/WRNS.
11. Ibid.
12. Christopher Warwick, *George and Marina the Duke and Duchess of Kent*, London: Weidenfeld & Nicolson, 1988, pp. 118–19.
13. RA MDKDH/MAIN/WRNS.
14. RA MDKDH/MAIN/WRNS/ROSYTH VISIT, 28 October 1940.

15. Young Women's Christian Association (YWCA), a movement of women working for social and economic change around the world. Today, it advocates for young women's leadership, peace, justice, human rights and sustainable development.
16. Women's Army Auxiliary Corps (WAAC).
17. Broadlands House, Romsey, Hants, was the home of Captain Lord Louis Mountbatten, RN.
18. Wooden fireplace peculiar to Scotland with Adam's mouldings, the design may have been by a young Scottish architect named Robert Adam but some of the fireplaces were initialled R&F, meaning the company of Ramage & Son.
19. The Official Papers of HRH Princess Marina, The Duchess of Kent, The Royal Archives, Windsor Castle; RA MDKDH/ARMFOR/WRNS/BROADCAST, 20 January 1941.
20. Prince Michael of Kent is married to former Baroness Marie Christine von Reibnitz of Austria, Princess Michael of Kent.
21. Miss Jocelyn Woollcombe, Chief Officer for the WRNS 1939; CBE 1944; Director of the WRNS 1946–50; DBE 1950.
22. RA MDKDH/MAIN/WRNS.
23. The Princess Mary (1897–1965), only daughter of King George V and Queen Mary, known as the Princess Royal 1932–65.
24. RA MDKDH/MAIN/WRNS.
25. Ibid.
26. Ibid.
27. Ibid.
28. Later Dame Mary Lloyd, Director of WRNS 1950–4.
29. RA MDKDH/ARMFOR/WRNS.

Select Bibliography

Written from the private papers of Her Royal Highness, Princess Marina, The Duchess of Kent, which papers are housed at the Royal Archives, Windsor Castle.

Fletcher, H. M., *The WRNS: A History of the Women's Royal Naval Service*, London: B. T. Batsford Ltd, 1989.

Warwick, Christopher, *George and Marina the Duke and Duchess of Kent*, London: Weidenfeld & Nicolson, 1988.

Watson, Sophia, *Marina: The Story of a Princess*, London: Weidenfeld & Nicolson, 1994.

Chapter 9

Hurricanes and Handbags

Women RAF Ferry Pilots during the Second World War

Mike Ryan

At the height of the summer of 1940, during the famous Battle of Britain, Royal Air Force (RAF) Spitfires and Hurricanes twisted and turned high above the streets of London, engaging the might of Hitler's *Luftwaffe*. How many people on the ground gazing up in awe at the spectacle that passed for daily life, ever spared a thought as to who actually delivered our pilots' aircraft to their air-fields? The answer is certainly, precious few, as the 'flyboys' who flew these aircraft were the heroes of the day, and nobody else. And yet, were it not for these mysterious people who lived in the shadows, our RAF would have ground to a halt in no time, as we had barely enough pilots to fly combat missions, let alone mundane ferrying flights.

So who were these secretive people who kept the RAF supplied with their aircraft? It may surprise even the modern reader to learn that many were actually young women, serving in a little known organisation called The Air Transport Auxiliary (ATA). Indeed, I only became aware of it through my late aunt Lil, who at one time during the Battle of Britain, volunteered for service in the organisation, following the tragic loss of her fighter pilot boyfriend, during a dogfight over southern England. Losing a personal, close friend in war is always hard to bear, but for my aunt her situation was particularly traumatic as she was at the time of her boyfriend's death on duty in the Operations room (Ops room) that was controlling his flight on that fateful day. He, of course knew this, and once hit, and knowing his demise was imminent, he bade her a last farewell over the radio, saying: 'Goodbye darling', just before it went silent.

It was a very moving experience for all concerned who were working in the Ops room that day. There were those who felt that my aunt had done more than her fair share and should now step down and take some time out to grieve and come to terms with her loss. Lil, however, would have none of it, and wanted to get back into the fight as soon as possible. She immediately put herself forward for flight training in the Air Transport Auxiliary, and was pleasantly surprised when her application was accepted. Her dream though was sadly dashed when her mother, who was also serving in the British armed forces, refused to sign her parental consent form as she felt the risks associated with a young girl flying an aeroplane in wartime were just too great. Another reason stemmed from her quite legitimate concern for the rest of her large young family, who were living on a farm in Ireland, without both their mother and their eldest sister. It was what could be described as a case of tough love for all the right reasons.

It was sometimes in similar situations where serious injury or the death of one's boyfriend, husband or other family member had occurred, that young women were encouraged to offer their services in wartime.

Initially, at the outbreak of the Second World War, the role of the ATA was as a delivery service for mail and medical supplies. However, it soon became apparent that their mission portfolio could be greatly increased to help reduce the pressure on both frontline RAF and Fleet Air Arm[1] (FAA) pilots, the FAA being the branch of the British Royal Navy responsible for the operation of aircraft. The ATA was therefore developed into a civilian organisation that ferried new, repaired, and damaged aircraft, between UK active service squadron airfields, aircraft assembly points, factories, Maintenance Units, and in some cases – scrap yards. The ATA also provided both an aircrew taxi service and an air ambulance capability. However, the ATA had no involvement in the transportation and recovery of carrier based aircraft.

Unlike the RAF and Fleet Air Arm, who insisted upon absolute medical perfection when it came to aircrew selection, the ATA were to their credit far more accommodating and generous in making medical allowances for those who could do the job but were not quite physically fit. The organisation recruited male pilots who were considered to be unsuitable for reasons of age or fitness for either the RAF or the FAA, and who were referred to somewhat humorously as 'ancient and tattered airmen', and which included pilots from countries neutral to the war. The experienced male fighter pilots were in great demand to fight the *Luftwaffe*, and carry out bombing raids over Germany, and could not therefore be spared for ferrying work. The physical handicaps in ATA pilots were ignored so long as he could still fly a plane. There were even one-armed, one-legged, short-sighted and even one-eyed pilots flying these aircraft, some of whom enjoyed playing tricks on their passengers once they had spotted that something was not quite right with the man at the controls.

As the war intensified, it became apparent that in order to supply sufficient numbers of pilots to fulfil the increasing demand in service, the ATA had to employ female pilots. In late 1939, Commander Pauline Gower was appointed to the position of organising the women's section of the ATA. Women pilots volunteered from Britain, the Commonwealth, Canada, New Zealand, the USA, Poland, Chile, Africa, and other countries. They came from all walks of life, with some twenty-eight countries being represented, and the majority were British.[2] Under Pauline Gower's command[3] were 166 female pilots, who at that time accounted for almost one in eight of all ATA pilots.[4]

ATA pilots were first introduced to military aircraft at the RAF's Central Flying School (CFS), Upavon, Pewsey, Wiltshire. The training course was progressive, with pilots starting out first on single-engine training aircraft. Generally, it was a case of learning the principles first, which was then quickly followed up by the practical phase which often involved the new rookie pilots ferrying aircraft of a particular class around, until they felt comfortable and competent enough to fly them without any problems. Once mastered, they would then return back to flight school to work on learning the next class up. Training was largely based around an individual's ability to progress rather than a fixed schedule, as there were cases where young pilots either did not want to fly larger aircraft types or simply were not up to the task.

Some 133,247[5] flying hours were amassed in school aircraft, during which the potential of each pilot was being assessed. Eventually a training programme that was unique to them was brought in that took account of all the various types of aircraft that they would have to fly. Pilots were then put forward for one of the 6,013 conversion courses[6] that were run as a means of preparing them for these types of aircraft. Those who were suitable went onto twin-engine aircraft. Eventually, they took on the demanding task of flying the massive four-engine class machines that were flown by the RAF.[7] Initially, female pilots were limited to flying non-combat aircraft such as trainers and transports, but eventually their portfolio increased to include fighters and bombers – but not large flying boats.

Pauline Gower's ladies were issued with an attractive uniform consisting of dark blue skirt or trousers, forage cap, light blue RAF style shirt, black tie, and a single breasted jacket with the ATA insignia in the centre of wings of gold thread. Badges of rank were gold bars on each shoulder. The press wanted photographs and tales of these glamorous girls, whose pictures brightened up wartime magazines and newspapers, and were a good advertisement in that they provided encouragement to other women and girls to join one of the services and do their bit for the war effort. Many of the women were already experienced pilots, having come from affluent backgrounds where their fathers had bought them a light aircraft or paid for private flying lessons.

One of the most remarkable aspects of the ATA related to its non-discrimination of women. Basically if a woman could do the job she got it, and women were also paid exactly the same rates as the men. For the period under discussion and even by today's standards it was a remarkable achievement, and marked the first time that the British Government had ever given its blessing for equal pay for equal work to an organisation that was under its jurisdiction. It contrasted sharply with the US equivalent, the Women Airforce Service Pilots (WASP), who received on average some 35 per cent less than their male colleagues for performing the same job.[8]

The credit for this modern, forward-looking ATA organisation must go to its Commodore, Sir Gerard d'Erlanger CBE, a director of the original British Airways, and later Chairman of BEA, and also BOAC, who suggested the formation of an aircraft ferrying organisation long before the outbreak of the Second World War. His letter setting out the basis for such an organisation dates back to 24 May 1938.[9] The ATA was initially placed under the financial and administrative control of British Airways Ltd, in August 1939, until it was taken under the control of Air Member for Supply and Organisation (AMSO) in October 1939.[10]

The first pilots to join the ATA were assigned to RAF Reserve Command, and then attached to RAF Flights for the movement of trainers, fighters and bombers, from factories and storage bases. To further enhance effectiveness, an entirely civilian ferry pool was set up at White Waltham airfield near Maidenhead, Berkshire, with operations commencing on 15 February 1940. On 1 May 1940, the ATA took over the role of ferrying military aircraft from their assembly points to the Maintenance Units, where their guns and radios were installed. There then followed a succession of control changes with the RAF Maintenance Command, first on 16 May 1940, and then the Ministry of Production on 22 July 1941.[11] Of interest is the fact that, despite the control changes, administration was always under the umbrella of British Airways. Another important date was 1 August 1941, as it marked the day the ATA took over all the ferrying jobs performed by frontline RAF combat pilots.

If a pilot was gifted, the sky was quite literally his or her limit. Essentially, if one equates the pilot's skills to vehicle transportation, they would one day be in an F1 racing car, and the next in an articulated lorry. It is important however to stress that no pilot was expected to be a total expert on every aircraft type – that would clearly have been impossible. Instead, pilots were given ferry pilot notes, which were little more than small cards in a ring binder that served as something of an *aide-memoire*. These notes told the pilot all he or she needed to know in terms of performance data and pre-flight checks, as once airborne, flying is flying, whether it is on one or four engines.

Landing is a different matter entirely. So as to make flying as simple as possible, ATA pilots were trained only to ferry and nothing else. They were expressly forbidden from performing aerobatics or blind flying, even if they were qualified to do so, as their mission was the safe delivery of aircraft. Of course there were isolated instances where pilots did show off, especially so when they were flying a high-performance aircraft such as a fighter. After all, if she had spent most of her flying career sedately moving about in a Tiger Moth, and she then suddenly got a chance to fly a machine capable of almost four times its speed the temptation for further adventure was sometimes too great to resist.

One particular example of this was the delivery of a Spitfire to a fighter base, where an officer on the ground took particular offence at a young pilot performing a barrel roll over his airfield. Determined to have it out with the young miscreant upon their landing, he was most surprised when the individual concerned took off their flying helmet to reveal a long mane of brown hair with stunning looks to match. He was apparently speechless. This officer was not alone in his surprise at seeing a young female pilot, flying what was in effect a state of the art fighter, as precious few men in that male-dominated society would ever have believed that such a feat would have been possible.

The ATA however, made such a scene possible, and it is fair to say that, had this wonderful organisation not existed, both the RAF and FAA would have seriously struggled to cope with the additional pressure that ferrying aircraft around would have brought upon them. Indeed, we are blessed to have had such an organisation during our time of need.

An insight into the level of operations during the war is to be found in the numbers involved. The ATA flew 742,614[12] flying hours, and delivered over 308,567 aircraft.[13] In addition, 883 tons of freight was carried by the ATA, along with 3,430[14] passengers. Air taxi movements accounted for a further 179,325[15] hours. Aircraft flown ranged from fighters to bombers, encompassing some 147 different types, including 360 Flying Fortresses, 9,326 Halifaxes, 29,401 Hurricanes, 9,805 Lancasters, 12,480 Mosquitoes, 26,176 Wellingtons and 57,286[16] Spitfires. In fact, ATA pilots flew more different types of aircraft than most operational pilots, and no doubt many had very interesting and highly qualified opinions as to which aircraft was best.

The women ATA pilots were therefore no amateurs when it came to flying, as each and everyone of them had had to prove that they were worthy of being pilots of highly precious aircraft that were critical to Britain's survival. God help any RAF pilot who ever attempted to chat up an ATA girl with tales of bravado and flying skill relating to his particular mount, as he may have got back as good as he gave. Nobody could ever accuse the ATA of discrimination or being sexist.

Flying of course was not without risk, and sadly fifteen of the female pilots assigned to the ATA lost their lives in the air, the most famous of them being Amy Johnson, who was a pioneer aviatrix. Proportionately, this was a greater loss than pilots in Fighter Command. Amy Johnson had set numerous long-distance flying records during the 1930s. On 5 January 1941, whilst ferrying an Airspeed Oxford for the ATA from Blackpool to RAF Kidlington, near Oxford, Johnson went off course in adverse weather conditions. When her plane ran out of fuel, she gallantly bailed out into the Thames Estuary but drowned.[17]

Speaking of the immense role that the ATA played during the Battle of Britain, Lord Beaverbrook once stated:

> Without the ATA the days and nights of the Battle of Britain would have been conducted under conditions quite different from the actual events. They carried out the delivery of aircraft from the factories to the RAF, thus relieving countless numbers of RAF pilots for duty in the battle. Just as the Battle of Britain is the accomplishment and achievement of the RAF, likewise it can be declared that the ATA sustained and supported them in the battle. They were soldiers fighting in the struggle just as completely as if they had been engaged on the battlefront.[18]

Another of the heroines of the skies was Diana Barnato (later Barnato-Walker), who was already a pilot at age 20, and her training was in Tiger Moths, a 1930s biplane, at the Brooklands Flying Club, Surrey. In early 1941 Diana applied to become one of the first women pilots of the ATA. In November 1941 she was admitted to the Elementary Flying Training School at White Waltham. Following a lengthy period of intensive flight instruction and tests in primary training aircraft, she joined her first ATA Ferry Pool (FP), No. 15 FP at RAF Hamble, Hants, in May 1942. She delivered low-powered single-engine aircraft from factory or repair base to storage units and to RAF and naval flying units. Following advanced training, she delivered several hundred aircraft – Spitfires, Hurricanes, Mustangs, Tempests and other high-performance fighter aircraft. After yet further training, she was qualified to deliver twin-engined aircraft – Whitleys, Blenheims, Mosquitoes, Mitchells and Wellingtons, normally flying solo. By 1945 she had flown eighty types of aircraft and had delivered 260 Spitfires. She developed her technical knowledge of aircraft, which enabled her to get out of a dangerous situation. On one occasion a

Typhoon she was flying began to break up in the air, but by nursing it with the greatest of care, she was able to bring it safely in to land. On arrival, she found that part of the tail had dropped off. Her flying competence was such that on one occasion she delivered five aircraft in one day.

One evening in 1963, in the officers' mess at RAF Middleton St George, the Wing Commander Flying, John Severgne, somewhat casually suggested that Diana might like to fly one of the RAF's new supersonic Lightnings. On 26 August 1963, following clearance from the Ministry of Defence, Diana took off, and reaching a speed of Mach 1.65 (1,262 mph), she became the first British woman to break the sound barrier.[19]

Notes

The author wishes to thank Mrs Mary (Minnie) S. Churchill, daughter of Sir Gerard d'Erlanger CBE, for providing figures on aircraft numbers, and Mr Simon Bird for his help on recommendations for extra material, which has enhanced this chapter considerably. Thanks are also extended to Mr Philip Mills, photographer.

1. The FAA service of the RAF had been formed on 1 April 1924, and encompassed RAF units that normally embarked onto aircraft carriers and fighting ships at sea. On 24 May 1939, control of the FAA was returned to the Admiralty. The aircraft carrier had replaced the battleship as the Fleet's capital ship, and its aircraft were now strike weapons in their own right.
2. Lettice Curtis, *The Forgotten Pilots*, Olney, Bucks: Nelson Saunders, 1985, p. 308.
3. Diana Barnato-Walker, *Spreading my Wings*, Sparkford (UK): Patrick Stephens Ltd, 1994, p. 42.
4. Curtis, *Forgotten Pilots*, p. 200.
5. Ibid., p. 308.
6. Ibid.
7. Figures for aircraft flights E. C. Cheesman, *Brief Glory: The Story of the Air Transport Auxiliary*, London: Air Transport Auxiliary Association, 2001. See Air Transport Auxiliary website.
8. Helena Schrader, *Sisters in Arms*, Barnsley: Pen & Sword, 2006, p. 32.
9. Cheesman, *Brief Glory*, p. 12.
10. Ibid., p. 17.
11. Air Transport Auxiliary, *Air Transport Auxiliary: Handbook [Reminder Book]*, White Waltham: ATA, 1945, pp. 5–7.
12. Figures from *Aviation Forum*; hpt://forum.keypublishing.com, January 2000.
13. Giles Whittell, *Spitfire Women of World War II*, London: Harper Perennial, 2008.
14. Curtis, *Forgotten Pilots*, p. 308.
15. Ibid.
16. Figures for aircraft flights, Cheesman, *Brief Glory*.
17. Kenneth Aitken, 'Amy Johnson (The Speed Seekers)', *Aeroplane Monthly*, 19/7, issue no. 219 (July 1991. See also Wikipedia).
18. E. C. Cheeseman, *Brief Glory of A.T.A.*, Leicester: Harborough Publ. Co., 1946, p. 208.
19. *Daily Telegraph*, obituary, 4 May 2008; *The Times* obituary, 8 May 2008; RAF website. Diana Barnato-Walker died on 28 April 2008, aged 90.

Select Bibliography

Air Transport Auxiliary, *Air Transport Auxiliary, Handbook*, White Waltham: ATA, 1945.

Cheesman, E. C., *Brief Glory: The Story of the Air Transport Auxiliary*, London: Air Transport Auxiliary Association, 2001.

Curtis, Lettice, *The Forgotten Pilots*, Olney, Bucks: Nelson Saunders, 1985.

Schrader, Helena, *Sisters in Arms*, Barnsley: Pen & Sword, 2006.

Walker, Diana Barnato, *Spreading my Wings*, Sparkford (UK): Patrick Stephens Ltd, 1994.

Whittell, Giles, *Spitfire Women of World War II*, London: Harper Perennial, 2008.

THE SECOND WORLD WAR:
SECRET SERVICE WORK

Chapter 10

British Secret Agents during the Second World War

Juliette Pattinson

Jos Mulder Gemmeke, a British-trained Dutch national who during the Second World War was a courier in the Dutch resistance, recalled the various strategies she used to ensure she was not discovered:

> You could change your hair, your clothes, you could charm a lot of people, flirt and I was then young so you could easily do that. Sometimes with a red hat I think, but it always worked ... When I arrived at a station, if I had luggage which was heavy and dangerous, I looked for a German soldier and asked him to carry my luggage and it always worked. He did it! ... I was smiling of course to the German officers. That was important too, to be very friendly.[1]

Jos recognised that being an attractive young woman could have its advantages when trying to fool German soldiers who were on their guard for resisters. Whereas men were suspected of engaging in clandestine activity, women were considered to be beyond suspicion and were thus rarely stopped and searched at identity document checks. Jos noted: 'A woman in that time was very important because they didn't look so much for women as for men of course ... As a girl you could do a lot more.' Women were much more mobile than men and were able to use the task of shopping as a cover for their movements. Jos recalled that she would often place weapons or a wireless set in her bicycle basket concealing them with food, flowers or knitting. The impression she gave was of 'a young girl who was travelling to a friend or something and I had to take a basket full with food and things for her grandmother. I played it like that.' Such displays enabled her to perform her resistance work unhampered by identity document checks and baggage searches, which would have revealed illegal items.

  This chapter examines the extraordinary wartime experiences of a remark-able group of ordinary young women like Jos, who were recruited by a British organisation to wage war against the Nazis. It uses published autobiographies, official documents, and interviews conducted both by myself and by the Imperial War Museum with surviving female agents to chronicle their wartime experiences, examining why they were considered suitable recruits, the training they undertook, their operational missions and for some their experiences during captivity.

Jos was recruited by the Special Operations Executive (SOE), which was established in July 1940, following the invasion of much of Europe and the withdrawal of the British Expeditionary Force from Dunkirk. There was a recognition that the rules of war had changed and that the only way to defeat Nazism was to engage in unorthodox or 'ungentlemanly' warfare. Acts of sabotage and subversion, which were given increased prominence in Churchill's war strategy, were perceived as a 'fourth arm' in addition to the established military services. The SOE was fully incorporated into plans to liberate Europe and received substantial funds to undertake its work. It was tasked with recruiting, training and infiltrating agents into western Europe who, would themselves enlist, instruct, and equip local civilians in order to conduct sabotage operations which hampered the German war effort. Roughly 10,000 men and 3,000 women were employed by the SOE. Most of the women were members of the First Aid Nursing Yeomanry who, as coders and wireless operators, handled the coded messages sent by agents from the field. Yet some women, like Jos, were recruited specifically for an operational role. She had worked for the resistance producing clandestine newspapers since the occupation in May 1940, when she was aged seventeen. In 1944, she was taken to Britain for extensive training before returning to the Netherlands. She was one of just three women who were recruited by the Dutch section. The Belgian section recruited two female nationals, and the French-led Gaullist branch of SOE, called RF section, sent eleven Frenchwomen into France between May and September 1944. However, it was the British-run F[rench] section which pioneered the use of female agents two years previously. In 1942, the new recruiting officer, Selwyn Jepson, decided that women possessed particular skills that might prove useful in undertaking clandestine work. His decision to recruit women was a controversial one and he recalled that 'there was a good deal of opposition from various quarters until it went up to Churchill'.[2] Having received official approval to recruit women, Jepson began interviewing women as well as men. Although the total number of women he recruited is unknown, thirty-nine women successfully completed their training and were infiltrated into France, along with 441 men. The women came from varied backgrounds: some were working class, while others had a more privileged upbringing; there were a couple of Jews, several Roman Catholics and a Muslim Sufi; some were in their early twenties, while others were in their forties; several were married with children, a couple were widows, one had been divorced and many were single. The one thing the F section women had in common was the ability to speak fluent French.

Letters inviting candidates to an interview were sent to individuals who were known to speak French. Some women had joined the Women's Auxiliary Air Force (WAAF), and their personal files noted their language proficiency. Others were recommended by those already recruited by the organisation. The interview, held in a London hotel, was conducted in French and, certainly, the first requirement was the ability to speak the language fluently so that they would be able to pass themselves off as French citizens. This would facilitate their undertaking clandestine work without raising any additional suspicions. Lise de Baissac, whose brother Claude had suggested that the SOE approach her, came from the French-speaking British colony of Mauritius: 'My French was perfect because it is my first language. It is my mother tongue.'[3] Odette Sansom was a Frenchwoman who had married a British man and thus made an ideal recruit, but even those who were British could be employed if their French was of a high standard. Claire Everett was a WAAF, had lived in France as a child and consequently 'was more at home speaking French than I was speaking English ... It just came naturally to me ... It was just the years I had lived there. And as a child I played with French children all the time.'[4] Many of the female agents had Anglo-French nationality, their British fathers having married French women after the First World War. Not only did they speak French fluently, but they had lived or holidayed frequently in France, and had inherited some of the physical characteristics of a stereotypical French appearance, such as dark hair, brown eyes, olive complexion and average height. Yvonne Baseden, for example, noted: 'I looked very French anyway, in those days particularly.'[5]

The prospect of returning to France was raised by the recruiting officer in the interview. This must have come as quite a shock to the female recruits. Despite being asked to engage in activities that were not considered appropriate for women to undertake, these women appeared to relish the opportunity. Noor Inayat Khan's personal file held in the National Archives, notes: 'she felt that she had come to a dead end as a WAAF, and was longing to do something more active in the prosecution of the war, something which would make more call on her capabilities and perhaps, demand more sacrifice'.[6] Women were just as likely as men to volunteer for dangerous duties. For the women that accepted the recruiting officer's invitation to join the organisation, the fact that they were women was irrelevant. Jos Mulder-Gemmeke remarked: 'you didn't think about being a woman at that time. That was not important ... they needed people and I wanted to help. I couldn't do anything else.'[7] Similarly, Nancy Wake, an Australian, who had married a Frenchman and who before joining the SOE had helped downed airmen escape back to Britain, asserted: 'I hate wars and violence but if they come then I don't see why we women should just wave our men a proud goodbye and then knit them balaclavas.'[8] A couple of the women had been widowed during the war and felt compelled to take their place. Yvonne Cormeau, whose husband had been killed in the Blitz, remarked: 'I think this was something my husband would have liked to do and as he was no longer there to do it, I thought it was time for me to do it.'[9] Violette Szabo wanted to take up arms to avenge her husband's death at El Alamein: 'it is my job. My husband has been killed. I am going to get my own back somehow.'[10] Both women were mothers to young children whom they risked orphaning by participating in the SOE, and yet motherhood appears to have been one of their key motivations, as it was for Odette Sansom: 'other people are going to suffer, get killed, die because of this war and trying to get freedom for my own children. Let's face it. So am I supposed to accept all this sacrifice that other people are making without lifting a finger in any way?'[11]

Those that impressed the recruiting officer with their ability to speak French were sent on a series of training courses held in stately homes that had been commandeered by the SOE. The first female recruits were sent on a women-only course, but following their success, those that were recruited later were trained alongside men. They were taught both armed and unarmed combat and silent killing techniques, given instruction in using a variety of weapons and shown how to use plastic explosive. The training reports of individual agents reveal that some women initially struggled but did progress. Madeleine Damerment 'has improved. Is now a fair shot with pistol and carbine, but is lacking in aggressiveness.'[12] Others were confident handling weapons: Francine Agazarian was 'by no means timid or gun shy ... never nervous with weapons'.[13] In addition to weapons instruction, recruits were expected to undertake rigorous physical exercise, negotiate obstacle courses and go for early morning runs. Forty-year-old Vera Leigh was the only woman on her course and reports from her instructors in January 1943 stated: 'She doesn't shun any part of the syllabus and goes in for everything with enthusiasm' and she 'certainly works hard to keep abreast of the others'.[14]

Agents also embarked upon parachute training, progressing from jumping from a tower, a lorry travelling at thirty miles per hour, a stationary barrage balloon, an aircraft in daytime, and then finally from an aeroplane at night. Yvonne Baseden recollected: 'The first jump is frightening and you do it because you're in a group of people and one person goes, so you go. It's a marvellous impression when you're sailing down having leapt from the plane .... Every time you have the same fear. That is natural.'[15] That at least one agent died when his parachute failed to open is a stark reminder that this was still a novel and highly dangerous activity in the 1940s, yet one that was clearly relished by adventurous women such as Yvonne.

Agents were also given basic instruction in Morse code and those that showed an aptitude underwent several months of specialist wireless training, being taught how to code and decode messages, how to send and receive messages in Morse code, and how to repair their wireless sets. Only a very few women were allocated the role of wireless operator; most were sent in as couriers. Wireless operating was perceived to be the most dangerous job and had an average 'life' expectancy of just six weeks. Indeed, several wireless operators, both male and female, were caught at their sets, direction-finding technology having pinpointed their location. Agents were made fully aware of the dangers they would face and were given a mock operational mission and interrogation to prepare them: 'We knew we were going into something pretty dicey' noted Yvonne Baseden.[16]

Having completed the training, agents prepared for their infiltration into France. They were given a cyanide pill in case they were captured. Several refused it and some like Claire Everett subsequently disposed of it: 'I flushed them down the loo when I got there.'[17] They also constructed a new identity. Their hair was cut in a French style, they were given some typical French clothes, and they were given forged documents issued in their cover name. Lise de Baissac chose the name Irené Brisse after a much-loved aunt, and pretended to be a young widow who had moved to Poitiers after the death of her husband.[18] Claire Everett remembered: 'My cover story was that I had been working in Paris at Louis Vuitton and I had contracted bronchitis or something and I was going down to stay with my cousin in the Sarthe to recuperate so I had the necessary clothes.'[19]

The first female agent to be infiltrated into France was Yvonne Rudellat, a grandmother, who arrived by boat in July 1942, while Andrée Borrel and Lise de Baissac were the first women to be parachuted on the night of 24/25 September 1942. Lise recalled:

A bit nervous, the two of us with our parachutes, very, very uncomfortable and when we reached the spot, there was a hole [in the aeroplane's floor] to open. She went first, she jumped and immediately afterwards, I jumped because if you wait one second, it's already too much. We drew a lot. She won. But I didn't mind really. I jumped almost at the same time. The reception committee took us to the middle of the forest and we waited there until early morning when the curfew was over. They took us to a safe house, friends of those who had received us, and gave us breakfast. I was only there one day and then I went off on my own.[20]

Lise's parachute jump was successful but not all agents' infiltration went so smoothly. Yvonne Baseden's first attempt to get to France was aborted because the signal flashed by the reception committee's torches was incorrect. This might have been a simple error or because the circuit had been penetrated. The group to which Madeleine Damerment parachuted had been compromised and she was received by a German-controlled reception committee and immediately arrested and later executed. Claire Everett parachuted safely into southern France in May 1944, but the canisters containing her belongings were blown off course and were subsequently picked up by German soldiers: 'So right away two things. (a) they knew a woman agent had been dropped and (b) I was stuck without any clothes except what I'd dropped in which was a grey flannel divided skirt, ski boots with hobnails in for landing and a sweater. And it was hot.'[21]

Returning to France, a country in which many had grown up, affected some of the women quite deeply. Claire Everett recalled: 'I remember when we were walking toward the safehouse feeling "this feels so good" and smelling all the wonderful smells from France and thinking I'm back home again.'[22] For Lise de Baissac, it was not until she had begun her work that she was struck by her love of France: 'when I was in Poitiers, alone and settled in my new job, I went into the countryside and I said "well, now I'm living on the soil of France." It was [pause] My heart was really [pause] I can still feel it. It was very moving. [Eyes fill up with tears] I had lived here in France, I was at home.'[23] The strong emotions she experienced still had the capacity to move her sixty years later.

Following their arrival, agents travelled to the area in which they were to operate and got to work. They contacted London to arrange parachute drops and trained Frenchmen in the use of various weapons. When I asked Claire Everett how she was perceived by the men in her resistance circuit, she replied: 'I was part of the gang. There was no question of me not being a part. It didn't matter. My sex had nothing to do with it at all.'[24] Similarly, Yvonne Baseden noted: 'I was just another member of the crowd. There didn't seem to be any difference at all. We were doing a job.'[25] Some of the female agents participated in acts of sabotage. Nancy Wake, whose resistance colleague asserted 'she is the most feminine woman I have ever met in my life, but in battle she's worth ten men', played a very active role on a number of occasions, ambushing German convoys, using home-made bombs, attacking the local Gestapo Head-quarters, and going into battle with German troops.[26] Agents were especially busy around the time of D-Day when all of their preparations began to pay dividends. Resistance circuits throughout France sabotaged railway lines, blew up bridges and ambushed German convoys making their way up to Normandy. A journey from southern to northern France that typically took two days now took up to a fortnight, which meant that the Allied soldiers landing on the Normandy beaches faced fewer troops – this undoubtedly saved many lives and possibly shortened the war by several months.

Activity intensified in the drive to liberate towns and villages from the occupiers. More and more people joined the resistance and extra weapons were needed. Yvonne Baseden's group was chosen to receive the first daylight parachute drop. On the morning of 26 June, Baseden sat in a ditch in the dropping ground with her wireless set and established contact with Britain, while 800 armed men from various local resistance groups were waiting to collect the canisters as they parachuted down. She remembered vividly the excitement they all felt as the planes flew overhead: 'I was jumping around, waving madly to them!'[27] Although the operation was a success, the day ended disastrously when German soldiers interrupted their celebratory lunch at their safehouse, a cheese depot. Baseden rushed to conceal herself in one of the spaces between the huge wooden circular stacks, pushing some planks of wood across to cover herself and a male colleague, while her male organiser hid in the false ceiling. They hid in the cramped space for over four hours, waiting for it to get dark so that they could attempt an escape. However, one of the soldiers started shooting randomly and one of his bullets hit her organiser who then took his cyanide pill. Baseden's hiding place was discovered and she was pulled out by her hair, punched and handcuffed. Baseden remembered:

> It was euphoria combined with this extraordinary happening. At least all that stuff had been distributed. For me, as a general reaction, I was thrilled because I had done what I wanted to do and I knew I was there because I had done that so I had a reasoning and I thought of all these other people who had been shopping in the street and all been rounded up and therefore I had really nothing to moan about.

She was placed in solitary confinement, was beaten up, her bare feet were stamped on and she was intimidated in an attempt to get her to contact Britain using her wireless set:

> They took me down to the cellar and left me there for about two days in the dark and then two officers came in and they said 'are you going

to tell us how to use the radio' and I said 'no' and one of them started shooting at my feet. They got me in the corner and they started with this revolver shooting around my feet. And the other stopped him.

As Yvonne's experience indicates, no concessions were made to female prisoners and she herself stated that her German interrogators regarded her as a resister, not specifically as a *female* resister. Once captured, women were not automatically shielded from torture because of their sex. Odette Sansom had her toenails extracted and a hot poker laid on her spine, and Eileen Nearne was repeatedly immersed in a bath of water until she lost consciousness. Genevieve de Gaulle, Charles de Gaulle's sister who was arrested for her involvement in the Resistance, asserted: 'I can affirm that women were treated the same as men. We were not favoured. If the Gestapo wanted some information, beatings, immersion in cold water, whatever they could imagine, was used on men or women.'[28] Yet female agents also experienced the threat of sexual assault and indeed there is evidence to suggest that some of the women were raped.

Seventeen of the F section women were captured either at their set, having been located by direction-finding vans, or as a result of betrayal or bad luck. One was arrested but after several weeks was released and another was equally fortunate in that she was one of fifty-two inmates who managed to escape from a French prison in September 1943. The other fifteen were deported to concentration camps. Yvonne Baseden recalled her arrival at Ravensbrück concentration camp for women:

> The procedure for being accepted at Ravensbrück – you went with the other women to the shower room and then you stripped and then you were passed onto another bunch of these German women and there were stacks of clothes in that one big room and you were just dished out enough to cover yourself with. I was never tattooed and my head wasn't shaved either. My number was 62,947. We were all in blocks of three-tiered bunks all pushed together, so we had to crawl in. I was up on the top tier. And we lived in the clothes we had on. You only thought day-to-day and what you were going to be able to find to eat. Because we had in the morning a crust of brown bread. And in the evening, that was all practically.[29]

Of the fifteen women arrested and deported to concentration camps, only Yvonne Baseden, Odette Sansom and Eileen Nearne survived. Yvonne and Eileen were never identified as SOE agents and pretended to be Frenchwomen who had become involved in the Resistance, while Odette asserted that she was married to the nephew of Winston Churchill. The other twelve women were either shot, killed by a lethal injection or died as a result of the camp conditions.

The women who served with the SOE risked a lot and almost a quarter of them were killed. They were well decorated after the war: the George Cross was awarded to Odette Sansom and, posthumously, to Violette Szabo, and Noor Inayat Khan and others were awarded MBEs, the *Croix de Guerre* and *Légion d'honneur*. They have been the subject of biographies, films, newspaper serialisations, television documentaries and museum displays, and have in many ways overshadowed male agents, of whom there were many more. Despite the public's fascination with the female agent, the women themselves clearly regarded the fact that they were women as irrelevant. Lise de Baissac was perplexed by the recent interest in the SOE: 'I turned the page a long time ago and I really wonder why all this fuss after so many years.'[30] Despite the organisation's ground-breaking decision to involve women, the agents regarded their participation as commonplace and unspectacular. Yvonne Baseden noted: 'I did think that it was some form of proof that women could do these sort of jobs more or less successfully. I thought it was quite a normal step forward for women.'[31]

Although most of the female agents following demobilisation got married and had children, they undoubtedly paved the way for women's more active involvement in military operations today.

Notes

1. Imperial War Museum Sound Archive (henceforth IWMSA) 18153.
2. IWMSA 9331.
3. Personal interview with Lise de Baissac, 2002.
4. Personal interview with Claire Everett (pseudonym), 2002.
5. Personal interview with Yvonne Baseden, 1999.
6. The National Archives, HS 9/836/5.
7. IWMSA 12297.
8. Elizabeth Grice, 'Return of the White Mouse', *Daily Telegraph*, 7 June 1994.
9. IWMSA 7369.
10. 'First British Woman GC: Fought Gun Battle Alone with the Gestapo', *Daily Graphic*, 18 December 1946.
11. IWMSA 9478.
12. The National Archives, HS 9/1654.
13. The National Archives, HS 9/10/2.
14. The National Archives, HS 9/910/3.
15. Personal interview with Yvonne Baseden, 1999.
16. Ibid.
17. Personal interview with Claire Everett (pseudonym), 2002.
18. Personal interview with Lise de Baissac, 2002.
19. Personal interview with Claire Everett (pseudonym), 2002.

20. Personal interview with Lise de Baissac, 2002.
21. Personal interview with Claire Everett (pseudonym), 2002.
22. Ibid.
23. Personal interview with Lise de Baissac, 2002.
24. Personal interview with Claire Everett (pseudonym), 2002.
25. Personal interview with Yvonne Baseden, 1999.
26. Personal interview with Nancy Wake, 1999.
27. Personal interview with Yvonne Baseden, 1999.
28. Margaret Collins Weitz, *Sisters in the Resistance: How Woman Fought to Free France 1940–45*, New York: John Wiley, 1995, p. 92.
29. Personal interview with Yvonne Baseden, 1999.
30. Personal interview with Lise de Baissac, 2002.
31. Personal interview with Yvonne Baseden, 1999.

Select Bibliography

Binney, Marcus, *The Women who Lived for Danger: The Women Agents of SOE in the Second World War*, London: Hodder & Stoughton, 2002.

Escott, Beryl, *Mission Improbable: A Salute to the RAF Women of SOE in Wartime France*, Sparkford: Patrick Stephens, 1991.

Foot, M. R. D., *SOE in France: An Account of the Work of the British Special Operations Executive in France, 1940–1944*, London: HMSO, 1966.

Jones, Liane, *A Quiet Courage: Women Agents in the French Resistance*, London: Corgi, 1990.

Kramer, Rita, *Flames in the Field: The Story of Four SOE Agents in Occupied France*, London: Penguin, 1995.

Pattinson, Juliette, *Behind Enemy Lines: Gender, Passing and the SOE in the Second World War*, Manchester: Manchester University Press, 2007.

Chapter 11

Sue Ryder and the FANYs of SOE

Jonathan Walker

Much has been written about the brave exploits of a number of women agents during the Second World War. Film and television has further fired the public's imagination. Most of these women worked under the auspices of the Special Operations Executive (SOE), trusted with the role of clandestine operations in enemy-occupied Europe. Many were also members of the First Aid Nursing Yeomanry, (FANY), and their role has become synonymous with that organisation. Yet, although the contribution of female FANY agents was undoubtedly significant, their numbers were small – some thirty-nine were engaged in actual operations in France, out of an estimated 2,000 women who worked at some time for SOE. Their dramatic stories have often overshadowed the great contribution of the other FANYs, who worked for SOE as coders, wireless telegraphist (W/T) operators, drivers and housekeepers. And it was this latter group, which included girls such as Sue Ryder, who were to fulfil valuable double roles as *confidantes* and counsellors to SOE's agents, particularly to those in the Polish Section.

As we have seen in Chapter 6, ironically, the FANY Corps was originally the inspiration of a man, Edward Charles Baker, who was wounded in 1898, during the Sudan Campaign. Following a delay in his rescue from the battlefield, he devised a plan whereby the injured could be speedily retrieved by mounted nursing auxiliaries. He finally formed a unit titled the First Aid Nursing Yeomanry Corps in 1907. The organisation floundered for several years and was then picked up and expanded by Grace Ashley-Smith, who modernised the unit, and although members maintained their first-aid and horsemanship skills, they dispensed with ideas of actually riding onto the battlefield.[1] The outbreak of the First World War gave a fillip to the Corps and although there was Army resistance to women driving the new motor-ambulances in France, the volunteer FANYs were employed by the British Red Cross Society to drive convoys of the wounded from the casualty clearing stations (CCS) to the Channel ports. They also assisted Talbot House (Toc H), the soldiers' rest house at Poperinghe, and with the canteens on the Western Front, but they will chiefly be remembered for their bravery in helping to evacuate the wounded in the face of the German Spring Offensive in 1918.[2] With the ending of the war came calls for the assimilation of FANYs into other women's units such as the Women's Auxiliary Army Corps (WAAC), but this was not accepted by its members. FANY was, after all, a volunteer organisation with its own uniform and creed of duty and sacrifice, though this was always tempered by a fiercely independent spirit. The Corps members considered themselves an elite who could always be counted upon to live up to the strengths and ideals of any officer corps.[3]

However, to survive, the Corps had to evolve, and during the 1930s, the emphasis moved almost entirely to the provision of transport. The official name was changed to the Women's Transport Service (FANY), but as war loomed again, the Corps faced being swallowed up by its much larger sister organisation, the Auxiliary Territorial Service (ATS). Although most FANYs were also compelled to join the 200,000-strong ATS, the Corps still managed to remain independent.

The social background of many of the FANYs was middle or upper-middle class. Because the Corps still recruited on personal recommendation, many of the applicants were known to existing FANYs from school days or social connections. These connections were not to be underrated as girls' boarding schools in the 1930s all fostered the more recently parodied qualities of British 'pluck', self-reliance and a stoic attitude in the face of adversity. However, this social exclusivity was never paramount; Violette Szabo, who was to become one of the bravest and most celebrated of the FANYs who operated in enemy-occupied territory, was the daughter of a Brixton car dealer. For all these strictures, the overriding requirements for those girls picked to work in SOE were 'quick brains and quiet tongues'.[4]

The creation of the SOE in 1940 boosted the fortunes of the FANY Corps, and they became inextricably linked. SOE was formed to assist Resistance units and sabotage operations in enemy-occupied countries. It had its own government minister and access to the Prime Minister, Winston Churchill. However the organisation was not without its enemies and even from its early days, it competed with the Foreign Office and the Secret Intelligence Service (SIS) for resources and manpower. It required large numbers of drivers, coders, wireless operators and even agents, but rather than draw these young women from the ATS (who were forbidden to use small arms), a strong link was established with FANY. Because FANY was a small, independent and volunteer organisation (as well as disciplined and uniformed) decisions as to its use and deployment could be made without having to confer with government departments. The Corps was also free of regulations that bound units like the ATS, and therefore would not be subject to 'questions in the House of Commons' – an event to be avoided by a highly secret organisation such as SOE. Such were the ties between the two organisations that, by late 1942, SOE was actually funding small allowances for its FANY volunteers from its own resources.[5]

The close relationship between the two organisations was further fostered by their senior officers. Lieutenant Colonel Colin Gubbins, who was initially Officer Commanding (OC) Special Training Schools of SOE, and would later command the whole enterprise, appreciated the quality and commitment of FANYs, and made every effort to enlist them. He knew one member of the Corps, Lieutenant (later Commander) Phyllis Bingham, as a family friend, and through her, established a recruitment link. It also helped that Gubbins's cousin, Captain Mary McVean was a senior FANY, involved in setting up Station XVIII in Hertfordshire, one of the early Polish 'holding bases' for agents.[6] The SOE/FANY bond was officially sanctioned by the Ministry of Labour in July 1941, and as SOE grew, so FANY numbers increased, and their threat of disbandment receded. The ties became so strong that of the 2,700 FANYs recruited during the war, an estimated 2,000 were attached to SOE. While many of the FANY signals personnel would be recruited direct from higher education schools, other volunteers came in by a more random, if not bizarre, selection method.[7] Pammy Leach (later Lady Niven) recalled:

> After a time working for the Red Cross in St James's Palace I was given an interview at the FANY HQ in St Paul's Vicarage in Knightsbridge. One of my elder sisters came with me. We both, of course, wore hats and gloves. One of the first questions Mrs Bingham asked me was 'Did you have a nanny?' Odd, I thought, but I told her that my younger sister had one and I loved her. 'Good – then you'll do what you are told.'[8]

Sue Ryder was another girl who would prove to have the right credentials. Born in 1923, at Scarcroft, near Leeds, into a prosperous farming family, she enjoyed a privileged upbringing, though it was not immune from the agricultural depression of the 1930s, when the family sold its estate and moved to their smaller farm in Great Thurlow in Suffolk. After attending Benenden School, she became a volunteer nurse in 1940.[9] A fine-featured and very small person, she nevertheless had huge reservoirs of energy and compassion and was always ready for some new challenge. So when the opportunity arose to enlist in FANY in late 1942, she swiftly applied. She initially undertook FANY training at Overthorpe Hall near Banbury and, once selected for SOE, was issued with khaki drill, Sam Browne belt and a leather cosh (those serving abroad would be issued with Colt automatics). She then took the established route; first, she signed the Official Secrets Act, and then was posted to SOE Station 17 at Brickendonbury House in Hertfordshire. She now came into contact with young escapees from enemy-occupied Europe, being trained by SOE as agents to be parachuted back into their mother countries.

SOE had set up separate country sections to assist resistance groups in all these occupied countries. Sue Ryder initially worked with the Czech Section, which had nurtured some twenty agents, all of whom perished in the aftermath of the successful assassination of the *Reichsprotektor*, Reinhard Heydrich in May 1942. She then saw unbroken service with SOE's Polish Section. At the height of its activity, some 250 FANYs were attached to this unit, engaged in catering, administration, driving and wireless operations.[10] The Polish Section was run by Major Mike Pickles and was, in turn, part of a wider grouping of Poland, Czechoslovakia and Hungary, run by the forceful and enigmatic Colonel Harold Perkins. The Poles enjoyed a certain kind of autonomy within SOE and, with the exception of parachute training, were allowed to organise their own courses, usually in Polish, and employ Polish instructors. These courses were run at stations set up in many of England's finest country houses, giving rise to the euphemism that SOE stood for the 'Stately 'Omes of England'. By May 1942, FANYs were serving at four different Polish stations, with the two most important courses (clandestine warfare and briefing) established at Audley End, near Saffron Walden, in Essex.[11] Ryder was moved between Stations 17 and 20, with other periods spent at 'holding stations'. These were safe houses, established within larger SOE training grounds or in isolated rural areas, where agents were held just before their missions. Within reach of secret SOE airfields, such as Tempsford, Polish agents might spend nerve-wracking weeks or months waiting for the right weather conditions or a change in the political or military situation of their indigenous underground, the Polish Home Army (*Armia Krajowa* or AK), before making their parachute jump.

Training for the agents who were to be parachuted into Poland was not without its dangers. Each would carry out a number of practice jumps at the Parachute Training Centre at Ringway, Manchester, and in one group a Pole recorded that two of his colleagues were killed, four suffered broken legs and one had a nervous breakdown.[12]

The first SOE flight out of Britain had taken place in February 1941, and missions continued on a regular basis. Once training was completed, and mission details confirmed, the actual jump would normally happen several days either side of a full moon. Ryder was now spending long hours in the company of her Polish charges and developed the greatest admiration for them. In a later testimony she said:

> Radio operators always seemed to have the worst time, because they had to carry these wretched receivers around with them and if they were caught, there was no way they could conceal them. Quite a lot of wireless operators were girls. Couriers also had a very difficult time as they had to break through the various frontiers in occupied Europe. We always had to check them before they left to make sure they had nothing incriminating on them. We had to make sure that all clothing labels were made in Poland and that there was nothing traceable to England. The Poles were, after all, almost reckless in their courage, unlike the Czechs who were more solid and cautious. The Poles always said, 'it was right to do it', whether they were going to lose or not – it just had to be done. They were like corks. The worse the situation for them became, they would pop up again.[13]

The young Polish agents were going to an uncertain fate. Although there would sometimes be an AK reception squad, agents often landed alone and had to make their way to a contact point or safe house. They might be weapons or explosives experts or wireless operators – the latter had a dangerous, if unglamorous role in the Polish underground. For once he was in occupied territory and had made radio contact with Britain or other resistance units inside Poland, he was liable to be detected by German listening posts. If he transmitted to one receiver for too long, a Gestapo snatch squad would pin-point his position and arrest him. Some had already been captured and tortured, but had managed to escape to Britain, where they had volunteered for further missions. Helping these young men to relieve their pre-mission anxiety was no easy task. Missions might be on, then suddenly cancelled, then on again and cancelled again. And while their emotions rose and fell, Sue Ryder and her FANY colleagues were charged with trying to reduce the tension. Yet, at one such holding station, Pollards Park in Buckinghamshire, Ryder found her work was most rewarding. After the FANYs had carried out their daytime role of driving, cooking, housekeeping, they would help the fraught agents relax. The FANYs would dance with their 'Bods', as the Poles were affectionately known and, if classical music became too melancholy, swing band records might lift the mood. Alcohol would also raise the tempo, but while the Poles were allowed wine, the FANYs had to make do with 'ersatz' orange juice.[14]

However, it was her role as listener and as counsellor to the agents that Ryder found most compelling:

> One had a tremendous admiration for the agents. They were young and energetic but we were only allowed to have platonic friendships and this rule was never broken. We were asked to keep an eye on agents who were under special strain, who might give way after capture. It was quite a lot to ask of people our age. Some agents were very frightened of what they were going back to, especially if they'd already been arrested by the Gestapo or the Soviets. We had one boy, 'Robert' who had been captured before by the Gestapo. He would pace up and down, dreading that he would be tortured again. I think he went back and was killed. Those Poles who had already had a spell in some gulag in Siberia would talk of cannibalism and that the Soviet system was on a par with the Nazi system. They had been released in 1941 as a result of the Sikorski-Maisky Pact. Many had suffered typhus and huge numbers had died.
>
> You knew you would never be called on to do this sort of work again. And you were with people who were under a sentence of death. Therefore, we FANYs did get to know people very well. They would talk about things you'd never discuss in normal life. It was rather like talking to people with a terminal illness. You would be told things you'd never normally hear. It was emotionally intimate and extremely memorable. It consumed one. It became a way of life.[15]

For FANYs used to the restrained and buttoned-up attitude of many British officers, the often emotional and highly charged nature of the Poles came as a refreshing change. While stories abounded of the sexual prowess and glamour of Polish airmen, and many British girls clamoured for their attention, the immediacy and danger of the SOE missions cast a more gloomy atmosphere over the Polish agents. Nonetheless, Gubbins was keen that relationships should not develop for fear that these agents might be distracted from their missions.[16] Even in this highly charged atmosphere, the FANYs managed to maintain their propriety, though they could not fail to privately despair at the plight of these young men, whom they would probably never see again. Ryder and her colleagues would sometimes be called upon to drive them to the airfield, where they would see them off and, if time allowed, wait for news of their mission. Hopefully the aircraft dispatchers would return with good news of a successful drop, with perhaps a final note from an agent to his FANY. Even then, there were thoughts of what would happen to the agent when he landed – arrest, torture or betrayal. Sometimes there was no news and the girls would return to a deserted holding station, full of memories. Pammy Leach, a good friend and colleague of Sue Ryder, who also worked at Pollards Park, remembered one night in particular:

> I met 33-year-old 'Alex' who had lived in Paris. He was incredibly kind to me and spent his last coupons on my new niece's dress. We had a happy time on my birthday – 7th February – and then his time came to be dropped. I knew that his parachute might not open as he was carrying a radio. I was in a room with five other girls and felt the only place I could be alone was in the bathroom. I imagined him falling all night.
>
> The crew reported a great success but I felt very strongly that 'Alex' had been killed. Three weeks later, in an effort to console me, Captain Podoski came from the HQ in the Rubens Hotel in London to tell me that 'Alex' had died a hero's death in Warsaw. I was surprised. Over fifty years later, at long last, there was a service in Westminster Abbey for the agents killed during the war. We were given a booklet with the names and if known, the dates of their deaths. My 'Alex' (whose surname I knew, although this was not allowed) had in fact died on the night of the 14/15 February – my night in the bathroom.[17]

This intense pitching of emotions was repeated for every batch of new agents. Yet the FANYs were expected to rally again and again. They were nearly all young girls, and if an ensign ever showed any sign of wavering, she was told to 'pull yourself together'. During leave, FANYs were expected to behave 'on all occasions as gentlewomen', which might allow their entry to cocktail bars in hotels or theatres, but saloon bars or public houses were definitely out of bounds.[18] However, although it was officially frowned upon, FANYs did sometimes liaise with their wards outside the base areas, if only to allow the Poles a glimpse of normal English life. Kazimierz Mazguy, a member of the highly secret elite squad, the Independent Polish Grenadiers, remembered a spell of leave with an SOE FANY:

> She was the daughter of a very grand Scottish family – they were whisky distillers – and one weekend she announced she was going home and would I like to meet her family. Well, the house was splendid. But everyone dressed for dinner and there I was in my old clothes. I was surrounded by lots of cutlery and so many different glasses. I was only the son of a miner and I had no idea what to use first. I was being trained to get myself out of tight spots but this was

terrible. However, the girl and her family pretended not to notice. They were so kind to me.[19]

Indeed, the tremendous emotional support that the FANYs offered the Poles, was never underrated. Senior Polish commanders knew their worth: 'You couldn't have found a finer type of Englishwoman anywhere. Cultured and friendly, hard-working and smiling, they created the relaxed happy atmosphere so necessary before the coming adventure.'[20]

As well as the FANY drivers, housekeepers and coders who worked for SOE, there were also a number of FANY members who went into action. The issue of sending women on active service continued to be a thorny problem. There was little precedent for women to be engaged in the operational end of intelligence work. Nurse Edith Cavell is reported to have had Secret Intelligence Service (SIS) links during the First World War, for which she paid a heavy price, but SOE's dispatch of women agents to France during the Second World War was indeed, ground-breaking. Within SOE there were mixed feelings but eventually Gubbins's view that it was perfectly legitimate to directly employ women in dangerous operations, held sway and was endorsed by not only the FANY Commandant, Marian Gamwell, but also the Prime Minister, Winston Churchill. When a potential woman agent was 'spotted' by SOE recruiters, she would be asked to attend for an interview at an anonymous flat near SOE Head Quarters in Baker Street, London. She might be a civilian, or already in the Services, such as the WAAF, and could be British or European. In fact, many of the celebrated heroines of SOE, such as Odette Hallowes (later Churchill), Violette Szabo, and Andrée Borrel were born in France. If accepted, the agent would then be afforded some cover. Unless she was already in the WAAF, the new agent usually became a member of FANY and immediately drew the uniform, which would act as a perfect cover whilst engaged in clandestine training.[21] It was also thought to afford them at least some protection in the event of their capture in occupied territory, as they could claim prisoner of war (POW) status. Out of the sixty-six FANYs who were trained for active service in occupied Europe, most operated as couriers (as men always attracted more attention from the enemy) or from 1943, as wireless operators. But of these, thirteen were captured and subsequently murdered by the Nazis.[22]

It was not only FANYs operating as agents who went abroad. A FANY contingent arrived in North Africa in December 1942, a month after the 'TORCH' Anglo-American landings in Morocco and Algeria. Their numbers increased to 250, providing many of the staff for the signals, stores and air operations that took place at the elaborate communications centre, known by the code name, 'Massingham'. Once the Vichy-French territories in North Africa were wrested away from the Axis, the Allies invaded mainland Italy in September 1943. Several months later, after the southern airfield of Brindisi had been secured, SOE set up a base at nearby Monopoli and a small unit of FANYs including Sue Ryder, were drafted in. The new mission for the SOE base was to provide specially adapted aircraft for relief flights to the Balkans and also to Poland – now a shorter return trip than the old routes out of Britain via Sweden or Denmark.

Again, Ryder was required to look after Polish parachutists, waiting to be dropped on SOE missions during 1944. From a villa in Latiano, she and her colleagues not only prepared and cooked meals for the Poles, but also arranged excursions and anything to distract the men from their worries. Described as a 'highly charged sparrow', Ryder packed a huge amount into each day, tearing around the countryside, sourcing scarce meat and supplies for her 'Bods'.[23] The girls looked after a succession of SOE personnel as well as Polish agents, and hosted the returning 'Operation Wildhorn III' party, which included the intriguer Józeph Retinger and Tomasz Arciszewski, a future Prime Minister of the Polish Government-in-exile.[24]

While FANY/SOE cooperation in Italy ran fairly smoothly at a local level, there was increasing frustration within higher command at the apparent stubbornness of FANY HQ to broaden its franchise. Major General William Stawell, Chief of Special Operations (Mediterranean), was moved to complain to SOE in London:

> We have had a spot of bother with Gamwell [Commandant] and the FANY organisation. She refuses to accept three of the girls in the last lot of trainees; they were already enrolled in the FANYs, but of course not finally approved ... I think we have reached the stage in the war where we cannot run a Corps on the lines of a ladies club, and within reasonable limits of course, the FANY Corps must take their share of the mediocre as well as the elite.[25]

Despite Stawell's concerns about a 'ladies club', the FANY Corps persisted in maintaining its high standards, particularly among those who served in the SOE Polish Section in Italy.[26] Mary McVean led a dedicated band that included not only Sue Ryder and Pammy Leach, but also Christine Hoon, Barbara Legge, Anna Foster, Sheila Muriel and Dippy Portman (who died tragically in an air crash in 1945). They kept up their support for the Poles throughout the agony of the Warsaw Rising in the summer of 1944, and consoled them as their underground resistance, the AK, collapsed during the following winter With the Soviet occupation of Poland, SOE had to wind down its operations and, as the war came to an end, the Polish FANYs dispersed.

Each girl in the Polish Section would have her own memories of the extraordinary events and some undoubtedly suffered from the burden of listening to the dark and brutal stories from occupied Poland. For those who wished to see the FANY contribution to the war recognised in print, the task would be difficult. In February 1946, a fire broke out in the offices on the top floor of the SOE HQ in Baker Street, which also contained the FANY Administration Section. Consequently, a large quantity of FANY records was destroyed, particularly those relating to women SOE agents.[27] During the 1950s and 1960s, Dame (later Baroness) Irene Ward MP, waged a campaign inside and outside of Parliament to secure the release of the surviving SOE papers, enabling the first public history of SOE to be written, as well as her own history of FANY.[28]

Some FANYs undoubtedly felt that the spirit of the Corps could be utilised to further other ends, such as relief or charity work – and after the war, there was no more deserving case than Poland. Sue Ryder promptly embarked on a crusade to help the dispossessed of that country, and employing her fantastic energy, she drove relief lorries back and forth between Poland and Britain, helping to alleviate suffering. She then set up a large number of care homes in both countries, which became the basis of the Sue Ryder Foundation. During this period she met Britain's most famous bomber pilot, Leonard Cheshire, who had engaged in similar charity work through his Cheshire Homes, and they married in 1959. Both converts to Catholicism, they embarked on a combined Christian mission, whose ideals were to survive Cheshire's death in 1992, and Ryder's death in November 2000.

The FANY Corps has survived and is now known as FANY (Princess Royal's Volunteer Corps). It continues to uphold the values of voluntary service and duty embodied by Sue Ryder and the FANYs of SOE.

Notes

1. Hugh Popham, *The FANY in Peace and War: The Story of the First Aid Nursing Yeomanry 1907–2003*, Barnsley: Leo Cooper, 2003, p. 6.
2. The early history of the FANY Corps is explored by Janet Lee, ' "I Wish My Mother Could See Me Now": The First Aid Nursing Yeomanry (FANY) and Negotiation of Gender and Class Relations 1907–1918', *NWSA Journal*, 19/2 (Summer 2007), pp. 138–58. See also, Janet Lee, *War Girls: The First Aid Nursing Yeomanry in the First World War*, Manchester: Manchester University Press, 2005, and Pat Beauchamp, *FANY Goes to War: An Englishwoman in the FANY Corps*, Burgess Hill: Diggory Press, 2005.
3. Popham, *FANY in Peace and War*, p. 48.
4. M. R. D. Foot, *SOE: An Outline History of the Special Operations Executive 1940–1946*, London: Pimlico, 1999, pp. 75–7.

5. 'Historical Development of the FANY Unit in SOE', Sir Colin Gubbins Papers, 3/2/57–83, Imperial War Museum, London (hereafter IWM).
6. Mary McVean had an important role within SOE as a cipher instructor. She later married Roger Cosyn, an officer in the Free French Forces. She was awarded the OBE in 1976, and died 4 September 2003. Ultimate sanction for FANY cooperation with SOE always lay with Commandant Marian Gamwell.
7. When SOE manpower was at its height of 13,000 in the late summer of 1944, this included an estimated 3,200 women; William Mackenzie, *The Secret History of SOE: Special Operations Executive 1940–1945*, London: St Ermin's Press, 2000, pp. 336, 719. Signallers and coders were often recruited from higher education schools because it was felt that they 'had not lost the classroom and lecture habit'; see 'Talk on BBC', undated, by Major-General Gubbins; also 'Draft of Speech to Cambridge University OTC', 26 October 1962, 4/1/1–10, both Gubbins Papers, IWM.
8. Lady Niven to author, 28 February 2009; also Lady Niven Memoir, File 05/76/1, IWM.
9. Her early life is covered, somewhat disjointedly, in her two autobiographies, *And the Morrow is Theirs*, Bristol: Sue Ryder Foundation, 1975, and *Child of My Love*, London: Collins Harvill, 1986.
10. Popham, *FANY in Peace and War*, p. 77.
11. Audley End was originally named SOE 'Station 61', and later 'Station 43'. This fine Jacobean house had been requisitioned by the Ministry of Works in 1941, and used by SOE for European agent training, finally being dedicated to training Polish agents in 1942. The FANY establishment at the base grew to eighteen.
12. George Iranek-Osmecki, *The Unseen and Silent*, London: Sheed & Ward, 1954, p. 23.
13. Sue Ryder Oral Testimony, ref. 10057, Sound Archive, IWM.
14. Lady Niven to author, 12 February 2009.
15. Sue Ryder Oral Testimony, IWM.
16. For a study of the social impact of Polish servicemen in Britain, see Adam Zamoyski, *The Forgotten Few: The Polish Air Force in the Second World War*, Barnsley: Pen & Sword, 2004, pp. 164–80. For relationships, see Major-General Sir Colin Gubbins to Donald Hamilton-Hill, 13 December 1966, 3/2/57–83, Gubbins Papers, IWM.
17. Lady Niven to author, 28 February 2009; also Lady Niven, 'Memoir', File 05/76/1, IWM.
18. 'Behaviour' in 'FANY Standing Orders', 05/62/1, Miss W. J. Holmes Papers, IWM.
19. Kazimierz Mazguy to author, 3 February 2009.
20. Iranek-Osmecki, *Unseen*, p. 25.
21. Pearl Witherington (later Mme Cornioley) was a WAAF who went on to become an actual network organiser in occupied France. Her personal SOE file can be found in HS9/355, National Archives, Kew, London.
22. Of this total number of FANY agents trained for the field, fifty-one were destined for France, eight for Holland, five for Belgium and two for Poland. See 'Historical Development of the FANY Unit in SOE', Sir Colin Gubbins Papers, 3/2/57–83, IWM.
23. Obituary, 3 November 2000, *Independent*.
24. For details of 'Operation Wildhorn III' and other Special Duties flights to occupied Poland, see Jonathan Walker, *Poland Alone: Britain, SOE and the Collapse of the Polish Resistance, 1944*, Stroud: History Press, 2008.
25. Major-General W. Stawell to C.D. (Gubbins), 16 June 1944, Gubbins Papers, IWM.
26. The FANY Corps as a whole made a significant contribution to the war, serving not only in North Africa and Italy, but also in the Middle East and Far East. The Italian interest is well

served by former FANY Ensign, Margaret Pawley (née Herbertson), in *In Obedience to Instructions: FANY with the SOE in the Mediterranean*, Barnsley: Leo Cooper, 1999.

27. Duncan Stuart (former SOE Advisor to the Foreign & Commonwealth Office), '"Of Historical Interest Only": The Origins and Vicissitudes of the SOE Archive', *Intelligence and National Security*, 20/1 (March 2005), p. 18. Since 1993, a steady stream of SOE material has been released into the public domain and deposited with the National Archives. Much of the original SOE material, particularly that relating to the Polish Section or papers referring to SIS matters, was destroyed after the end of the war. Nonetheless, documents released from other country sections, although heavily 'weeded' and erratic in quality have allowed a number of SOE country section histories to emerge. For details of these publications, as well as an assessment of SOE studies, see Mark Seaman, 'A Glass Half Full – Some Thoughts on the Evolution of the Study of the Special Operations Executive', in a special SOE edition of *Intelligence and National Security*, 20/1 (1 March 2005), pp. 27–43.

28. Dame Irene Ward, *F.A.N.Y. Invicta*, London: Hutchinson, 1955.

Select Bibliography

Foot, M. R. D., *SOE: An Outline History of the Special Operations Executive 1940–1946*, London: Pimlico, 1999.

Popham, Hugh, *The FANY in Peace and War: The Story of the First Aid Nursing Yeomanry 1907–2003*, Barnsley: Leo Cooper, 2003.

Ryder, Sue, *Child of My Love*, London: Collins Harvill, 1986.

Walker, Jonathan, *Poland Alone: Britain, SOE and the Collapse of the Polish Resistance, 1944*, Stroud: History Press, 2008.

Chapter 12

Women with a Secret
Photographic Interpretation

Christine Halsall

High on the banks of the River Thames near Henley stands an imposing hotel, which, during the Second World War, housed the Allied Central Interpretation Unit, the headquarters of wartime Photographic Intelligence. Among those who worked there were a significant number of women who, collectively, held the secret of the war-winning part their organisation played in the Allied victory. They were members of one of the first truly joint service units in which Army, Navy, and Air Force personnel drawn from Britain and the Allied countries, worked together to provide intelligence from aerial photography.

The history of photographic interpretation is inextricably linked to the development of military aviation. In 1858, the first aerial photographs were taken over Paris from a camera attached to the basket of a tethered balloon. Aerial photographs were taken from balloons in 1883, by an officer of the Royal Engineers and during the Boer War, which resulted in a great expansion in military ballooning. During the early years of the twentieth century, powered aircraft superseded balloons, camera design advanced, and film began to replace glass plates. The first British military aviators to practice photography from aeroplanes were pilots of the Royal Flying Corps in 1913.

The First World War saw photographic reconnaissance (PR) and photographic interpretation (PI) firmly established as an important source of intelligence. The human eye and mind, being subjective, cannot retain in detail everything it sees, but the camera produces a permanent, objective record. For the first time in warfare, a powered aircraft with a camera could 'see over the hill' and obtain an aerial photograph from which information on the enemy's dispositions and resources could be extracted. By the end of the war, although photographic intelligence was recognised as indispensable, it was kept principally for battlefield use, due to the technical limitations of cameras and the restrictions on the range of aircraft. The inter-war years saw little interest shown in PR and PI. While the Army trained a number of officers in photo reading, the three Armed Services had only a handful of PIs between them. In 1939, the aircraft assigned were slow, low-flying and of relatively short range.

The actions which caused photographic reconnaissance and interpretation to become vital intelligence assets were brought about by an unconventional Australian pilot named Sidney Cotton. From the summer of 1938, Cotton was employed by the Secret Intelligence Service (MI6), to take covert photographs of the build-up of armaments in Germany. He flew there frequently, ostensibly for business reasons, all the time using cameras hidden within his aircraft to take clandestine photographs of military installations, airfields and the German Fleet. These provided invaluable intelligence on German capabilities and locations not available from any other source.

With the outbreak of war, Cotton and his aircraft were absorbed into the RAF as the Photographic Development Unit (PDU). He proved conclusively that, to take the required photographs and to escape enemy aircraft, reconnaissance aircraft had to fly faster and higher than ever before. With difficulty he acquired some of the prized Spitfires just being delivered to fighter squadrons and recruited experienced pilots to fly them at heights up to 34,000 feet.

Cotton applied the same aggressive attitude to achieving quick processing and accurate interpretation of his photography. Brushing aside the lengthy delays in official procedure, he took the film instead to a civilian establishment, the Aircraft Operating Company (AOC), in Wembley, London. It employed skilled interpreters and produced accurate, timely reports for civilian surveyors, geologists and the like. This was just the service Cotton required for his small-scale photography taken at high altitude. Using the Swiss photogrammetric machines owned by the AOC, the process could be adapted to military requirements and enabled him to present accurate reports with photographs within a few hours of a sortie being flown. Although Sidney Cotton's unwillingness to conform to RAF rules and regulations caused him to be dismissed from the service, his legacies were the PR flying techniques and the interpretation procedures that proved so successful for the Allied Central Interpretation Unit (ACIU).

In 1940, the RAF took over the AOC, and following damage in the Blitz the unit moved to a requisitioned Victorian mansion called Danesfield House near Henley-on-Thames. It was here, on 1 April 1941, that the Central Interpretation Unit (CIU) whose Air Force Station name was RAF Medmenham came into being. It was redesignated the ACIU in May 1944, when the Americans joined the Unit.

Mollie Thompson was one of the first to join the Women's Auxiliary Air Force (WAAF) after it was formed in June 1939. She was working in the

Research Department of the Portland Cement Company, having graduated two years earlier from the University of London with a BSc (Economics). After a required six months in the ranks she was ordered to report to the Air Ministry for training on the first of the many wartime courses held to teach and practice the principles and techniques of photographic interpretation. Mollie, who knew nothing of photography before the war, assumed that she was picked for training because her degree studies had included map making and industrial development. Much of this fitted neatly into PI work, as did the experience of the geographers and archaeologists who had used aerial photography in their previous work. It was perhaps harder to recognise what skills the painter, the historian or the journalist brought to photographic interpretation. The answer was a keen eye for detail, visual memory, patience and curiosity.

Familiar objects, seen from above, become unfamiliar due to a loss of perspective and the student in PI spent many hours learning to recognise familiar objects from an unfamiliar angle. 'Size, shape, shadow, tone and associated features' became a mantra, which PIs repeated in their sleep. The use of stereoscopes to obtain a three-dimensional image, familiarity with scaling, mathematical tables, slide rules and measuring instruments all played their part. With this training complete the PI could identify places and objects and prepare a report noting anything unusual that required further investigation.

One of the most important techniques used by PIs was to note changes over a period of time: the principle of comparative cover. Regular comparisons of an airfield, for example, might show attempts to camouflage particular buildings or the disappearance of a number of aircraft. The PI would immediately ask 'why?', and further sorties would be mounted to discover the answer.

To prioritise the examination of the many thousands of photographs, a three-phase system of interpretation was adopted. When a reconnaissance aircraft landed after a photographic sortie, the films were immediately unloaded and processed. Interpreters based at the airfield examined the negatives for high-priority targets and sent teleprint answers on specific questions to the appropriate headquarters. This First Phase Interpretation could result in an immediate response. Eve Holiday, one of the many women PIs posted to a reconnaissance airfield, spent several months at RAF Wick, in the far northeast of Scotland, from where a daily watch was kept on the German Fleet in Norwegian waters. Eve was on duty with David Linton, a geographer PI, in May 1941, when the PR pilot landed with his photographs of six large ships preparing to move. The largest vessel was identified as the infamous German battleship *Bismarck*, a massive threat to the Atlantic supply convoys. As a result of the PI identification and immediate report, an epic chase by Royal Navy ships ensued and *Bismarck* was sunk six days later.[1]

Mollie Thompson passed her course in 1940, and was posted to Wembley to join Second Phase Interpretation, which dealt with a huge volume of diverse work. After processing of the prints from all photographic sorties flown, these were plotted on to maps, to identify their locations and ensure quick retrieval at a later date. The interpreters then examined them to construct an overall view of enemy activity. The subjects covered were wide ranging, and recognition skills were fully tested; the photographs might relate to military, industrial or economic subjects. A situation report was prepared twice a day, and sent to relevant Headquarters with any untoward activity flagged up. Throughout the summer of 1940, when Britain ceased to have a footing in Europe, PIs reported daily on the build-up of barges and troops gathering at Channel ports. The peak was reached on 17 September when the Prime Minister Winston Churchill told Parliament that 1,700 barges and 200 large ships were poised to invade Britain. Aerial reconnaissance provided the only means for such detailed assessment of enemy activity. Fortunately at the beginning of October the PIs could report that the barges were dispersing and the danger of invasion had passed.

Third Phase Interpretation was concerned with longer term, strategic analysis. It was divided into specialised sections, each designated by a letter of the alphabet and headed by a senior PI, whose team kept a long-term watch on their specific subject. Several Third Phase Sections were commanded by women.

When the CIU moved to Medmenham in 1941, Mollie Thompson was appointed head of 'E', the Camouflage Section. In 2009, she wrote:

> I do not remember any tinge of 'the old boy network' or 'the glass ceiling' towards women working at Medmenham. As far as the interpreters were concerned you did your job, you were capable and whether you were a man or a woman did not matter.[2]

Camouflage is based on the principle that you will not attempt to hit an object that you cannot see, so it is made to 'disappear' from view by merging with its surroundings; such as a ship in disruptive paint blending into the colours of the sea. Overlapping with camouflage is the art of deception which deceives the enemy into assuming the function of an object when, in fact, its purpose is something completely different. Decoys, where complete replicas of operational airfields, factories or gun emplacements were built some distance away from the real thing, were a much-used form of deception. These could fool the enemy into attacking the wrong site. The only effective tool in detecting these enemy strategies was aerial photography. Mollie's Camouflage Section helped to brief Allied aircrew and improve the accuracy of missions by ensuring that bomber crews were not led astray by dummy airfields, concealed factory sites, and mock burning buildings. Mollie also lectured at the School of Inter- pretation, and offered advice to the British camouflage designers.[3]

Eighteen-year-old Hazel Furney was another early WAAF entrant. Pay parades at RAF Farnborough were held in an old aircraft hangar where she learnt how to shout out the 'last three' of her service number and collect weekly wages of seven shillings.[4] She became a cook, and remembers mixing up great troughs of plum duff or making yards of sausages before being promoted to sergeant butcher. After being selected for PI and passing her exam, Hazel was posted to RAF Medmenham and joined 'L', the Aircraft Section, which kept a continuous watch on enemy aircraft production. New types and modifications were identified while still in prototype form, later on in production, and finally when they became operational.[5]

The head of 'L' Section was Constance Babington Smith, who had become fascinated by aeronautical matters several years before the war. She wrote articles for *The Aeroplane* magazine, while also designing hats for the fashion- able milliner, Aage Thaarup. Early in 1942, while examining photographs of the German Heinkel works in Marienehe, Constance found the first image of the He280, the first twin-jet aircraft in the world. This led to an intensive search to find more jet fighters that might go into large-scale production. The giveaway signs of jet aircraft activity were the scorch streaks that showed up on grass airfields. Within a year the new Me163, the first and only rocket-powered fighter, was found at Peenemünde, a village with a seaport on the edge of a long sand-spit in the northwestern part of the island of Usedom, on the Baltic Sea coast of Germany, and another twin-jet fighter, the Me262, was sighted in early 1944. Hundreds of these were built before the end of the war and provided a serious threat to Allied PR pilots who had held the lead in the speed and altitude capabilities of their aircraft for most of the war. The PR pilots had to develop special tactics to evade the enemy jets by exploiting their weaknesses: enormous turning circles and short endurance. The perseverance of Constance and her team and their search for the unusual over many months had revealed these new aircraft and provided valuable technical intelligence.

One of Hazel Furney's fellow PI students was Sarah Oliver, better known as Sarah Churchill, a daughter of the Prime Minister Winston Churchill, who had served as an aircraftswoman plotter for six months before training as a PI. She was then posted to Medmenham for Second Phase work where her specific responsibility was to keep a daily watch on Kiel Harbour, to identify the German vessels in port and monitor their movements. In the summer of 1942, with the build-up to the North African landings under way, a new section was formed as part of Combined Operations. Sarah transferred to this inter-Allied, inter-Service team, and worked intensely for several months on preparations for the top-secret 'Operation Torch'.

On 7 November, after the rush at Medmenham was over, she went on leave to nearby Chequers, the country residence of British Prime Ministers. As the clock struck 1.00am, Churchill gravely announced:

> 'At this very moment six hundred and forty-three ships carrying Allied troops are approaching the shores of Africa.'
> 'Six hundred and forty-four', said Sarah.
> 'What's that?'
> 'I've been working on "Torch" for months.'
> 'Why didn't you tell me?'
> 'I was told not to mention it to anyone.'[6]

Winston later told this story to Mrs Roosevelt, the US President's wife, who used it in lectures in the USA to illustrate how conscientious British women were about security. It was an attitude that permeated Medmenham and all other interpretation units; friends might be working in adjoining rooms, yet never spoke of what their section was working on at a particular time. This attitude to secrecy stayed with them even when the war was over and they returned to peacetime lives.

While Constance was concerned with searching for jet-plane prototypes, Ursula Powys-Lybbe was keeping a watch on enemy airfields. Before the war Ursula had been a professional photographer, first running a studio in Cairo and subsequently establishing a business in London. After a brief spell as a driver for the Auxiliary Fire Service, she joined the WAAF, and served her regulation six months as a records clerk before training as a PI. Later on she was put in charge of 'C', the Airfields Section at Medmenham which supplied detailed information on the state and dispositions of the enemy's airfields, essential to the planning and carrying out of all operations. Expansion and modification, such as the lengthening of runways of existing airfields and construction of new ones, was closely watched, numbers and types of aircraft constantly checked and details of serviceability and capacity tabulated.

Born in 1892, Dorothy Garrod had read history at Cambridge University, long before women were awarded degrees. During the First World War, in which all three of her brothers died, she served in France and Germany with the Catholic Women's League. She spent the inter-war years on archaeological excavations in Palestine and teaching at Cambridge. Her appointment to the Disney Professorial Chair of Archaeology was announced just before the outbreak of war, making her the first woman to become a professor in any field at either Oxford or Cambridge Universities.

Her applications to join Air Intelligence were consistently refused on the grounds of her age until, with the help of fellow archaeologists, an exemption clause was found for those individuals who had served between 1914–18. On 5 May 1942, her fiftieth birthday, this remarkable woman reported for duty at ACIU. Working initially in Combined Operations with Sarah Churchill, Dorothy then moved to 'F', the Communications and Transportation Section, that provided detailed reports on enemy rail, road and waterway movements and traffic concentrations. The section also provided reports on the location, layout and vulnerability of marshalling yards, depots, bridges, aqueducts and locks. Assessments were made of the traffic interruption following Allied attacks and the speed with which facilities were restored to use. It could also provide more light-hearted information; while compiling her daily report on troop movements, Dorothy followed the journey of a German circus on its wartime travels and was delighted when she identified the arrival of a new baby elephant, clearly visible on the photography!

In the spring of 1942, Sophie Wilson and two other women students were coming to the end of their geography and surveying degree studies at Cambridge when the head of 'W' Section at ACIU visited to recruit potential PIs. Finding that the male students had already been selected by the Army, it was pointed out to him that the three females had completed exactly the same course, including work on the 'Wild' Photogrammetric Comparator. They were promptly instructed to join the WAAF, and on arrival at Medmenham a few weeks later were immediately put to work on the production of maps for the imminent invasion of North Africa. The main task of 'W' Section was the production of maps and data ordered by the various Field Commands through the Directorate of Military Survey. The urgency of the requirements, due to rapid advances in the field, necessitated a high rate of map production over a long period. Sophie's two friends remained in the mapping part of 'W' while she moved to contouring work in conjunction with 'V', the top-secret Model Making Section where artists and sculptors constructed models for every branch of all three services. These ranged from recognition models of enemy war equipment to terrain models used for the planning and briefing of all large-scale landing operations and practically every special bomber and commando task. Sophie contoured target areas to provide accurate heights, calculating the declination and altitude of the sun to show how it would fall on a particular area. This gave pilots an accurate, three-dimensional view of what they would see on different bearings as they approached the target area. The work was demanding, requiring great skill and meticulous attention to detail. She summed it up many years afterwards: 'You had to get it right; lives depended on what you did.'

In 1943, Margaret Hodgson was the first Auxiliary Territorial Service (ATS) PI to join 'B', the Army Section, which provided strategic military intelligence on Europe. In addition to Army personnel it was staffed by US, Canadian and RAF PIs as the shifting requirements and priorities of operations demanded. Two years before Margaret's arrival, Mary Winmill, one of the earliest Women's Royal Naval Service (WRNS), had served as a PI for some time in 'A', the Naval Section, that dealt with all subjects connected with naval and merchant shipping. In 1944, women PIs from the USA arrived, one of whom was Lilian Kamphuis, a college student who had joined the Women's Army Air Corps (WAAC) after Pearl Harbour. She spent seven months at Medmenham before being reassigned to a unit in France.

As the Allied advances progressed through North Africa and from Sicily into Europe, Photographic Interpretation Units (PIU) were established alongside reconnaissance bases to provide a similar function to Medmenham. Hazel Furney was posted to an Anglo-American PIU in Algiers with other women including Ann Whiteman, a historian and Oxford don, and Dorothy Colles, a portrait painter. They were the first Allied servicewomen to serve in North Africa. A few months later, they moved to Tunisia, working on the planned invasions of Sicily and Italy. In December 1943, following the Eighth Army landings, they were flown to San Severo, a PIU in Southern Italy.[7]

Other women PIs served in PIUs in the Middle East and India, where they worked on Allied plans for the invasion of Japanese occupied territory, to be activated after the war in Europe was won. The large PIU in New Delhi included a school where experienced women PIs, such as Ann McKnight-Kauffer, who had been one of the earliest entrants at Wembley in 1939, lectured on the intelligence to be gained from H2S navigational radar imagery, a new and growing asset.

The operational planning for the Normandy invasion and subsequent advance through Northwest Europe demanded extensive work in every section. Information on enemy defences, depots, ordnance dumps, prisoner of war camps, underground factories and transport was needed. In preparation for the beach landings, and in addition to topographical intelligence, the vetting of ground information against air photographs and the provision of countless briefing photographs, annotated maps and defence overlays was required.

By April 1943, the existence of the threat of V-weapons had been recognised and every PI who could possibly be spared from other duties was involved in a search to identify the nature and type of weapons, where they might be produced, and from where and how they might be launched. Peenemünde was identified as the principal research facility and connected with production of the V-2 Ballistic Rocket. Several enormous concrete constructions in

Northwest France were also believed to be associated in some way. All were subjected to massive and disruptive bombing. Photography of the whole French coastal strip and intensive interpretation resulted in the identification and destruction of ninety-six launch sites but only late in 1943 was a V-1 seen for the first time at Peenemünde.

The German 'Vengeance' weapons programme to develop secret weapons was seriously delayed, but reacting to the D-Day landings in June 1944, and using temporary launch sites with London as the principal target, over 9,000 V-1 Flying Bombs and V-2 Rockets were launched, causing over 24,000 dead and injured. Had it not been for the timely identification of the V-weapons and their sites by the ACIU, London could have been facing the delivery of 2,000 flying bombs every twenty-four hours. Photographic reconnaissance and interpretation played a critical part in the defeat of the V-weapons and the retrospective identification of the first V-1 by Constance Babington Smith's team was notable in this respect.

Millions of aerial photographs were interpreted during the Second World War. Records show that up to half the interpreters were women, dating from the early days at Wembley. Many served overseas in PIUs and as heads of sections, and some lectured on PI courses and in America. The work of film processing, typing, teleprint operating and librarianship was predominantly carried out by women. They also worked as photographic plotters, supporting a system which could retrieve photographs of anywhere in the world in a matter of minutes.

In 1938, General von Fritsch, was dismissed from the office of Commander-in-Chief of the German Army, having fallen out of favour with the Nazi regime. Shortly afterwards he is alleged to have forecast that the side with the best photographic reconnaissance would win the forthcoming war. In the event none of the Axis powers used their reconnaissance and interpretation capabilities to the same extent as the Allies.

The success of Allied photographic interpretation was in part due to the decision to use civilians, from both scientific and artistic backgrounds and with a wide range of experience and skills, as interpreters. They brought with them extensive knowledge from diverse occupations and converted that knowledge to military use. Promotion to officer status gave them, and their reports, a necessary level of authority. Wartime Medmenham resembled more of an academic institution than a military unit, and women played a major role in this enterprise. Few groups of women have had the opportunity to live so close to the heart of great events and to have contributed in such a significant way to the eventual Allied victory.

Notes

1. Constance Babington Smith, *Evidence in Camera*, London: Chatto & Windus, 1958.
2. Mollie Chadsey, correspondence with the author in 2008–9.
3. Ursula Powys-Lybbe, *The Eye of Intelligence*, London: William Kimber, 1983.
4. Today's equivalent is 35 pence.
5. Hazel Scott, *Peace and War*, London: Beacon Books, 2006.
6. Babington Smith, *Evidence in Camera*.
7. Scott, *Peace and War*.

Select Bibliography

Medmenham Collection Archive is the major source of unpublished manuscripts, correspondence, and photography used in the compilation of this chapter. The author also benefited from correspondence with Mollie Chadsey in 2008–9.

Babington Smith, Constance, *Evidence in Camera*, London: Chatto & Windus, 1958.
Powys-Lybbe, Ursula, *The Eye of Intelligence*, London: William Kimber, 1983.
Scott, Hazel, *Peace and War*, Beacon Books, 2006.

Chapter 13

'Station X'

The Women at Bletchley Park

John Lee

The absolute secrecy surrounding the work at Bletchley Park, where British cryptographers during the Second World War broke most German military codes (and much Italian and Japanese traffic besides), began to be lifted in the mid-1970s. The remarkable achievement of mastering the technique of discovering the daily settings for the complex German encoding machines (Enigma and Lorenz), thus enabling the Allies to read vast amounts of material that the Germans thought was perfectly secure, is now quite widely known. A number of books, memoirs and television documentaries have added greatly to our understanding of the importance of this work, and that understanding has survived the blandishments of one or two Hollywood movies that have seriously distorted the work done.

But despite the well-meaning intentions of books, visual records and a wonderful museum run by the keenest of volunteers, it is still a battle to appreciate the extraordinary contribution of women to the successful running of Bletchley Park. It is tempting to concentrate on the brilliant work of some famous individuals – mathematicians like Alan Turing, Gordon Welchman and John Jeffreys; linguists like Alfred Dillwyn ('Dilly') Knox and Alistair Denniston; physicists like John Twinn. But the amazing deductions made by these and many other intellectuals and academics would have been overwhelmed by the sheer volume of material to be worked on if it were not for the huge support they received from the rank and file personnel of Bletchley Park, which was principally provided by women.

The very first intake of workers at Bletchley Park was 46 per cent female (67 out of 146) and by the war's end they made up between 66 and 75 per cent of the total workforce, depending on the interpretation of 'workforce'. At least 6,600 women made a direct contribution to the daily deciphering of enemy messages.

It is a sign of how the likelihood of a new war with Germany was on many people's minds that Admiral Sir Hugh Sinclair reputedly used £7,500 of his own money in 1938 to purchase the nicely secluded, but in handy distance of London, Buckinghamshire manor farm of Bletchley Park in Milton Keynes for the British secret intelligence service, MI6. He 'rescued' it from a group of businessmen who were planning to demolish the house and develop the site commercially. It was in August 1939 that 'Captain Ridley's shooting party' took residence – a code name for the advance party of the Government Code and Cypher School that was to colonise the house and its grounds.

It was known that the German military had adapted the commercial encoding machine called Enigma for their own use. Its complex interplay of five wheels, of which three were in use at any one time, each containing twenty-six letters, and using a transmitting and a receiving keyboard and an electrical plugboard, could generate 150 million million million encryptions. The sending and receiving machines were configured identically, using three-letter settings for the wheels in use that were changed every day, and messages were then broadcast in Morse code.

Before the Second World War started, Polish military intelligence had done a great deal of work to replicate an Enigma machine and, with French help, this was passed to the British. The British then went on to invent a machine called a 'Bombe' that took a coded message, running it through a complex series of wheels with the same number of letters as Enigma, and then testing all the possible combinations until it began to produce a German text message. The trick was to discern what the three-letter setting was for the day the message was transmitted. This involved a great deal of fiendishly difficult cryptography, looking for repeated patterns of letters, and the task was occasionally aided by some lapses by bored German personnel repeating standard messages with little attempt at concealment. 'Nothing to report' and 'Heil Hitler' were soon identified as such phrases, as were daily weather reports in identical format.

The encoded message was transmitted in blocks of four letters and part of the skills acquired by the codebreakers was in getting used to the style of message. The first and last groups of letters contained various bits of information identifying the sender and recipient, and most importantly the daily setting for the Enigma wheels. It was found that enthusiasts for crossword puzzles had a great aptitude for spotting these sorts of conundrum. Reading endless streams of garbled letters, looking for the vital three letters was a huge task. It was the 'mechanisation' of this process with the 'Bombes' that speeded up the process and led to so many vitally important decryptions. The resulting intelligence, called 'Ultra', could only ever be ascribed to a 'Most Secret Source'. Even the British military commanders receiving this valuable information could never be told that it was coming from the daily breaking of the enemy codes. Nor could the Allies do anything that would make it clear to the enemy that they were reading their messages on a daily basis. Nothing could be done to alarm the enemy or shake their belief that their codes were unbreakable. They had to be encouraged to go on using the same method of transmission.

The first requirement was to capture the coded messages sent by Morse code between German military, state and economic organisations. The British maintained a number of listening facilities, called Y Stations, where endless shifts of very patient and dedicated personnel endured hours of white noise and background interference to write down outwardly meaningless Morse code messages. Great care was demanded to take down this raw data. The odd missed letter was understandable but too many would make the decryption vastly more difficult. There was only one chance to capture the message, usually of a fairly routine nature, but a sudden increase in traffic signalled a major operation developing, and then tensions ran high. Joan Nicholls, who added two years to her real age to enlist in the ATS at '17', worked at Hut 6 Bletchley Park, which housed an intercept station. 'They would tell us if they wanted them double-banked, two people to take them, or if one good-quality operator would be sufficient.'[1] As many as 10,000 people may have worked in these listening stations and 75 per cent of them were women of the three services – Women's Royal Naval Service (WRNS), Women's Auxiliary Air Force (WAAF) and Auxiliary Territorial Service (ATS). Without them there would be nothing on which the more well-known codebreakers could display their undoubted genius.

The coded messages were delivered by courier to Bletchley Park, and parcelled out to the various huts to be worked on. Large numbers of so-called copy typists had to prepare the messages for analysis. In Hut 6 a carefully selected group of women graduates recruited by Stuart Milner-Barry from Newnham College, Cambridge (where his sister was vice-principal), looked for patterns in the messages, knowing that the first and last groups of letters sig-nified the Enigma settings for the day, with perhaps a call sign and frequency, and an indication of who was sending the message. Mavis Lever, a student of German at University College London and one of 'Dilly' Knox's team (nine out of ten of whom were women), found herself listening to one young German signaller who regularly used his girlfriend's name for a four-letter setting as well as certain German obscenities. She later recalled, 'I am the world's expert on German four-letter dirty words!'[2]

No less than 210 'Bombe' machines were operated by an overwhelmingly female staff, where the coded messages were decrypted and turned into

German text. It is known that 1,679 Wrens worked on these machines. How ironic that when they first came to Bletchley Park 'it was doubted if girls could do the work. The final compliment shows how successfully this experiment worked out.'[3] These young women had to set up the Bombe as if it were an Enigma receiving machine, using the settings deduced by the codebreaking staff in the various huts (each working and specialising in a particular type of traffic – army, navy, air force, etc.). The Bombes then ran through endless combinations of settings until the text emerged as readable German. The operators had to let the machine process the message, which took about seventeen minutes, and then check the text to see if it was readable German. If the codebreakers had successfully identified the daily settings, this could be quite straightforward. If they had been only partially successful, then it was down to the machine operators to identify how much of the message was coming out as readable and they, as their experience developed, could then make adjustments of their own and keep running the machine through its seventeen-minute cycles to complete the task.

This text then went for translation, where large numbers of Foreign Office personnel and university graduates were employed. There had been a special drive to recruit young women who had lived, worked or studied in Germany in the 1930s. One Australian in London, Elizabeth Agar, described her 'interview' at the Admiralty. One officer asked, '*Konnen Sie Deutsch sprechen?*' to which she replied, '*Ja, ich kann ganz gut sprechen*', and was told 'You'll do.'[4] This was not a simple job for the linguists as often there were missing bits of text that needed a good deal of interpretation. And finally the translated text went for analysis by military intelligence experts.

The working conditions were very demanding. The machines generated great heat when running at full capacity and the huts had been thrown up quickly and lacked any sort of comfort. The women had to clean the carbon brushes at each wheel, and make many fine adjustments to the filaments to make sure there would be no short-circuiting. An added hazard was the generation of static electricity and many shocks were felt until rubber mats were provided for both sides of the machines. The huts were surrounded by six-foot-high blast walls, which reduced air circulation still further. They were stifling in the summer and freezing in the winter. One hut alone contained ten Bombes; it was known as the 'Hell Hole'. In the summer what began as official permission to remove jackets and work in shirt-sleeve order would, in an all-female working environment, see more and more clothing removed. There are accounts of young men entering rooms where the machines were working at full tilt like furnaces and fleeing in embarrassment before an array of scantily clad young women. Innocent days! And in the depths of winter the women working side-by-side in Huts 3 and 6 (on German army and *Luftwaffe* material) devised an ingenious tunnel between the buildings to avoid carrying material outside. A pulley system saw material transferred to the relevant hut on a handy tea tray! When the blasts of winter wind saw the material blown about, the girls soon jury-rigged a set of doors at each end of the tunnel with loud thumps announcing each time material was ready to be hauled across. It sounds all very Heath Robinson and a typically British way of 'muddling through', but it was the work of intelligent young people doing everything they could to speed up their work and thus increase their efficiency.

The work itself was demanding, being highly repetitive but still requiring great concentration. All personnel found that with increasing experience, they could start to recognise repeating patterns in the material they handled and assess the relative importance of certain messages. Winnifred Stokes recalled:

> As I had been a typist in civilian life I was told I was to be one of the many operators of the Enigma machine. Hours of setting them up with wheels in different sequences as instructed, hoping that the typed up text would appear in German. If, and when, it did the Shift Leader had to be notified immediately so that all the messages received on that frequency could be typed up as quickly as possible with the wheel setting that had been used. This was when you felt you were really contributing something.[5]

Of great importance was the Intelligence Index built up in Hut 3. Here, another 570 Wrens transferred all captured data onto card files, and these experts began to build important data on enemy personnel, installations and operations, with a careful cross-referencing that was a mine of information for British military planners.

Another 400 WAAFs worked in the Communications Centre, and there were many more women involved in the important duties of collecting and delivering the staff from the several villages in the surrounding three counties and the dozen or so stately homes and country mansions, like Woburn Abbey and Gayhurst Manor, that housed the workforce. Later in the war, special camps of Nissen huts were set up for the servicewomen. These drivers of the Motor Transport Corps (MTC), and First Aid Nursing Yeomanry (FANY), played their part in the success of Station X, without ever having the faintest idea of the importance of the work being done there. Three eight-hour shifts each of 2,500 people, with another 2,500 on hand to cover shift changes and the granting of leave, had to be processed every day. Of the 6,600 women working in the Government Communications Headquarters (GCHQ – as the code-breaking side of Bletchley Park was officially known), 2,600 were Wrens,

400 ATS, 1,100 WAAF and some 2,500 were civilians, seconded from the Foreign Office.[6]

There were so many WRNS personnel on site that in December 1942 they set up their own naval establishment – 'HMS Pembroke V'. Besides administering to the needs of the Wrens working the Bombes and Colossus, they ran a cafeteria that served a thousand meals a day. Here was, of course, a veritable army of cooks, cleaners, laundry workers, medical and dental staff, and drivers, who all made their contribution to the smooth running, and hence the success, of Bletchley Park. These humble but essential workers also deserve to be remembered.

What comes out repeatedly in all the memoirs is the absolute secrecy maintained by all people working there. It was difficult to be always working on one small aspect of the problem and never to be told what the bigger picture was. Yet all were imbued with a sense of the importance of the work they were doing. Even as they typed the messages most of the women did not know they were from broken German codes. Julie Lydekker, a clerk in Josh Cooper's Air Section said, 'We knew nothing about Enigma at all until long after the war.'[7] Susan Wenham, a codebreaker working in Hut 6, explained:

> It was a very curious organisation. We were very, very departmental-ised. You never discussed your work with anyone but your little group that you worked with. I hadn't a clue what was going on in the rest of the Park and nobody else had a clue what we were doing, except the real high-ups. It was a curious world of its own.[8]

Jean Campbell-Harris (later Baroness Trumpington) later recalled in a television interview how she, being fluent in German and French, was recruited into the Foreign Office as a cipher clerk and was transferred to Bletchley Park. She and six other women spent all day in one room typing German naval messages onto teletape and, while admitting that they had no idea of the purpose of this tape, said they couldn't help but sense its vital importance. When pressed by people in the surrounding area about what went on at Bletchley, they devised a cover story that they were the office that decided who got what medals. She said it made them very popular with some service personnel, especially officers, but usefully diverted any more questions.

The first real successes for the codebreakers came as early as April 1940, when they read many of the German messages relating to the invasion of Norway. The surge in the number of messages during major operations gave them so much more material to work on and more opportunities to crack the daily settings. Now the various huts waiting to work on messages were said to get 'tetchy' if the daily settings were not revealed to them by breakfast! The sheer volume of material they processed during the German conquest of France (May–June 1940) saw the huge increase in staff and facilities at Bletchley Park. Tracking German *Luftwaffe* activity during the Battle of Britain was important, but many people agree that the most vital work of all was the ability to read the German naval messages that told where the submarine 'wolf packs' were lurking during the battle of the Atlantic. The one great fear (and Winston Churchill said it was his greatest fear) was that the sinking of Allied shipping by the dreaded U-boats would starve Britain into submission. The work of Huts 4 and 8 at Bletchley (which specialised in naval intelligence) enabled the convoys to avoid the worst attacks and their escorts to inflict damage on the attacking submarines. There was a moment of severe crisis in February 1942, when the *Kriegsmarine* (German navy) introduced a fourth wheel into their daily settings. This exponential increase in the possible number of encryptions caused a 'blackout' in the ability to read naval messages that lasted for most of the year, and was grievously expensive in shipping and seamen's lives. The capture of a codebook from the scuttled U-559 gave Hut 8 what it needed to start cracking the daily settings again. It was December 1942 before the elated news, 'We are back into the U-boats', was announced.

As has been seen in Chapter 12, a photographic reconnaissance pilot photographed the great German battleship the *Bismarck*. The crucial cooperation between the services was demonstrated as the last voyage of the *Bismarck* was tracked by Ultra until she was sunk by British ships and aircraft. Ultra decrypts kept the Allies in North Africa fully informed of General (later Field Marshal) Erwin Rommel's difficulties there. There were difficult decisions to be made about how much information to pass to the West's Soviet allies about German operations in Russia without giving away the big secret about the breaking of the Enigma code. Once the Allies had re-entered Europe in June 1944 via the Normandy beaches, Ultra decrypts kept the Allies one step ahead of their determined foe. As the breakout from the Normandy beachheads came in August, Bletchley Park was reading 18,000 German army messages a day, and read a total of 40,000 important messages a month.

We must remember that, besides all this German traffic, the Italian and Japanese codes had to be worked on. Teams of Bletchley Park experts, especially the WRNS Bombe operators, were sent overseas to work on Japanese material in the Far East.

In August 1941, a message was picked up in transit from Athens to Vienna of a quite different order. It was sent by the German's Lorenz machine, used only for traffic between the highest authorities of the Nazi regime. It had twelve wheels and the number of encryptions was incalculable. In 1943, Alan Turing led the team of brilliant intellectuals that devised the world's first digital computer, the Colossus, to deal with the problem. Using the basic equipment of a Post Office telephone exchange, they devised a Mark I that used 1,800 valves to power the search engine (a Mark II would use 2,400 valves). Before long it would take just four and a half hours for Colossus, and its WRNS operators, to find the daily settings for Lorenz message machines. A total of ten Colossus 'computers' were built.[9] A team of 270 Wrens, under civilian technician guidance, were solely responsible for Lorenz decrypts.

At Bletchley Park, with its concentration of mostly young wartime personnel, there was much thought given to the maintenance of morale. Its concert parties were legendary; there was also a very able Drama Group and a very fine choral society that both made a contribution to the local entertainments. Monthly dances were greatly appreciated and a trip to Bedford to hear Glen Miller was a rare treat. There were, of course, irrepressible high jinks. Sarah Norton, who had been promoted from the Naval Index Room to translating German decrypts, recalled launching Jean Campbell-Harris in a large, wheeled laundry basket, normally used to move secret files down a long corridor in one of the newly built blocks. She was aghast to see her crash through some swing doors and end up in a men's loo! Sadly this watch had to be split up amongst more sober workers but, apparently, not for too long.[10]

Bletchley Park kept its secret so well that it was never deliberately bombed by the enemy. One German bomber did offload its cargo and bombs fell in the nearby churchyard, one exploding right next to a hut full of Wren typists. The hut is said to have physically moved one metre on its foundations but the Wrens carried on working. There were the inevitable jokes about 'whether you felt the earth move for you, darling'!

After a visit to Bletchley Park on 6 December 1941, Prime Minister Winston Churchill described how much he valued 'The geese that laid the golden eggs, but never cackled'. He received a daily synopsis of important intelligence from Station X. Patricia Chappell worked on the 'Naval Headlines' for the Prime Minister, where she specialised in news from the Eastern Adriatic and the Balkans. Assessments at the end of the war have suggested that it shortened the duration of the war by between eighteen months and two years, and hence saved the lives of anything up to twenty-two million people. Besides the astonishing level of intellectual genius and organisational innovation displayed, stands the total and remarkable level of secrecy achieved and maintained by the workforce for decades. The story that a husband and wife each went out to work every day not knowing that they were in different huts at the same facility is entirely believable. What is needed now is wider recognition of the vital contribution that women made to the success of Station X at Bletchley Park.

After the war, British military intelligence, with an eye to having to soon be cracking Soviet codes and ciphers, wished to continue to conceal the fact that it had been so successful in reading German secrets on a daily basis. Station X was closed and the Colossus and Bombe machines were broken up. (As an aside this meant that the British failed to take out a patent on their digital computer, which huge economic benefit was left for America's IBM to acquire.) The departing staff were sworn to secrecy under the Official Secrets Act. The site was used by various commercial enterprises and as a teacher training college, with nobody knowing anything of the history of the establishment. It was vacated by 1991, and stood in danger of demolition. The Bletchley Archaeological and Historical Society began to trace veterans, and gathered 400 to a meeting that was almost like a farewell party. But this stimulated a movement to preserve the historic site that was taken up by Milton Keynes Council. Now, under the auspices of the Bletchley Park Trust, a wonderful and expanding museum opened in 2004 to preserve the memory forever. A visit by Sue Black of the British Computer Society has led to calls for the increased recognition of the part played by the women of Bletchley Park. Together with her BCS colleague, Dr Jan Peters, the BCS Women group is recording the memories of these women for posterity. In a similar way, Gwendoline Page, a wartime Wren who worked at Bletchley Park has done excellent work, recording and publishing the memories of those WRNS who 'kept the secret'.

Notes

The author wishes to thank: HRH The Duke of Kent KG GCMG; Jean, Campbell-Harris, Baroness Trumpington; and Sue Black of the British Computer Society, for their assistance with guidance and material in the writing of this chapter.

1. Michael Smith, *Station X: The Codebreakers of Bletchley Park*, Basingstoke: Macmillan, 1998, p. 51.
2. Ibid., p. 33
3. Brian Oakley, *The Bletchley Park War*, Milton Keynes: Bletchley Park Trust, 2006, p. 32.
4. Gwendoline Page, *They Listened in Secret*, London: Reeve, 2003, p. 121. She was asked, 'Can you speak German' and she replied 'Yes, I can speak it well.'
5. Gwendoline Page, *We Kept the Secret*, London: Reeve, 2002, p. 27.
6. Ibid., p. 32.
7. Smith, *Station X*, p. 36.
8. Ibid., p. 37
9. An astonishing replica has been built at Bletchley Park by Mr Tony Sale and his team, working from old photographs and some partial wiring diagrams that survived the post-war destruction. It was officially opened by HRH Duke of Kent in July 2007
10. Smith, *Station X*, p. 96.

Select Bibliography

Oakley, Brian, *The Bletchley Park War: Some of the Outstanding Individuals*, Milton Keynes: Bletchley Park Trust, 2006.

Page, Gwendoline, *We Kept the Secret*, London: Reeve, 2002.

Page, Gwendoline, *They Listened in Secret*, London: Reeve, 2003.

Smith, Michael, *Station X: The Codebreakers of Bletchley Park*, Basingstoke: Channel Four Books/Macmillan, 1998.

THE SECOND WORLD WAR:
THE EASTERN FRONT

Chapter 14

Women in the Siege of Leningrad

Tatiana Roshupkina

It seemed that nothing could spoil a long anticipated holiday, when a 9-year-old girl who lived with her parents in a flat in Leningrad arrived one hot summer's day, accompanied by her mother, at the former Finnish resort, Terijoki, on the Gulf of Finland, 50 km from Leningrad (now St Petersburg). This beautiful spa area known as the Northern Riviera with its sandy beaches, cedar forests, and wooden cottages, had belonged to Finland prior to 1939. A town on the border with the Soviet Union, it once rose to glory as the capital of the short-lived Finnish Democratic Republic (December 1939 to March 1940), to be later ceded under the Moscow Peace Treaty to the Soviet Union, together with about 9 per cent of the pre-Winter War Finnish territory, and eventually, in 1948, losing its original name to the Russian-sounding Zelenogorsk.

It was June 1941, and the little girl on vacation was my mother, Tatiana (who is today Mrs Chernysheva). She came with her mother, Varvara Sysoenkova (*née* Schedrina) to spend the summer at her uncle's cottage. Uncle Nikolai Schedrin, Varvara's brother, was a military man, who stayed in Terijoki with a small military unit. Like many of his comrades-in-arms, he had a beautiful carved wooden cottage facing the Gulf of Finland.

Despite the Blitzkrieg and crushing advance of the Germans into Western Europe, the Russians, having been lulled into a false sense of security by the Hitler–Stalin Non-Aggression Pact of 1939, known as the Molotov–Ribbentrop Pact,[1] were enjoying the first summer month of 1941. All rumours of the deployment of German divisions along the Soviet Union frontier were dismissed by the media, and branded as absurd propaganda.

The country did not expect to be attacked, and was not prepared for war. For this reason, a prolonged, distant noise at dawn, on the 22 June 1941, was mistaken for a heavy thunderstorm by the unsuspecting Varvara and Tatiana. But seeing the Gulf of Finland in the morning, full of stunned fish, floating with their silvery bellies up, revealed the grim truth; the country had been attacked, and war had broken out. The noise they heard was the heavy bombing of Kronstadt, a Russian seaport town on Kotlin Island, 30 km west of Leningrad, near the head of the Gulf of Finland. It was the early start of Hitler's battle plan, Operation Barbarossa, aimed at the rapid conquest of the European part of the Soviet Union.

The plan envisaged launching offensives in three major directions, using dedicated German army groups: Leningrad (Army Group North) Smolensk-Moscow (Army Group Centre) and Kiev (Army Group South).[2] The overall objective of the plan was to destroy Soviet forces in the area up to the Urals by the autumn of 1941, with the help of 183 divisions, 3,350 tanks, 7,184 guns and 1,945 aircraft.[3] Leningrad's fate was clearly defined in this plan. This city was the main strategic goal of Army Group North under the command of Field Marshal Wilhelm Ritter von Leeb, and it was intended to be wiped off the map, together with about 3,000,000 of its citizens. Army Group North had twenty-one divisions at its disposal, five of which were mobile, and was thought to be able to carry out its task well without the help of other groups, and later even to help Army Group Centre in a push to Moscow.[4] So sure was Hitler of his victory over the legendary city, and indeed the whole of Russia, wrongly believed by the Germans to be 'a colossus with feet of clay',[5] that he had sent out invitations to celebrate Christmas 1941 in vanquished Leningrad. Little did he know that a planned ninety-day operation would turn into one of the longest sieges in history, lasting 900 days, and resulting in the defeat of the German troops.

For Varvara Sysoenkova and her daughter Tatiana, remaining on former Finnish territory, with Finland fighting on the side of Germany, was much too dangerous. Nikolai was a commissar, a military-political Army officer, and using his influence was able to secure Varvara and Tatiana standing room on a heavily overcrowded train in a stampede of people who were eager to reach Leningrad.

Today, Tatiana still remembers that Leningrad greeted them with chaos at the railway station. Those called to the colours, and volunteers, surrounded by sobbing relatives, were getting on military trains heading to the fighting at the front. Screams filled the air, panic engulfing the ones who stayed. What would the future hold?

Varvara took Tatiana back to their home which was house 15/17, Flat 6, Steklyannaya Ulitsa (Street), Leningrad. Tatiana's father, Fyodor Sysoenkov, had been drafted into the army in the early days of war, and was tragically killed in the battle of Smolensk in the autumn 1941.

With the men away at war the remaining population, who were mostly women, were immediately mobilised for constructing fortifications along the northern and southern city borders. Up to 500,000 people worked on fortifications every day – women, teenagers and the elderly. Time was at a premium and, following the order from the Supreme High Command General Head-quarters, the armed forces from the Northern Front were enlisted to help civilians in building a fortification belt in the Southwestern part of Leningrad.

No one complained of the hard working conditions. People were united in their fervent desire to save their beloved city. Apart from fortifications along the perimeter of Leningrad, citizens built a large number of air raid shelters (over 4,600 of which were ready by 20 August 1941); anti-tank entrenchments, ditches covered with steel 'hedgehogs', and barbed wire entanglements were placed at the approach routes to the city. In all 190 km of timber barricades, 635 km of wire entanglements, 700 km of anti-tank ditches, 5,000 earth-and-timber emplacements, and reinforced concrete weapon emplacements, and 25,000 km of open trenches, were built by civilians.[6]

Varvara was among the first women to work on defence line fortifications. She worked a ten-day shift, followed by one evening off. She was allowed a short time off to see her young daughter Tatiana, who was at home with an elderly grandmother, Ekaterina Schedrina. Families with only one child were not permitted to leave the city, so evacuation was out of the question.

Women's tasks were to dig trenches with shovels, carry heavy timber beams and stones (several women at one time) and perform other heavy manual labour. Every finished stretch of entrenchment was greeted with relief. Those working on fortifications were provided with basic meals. They slept in the shelter tents put up on the site where they were working. Rest time was reduced to a minimum, and they worked up to twenty hours a day. With the enemy fast approaching Leningrad, all effort was consolidated to ensure the required defence of the city.

With the first casualties arriving, Varvara was sent to work in a field hospital. She was a petite woman of delicate build, and it was considered that she could be of more help nursing wounded soldiers and civilians who, even at the height of fighting at the city borders, continued to work on fortifications.

From the start of the war the women of Leningrad had to learn how to become snipers, communications operators and reconnaissance scouts. They took up posts in Air Raid Patrol (ARP), the militia and the Navy. They worked in hospitals and factories, and in public transport, driving trams through the city under heavy shelling, risking their lives. Industrial plants were converted to military production to make ammunition, tanks and ships for the Navy, and women constituted nearly 75 per cent of the workforce.

For Tatiana, the autumn of 1941 began with a return to school. Classes took place in the basement, which also served as a shelter where children could remain during the air raids. They were issued with gas masks, and asked to help the city by being vigilant, and report any suspicious activity, like seeing someone sending signals to guide the enemy to the right targets for air attacks.

Many places in Leningrad were camouflaged. For example some bridges looked like innocent rows of wooden houses, and the spires of major cathedrals were covered with sackcloth and sand bags. Thanks to these measures, nearly all the bridges in Leningrad remained intact during the war, but some of the historic buildings were not so lucky. The famous Palace of Empress Catherine the Great (1729–96) at Tsarskoye Selo, and the Peterhoff Palace were destroyed. The beautiful Amber Room in Catherine's Palace, which had been a present to Peter the Great from the King of Prussia in 1716, was stolen by the Nazis. After the war, both palaces were painstakingly restored, and the Amber Room reconstructed in 2003, with the financial help of the German company, Ruhrgas.

In early September 1941, the Leningrad Zoo was hit by a bomb, killing many animals. For several days, Tatiana was haunted by the blood-curdling screams of a mortally wounded elephant. Chaos and fear settled in her mind. She was confused and frightened by the whole situation. Her parents were away; she felt lonely and anxious; and her daily trips to school were far from being safe.

By 8 September, Leningrad and its suburbs were completely surrounded by German forces. It was the start of a 900-day siege, 'the iron ring of Hitler had closed'.[7] All ground supply routes were cut off, and the remaining air supply route was constantly under attack by the Germans. The city authorities faced an acute problem of providing the citizens with food. The population of Leningrad had increased considerably due to the influx of refugees. The stocks of food for the city could barely stretch for just over a month. All food stores were emptied within a short period of time, and many were closed completely. The people themselves stored as much food as they could but that would last only for a limited period of time.

Food rationing seemed to be the only equitable option, and although it was introduced as early as July 1941, initially the amount of food and its variety, however basic, could help people stave off hunger. Many families still had some stocks of cereals, sugar and even butter in their homes. An average Leningrad citizen was entitled at that time to 600 grams of bread a day, if in employment, and their dependants were rationed to 400 grams a day.[8] Citizens were also given small quantities of meat, 400 grams a month for their dependants, cereals, fats and sugar. However, by 20 November, the food allowance had been sharply reduced, and there was little else available apart from bread. Factory workers' rations shrank to 250 grams of bread a day, and office workers and non-working dependants and children got only 125 grams a day. Bread was heavily adulterated with sawdust, cellulose, and cottonseed, and contained less than 250 calories. Very little other food was available for distribution, other than some lentils, cereals, to the amount of 400 grams per person per month, and hardly any fats or meat were available.

In November 1941, on the initiative of Andrei Zhdanov, a Soviet politician who was in charge of the defence of Leningrad, a stretch of road known as 'A Road to Life' was constructed across the frozen Lake Ladoga, which provided the only link with the unoccupied Russian territories to the Northeast of Leningrad. An unusually severe winter of 1941–2 claimed the lives of many weakened people in the besieged city, and, ironically, the same frosty winter facilitated the transportation of heavy loads of food, ammunition, fuel and vaccines, over a thick layer of ice that had formed on the surface of the lake due to extremely low temperatures of minus 35–40 degrees. Heavily loaded trucks moved slowly over the ice, pulling sledges that were used to even up the weight distribution, and which were piled high with bags of flour, tinned meat, cereals, milk, and egg powder, fats and sugar. Precarious weather conditions made every journey across the lake a daunting task. Strong winds weakened the ice in places, creating treacherous conditions for the truck drivers and the horses that were also used as load carriers. The road was under constant bombardment by the Germans, and quite often trucks with a precious load would be seen sinking through holes in the ice. The most dangerous parts of the road were pegged, and there were service stations set up across the whole length of the lake. These stations were staffed by women who were traffic wardens, doctors and signallers. They offered first aid to the wounded and passed information on all traffic accidents from post to post. They also made regular walks about the area in search of stray travellers in need of help. Despite the self-sacrifice and dedication of the people on the Ladoga route, the 1,200-tons-a-day[9] minimum food delivery target was not often met, and the population of Leningrad continued to die of starvation.

During her short visits home, Varvara made sure she brought her family some salt in a matchbox. It was remembered by Tatiana as dirty grey crystals, some of which were scourings from the pots in the hospital where her mother worked, and where soup was made in the kitchen. The muddy liquid provided at least some nutrition for her emaciated daughter Tatiana, and the elderly Ekaterina, and salt helped prevent scurvy, a plague amongst the starving people.

To stop scurvy reaching epidemic proportions, scientists at the All-Union Vitamin Scientific-Research Institute (VNIVI), developed a conifer-sourced vitamin C preparation. Leningrad was surrounded by beautiful conifer forests, and pine needles were an excellent material for this purpose. Some women volunteered to help collect pine needles, and soon conifer extract, mixed with acetic or citric acid, still stocked in confectionary plants, found its way to hospitals, the front line and civilian households. However, due to the laborious nature of its production, the latter were given a lower priority.[10]

Varvara used to go to a black market to exchange some valuables for bread and *zhmykh*, a cake made of sunflower seeds left over from oil extraction, which was normally used as feed for livestock. One could get a 600 g or 1 kg loaf of bread in exchange for some table silver or gold jewellery, or high-quality warm clothes – or in the early months of the siege for money. The best deal could be struck with *remeslenniki*, teenagers, from the tradesmen's schools. These schools were set up at major factories and plants to teach youngsters an industrial trade. During the war, they helped produce ammunition, mines and mortars, as well as explosives. Some of these boys formed gangs, and roamed the city streets[11] attacking vulnerable people and stealing their ration cards. One such school was near Tatiana's house.

One late November morning, shortly after Tatiana's tenth birthday, which passed unnoticed, her grandmother Ekaterina was too weak to get up at 6.00am, the time announced on the radio to go to the shops and queue for hours to get the daily ration of bread. She promised to join Tatiana later, but never turned up. It later transpired that when she left the house, Ekaterina was attacked by a gang of *remeslenniki*. She fought to hold onto her ration card with all her remaining strength but she was savagely beaten and the card was stolen from her. On her return from the shops, Tatiana found her grandmother semiconscious in the flat. A neighbour had found her and had helped her home. Ekaterina died a few days later from her injuries. Varvara had to remain at her job in the hospital and Tatiana was alone in the flat with her grandmother's dead body for a week, until her mother's next short visit home. With the help of the same female neighbour, Varvara rolled Ekaterina's body into a Persian rug and tied it with cord. She placed it on a sledge and the two women pulled the sledge along the dark and cold city streets to a common grave at the local cemetery. There Ekaterina Schedrina found her last resting place; her attackers were never found or brought to justice for her manslaughter.

Little Tatiana was now left entirely alone in the flat, and her school was closed. Varvara settled her daughter on a windowsill in the kitchen, the warmest room in the house. The sill was wide enough to accommodate a child. Varvara made a bed for her with a mattress, pillow, and a few blankets, and there she stayed for many days and nights. The sill became her home. She kept her favourite books there, and read them during the day, when she felt strong enough to do it. She missed going to school and missed her schoolfriends. She tried to learn poems by heart to keep her mind alive but had to abandon this idea due to constant fatigue and hunger.

Varvara gave her daughter tasks to carry out in the flat to keep her mind off hunger, and to make her days pass more quickly. During the day, Tatiana was busy building a fire in the stove with logs, initially supplied by the house caretaker, and making herself the occasional cup of tea, which in reality was just boiled water. She also rummaged in the general waste bins in the streets, searching for herring heads, which, when cooked, could pass for fish broth. Higher rank officials and blue-collar workers were on a special ration, and food waste from their kitchens was a coveted treasure from the bins.

When her mother was due for some leave at home from her job, Tatiana made trips outside to bring home as much snow as she could. She placed it in the bathtub to melt, and it was used for washing both herself and the clothes, using whittled bars of soap brought by her mother from hospital. Varvara also washed the floor in the kitchen where her daughter stayed to protect her from infection. Other rooms in the flat where their furniture was stored were kept locked, and opened only when they needed more fuel for the stove. They chopped it up and burnt it, including some beautiful Viennese chairs, book-shelves and the books from their vast library.

For Tatiana, the nights were hard to endure. Blackouts were compulsory, and she curled up on her makeshift bed in the kitchen windowsill in pitch darkness, behind the closed curtains, trying not to miss a radio announcement of a coming air raid. When a raid was announced, she would crawl underneath the kitchen table, and stay there until the attack was over. Sometimes the announcement was not verbal, but the raid could be detected with a metronome, which was highly sensitive to sound or vibration. Fast beating signified an air raid was coming, and it decreased with the end of the attack.

When her grandmother was alive, Tatiana used to go to a shelter during the air raids. Shelters were very damp places, hastily built to ensure at least some protection. Water constantly dripped from the ceiling, and could reach up to one's knees. Shelters were packed, and it was impossible to move one's arm or leg if it was caught in some awkward position. With her grandmother dead, Tatiana stopped going to shelters altogether. Even today, she experiences panic attacks if surrounded by a crowd of people, and feels claustrophobic in small rooms.

During one of the air raids the roof of Tatiana's house was partially hit by a shell, which damaged a corner of the kitchen. Crumbling plaster pulled the wallpaper down, and formed a sinister-looking shape, resembling the face of an old man. Tatiana spent evenings pressing her nose to the window glass to avoid looking at the gaping corner until she drifted into sleep. She wished her mother was there.

A view from the window revealed the Finland Railway Bridge, camouflaged with wooden boards and windows and doors painted on them to make it look like a street full of houses, and a twelve-storey bakery plant. Every now and then, Tatiana saw a flickering light on top of the building, followed shortly afterwards by an air raid. A traitor was sending signals to attract the bombers to the right place. This meant yet another ferocious attack, killing more people, littering the city with more dead bodies.

Tatiana was used to dead bodies. They were everywhere – in the streets, in bread queues, where people dropped, unable anymore to stand for hours. If anything, they were a welcome sign of getting your ration of bread sooner. The dead body of her grandmother had not frightened her. She could not grieve over the death of her grandmother. She accepted it without question. Death was a familiar thing to her – dozens of people in the city were dying of starvation and hunger-related diseases every day. 'In the besieged city … a multitude of families were wiped out completely.'[12] Tatiana's mind was fuzzy, her senses dull; there was only one desire left – to get her bread at the distribution shop and gobble it down there and then. She never took bread home. Her hunger was too strong to survive a seemingly endless trip. Also, she feared being attacked by *remeslenniki* and other criminal types, preying on solitary and vulnerable people, who would steal her bread.[13]

The whole city looked more dead than alive. Shuffling, slow figures with bluish, haggard faces or cheeks puffed and bloated with hunger, filled the streets of Leningrad. People left their houses mostly to see to their immediate needs – queueing for bread, going to the water-pumps to take some drinkable water home. Many took their dead relatives on sledges to the burial places. There were no horses, dogs, cats, birds, or even rats in the city. All animals and birds were eaten in this shell of a city, populated with ghost-like people. By the end of 1941, 19,984 citizens of Leningrad had died of starvation.[14]

Food deprivation and constant shelling proved to be too much for the psyche of some people, driving them to atrocious activities such as cannibalism. Markets were selling *pirozhki* (pasties), stuffed with meat of a dubious nature. Some cannibals were just after cadaverous meat, and used to dig up fresh graves and cut strips of flesh from the buried bodies. Others turned into murderers, and attacked people in the dark lanes with an axe or a hammer. Cannibals rarely acted individually, but were organised into groups. The city authorities were aware of their existence, and by early 1942, 886 cannibals were prosecuted and convicted for the gruesome crime.[15]

Hunger and shelling plagued the city for days on end. Massive air raids and artillery bombardments racked the city for many hours at a stretch, and up to five or six times a day, and seven times at night. The air was thick with smoke from incendiary bombs, and with dust and fumes from the burning buildings. The first shelling of the city took place on 4 September 1941, and over the next three months, Leningrad was hit with 2,296 artillery shells. During the period from 28 October 1941 to 11 November 1941, 190 incendiary bombs and 97 blast bombs were dropped on the city. The longest air attack took place on 7 October 1941, and lasted for six hours and ten minutes.[16] The main targets for bombing were major plants, power stations, factories and waterways, chosen in an attempt to bring the city to a standstill. The water mains were damaged in 5,609 places in different parts of the city.[17] Once a sugar refinery in the area where Tatiana lived was blasted by a bomb, and burnt melted sugar was quickly picked up off the street by starving people – it provided what seemed like a wonderful treat. To her utmost delight, Tatiana managed to take home a few molten lumps of bitter-tasting burnt sugar.

The first two months of 1942 proved to be the hardest for the citizens of Leningrad. In February, heavy bombing of the Ladoga route made it impossible to reach the city for a whole week, and the besieged people were left without any food supplies. To exacerbate the already perilous situation, all the functioning water mains within the city froze in sub-zero temperatures. Melted snow was the only source of water at that time. A bitter winter and famine made the death toll reach unprecedented levels, and 256,386 people died of hunger and cold that year.[18]

The late spring of 1942 brought some relief in the form of an improved food supply. Children in Leningrad were given a one-off treat of a chocolate bar and a tiny piece of horse meat. Varvara and Tatiana went together to the shop to collect it. On the way home, Tatiana could not control her hunger any longer. As they walked along, she slipped the small piece of meat out of her mother's shopping bag and walking behind her, ate it raw. When they arrived home her mother was reduced to bitter tears by the discovery. Varvara did not scold Tatiana, she knew that she had been reduced to it by hunger, and she took her in her arms and kissed and hugged her.

The city's plight struck a deep chord in the hearts of caring people in other countries. That spring, women from Airdrie and Coatbridge in Scotland sent through diplomatic channels a book containing 5,000 messages of support to the women of Leningrad. In return, they received an album with 3,000 messages and sketches of Leningrad from the female writers, painters, and scientists of Leningrad. This album is today kept in the Mitchell Library, Glasgow.

Despite the dismal mood in the city, the theatres and libraries remained open during the siege, and the attendance rate was adequate enough to justify the efforts of their struggling staff. People needed places where they could escape to from the grim reality of their life.

That March, it became obvious that the city's defences needed an injection of new blood, and many more women volunteered to join the defence ranks. This movement continued well into the autumn of 1943. During the period from 15 March 1942 until 10 October 1943, 17,473 women were trained in how to use automatic rifles and machine guns, and to fire mortars.[19]

For Tatiana, the spring of 1942 had brought about a severe deterioration in her health. Her whole body was swollen, and she could not get into any of her usual clothes. Her gums were inflamed, and she was very weak. Her only activity at that time was going to a local cemetery to pick spring grasses used for making vegetable cakes. The grass was then mixed up with linseed oil, and fried and eaten. Varvara reported her daughter's condition to a local doctor, but nothing could be done until Stalin's Directive of 5 July 1942 permitted families with one child to leave the besieged city.[20]

On 5 October, late at night, Varvara and Tatiana slipped quietly out of their flat, and left the city, crossing the Road of Life. They travelled in a heavily overladen boat, under incessant bombardment by German planes.[21] Bashkiriya, a Soviet republic situated between the Volga River and the Urals Mountains, was their evacuation destination, but fate would bring them instead to Siberia. On the way to Bashkiriya, their train was destroyed in an air attack, and they were picked up by another train that was heading for Siberia.

The siege of Leningrad continued until 27 January 1944. When it was over, there were approximately 600,000 citizens left in the city.[22] Many thousands had been evacuated, and 641,803 people died of starvation. The total death figure reached about 1,000,500. An eternal flame at the Piskarevskoye Memorial Cemetery serves to remember all those who died during the siege.

It is impossible to underestimate the role of women in the days of the siege. They were trained in the use of firearms to fight the enemy at the front line; they patrolled the city streets day and night, ready to help the wounded and frail; they sewed enormous numbers of sandbags to protect historic monuments from air attacks. Many members of the female staff at the Hermitage museum lived in the basement, and were always ready to extinguish fires from the incendiary bombs that the German planes dropped, in order to save the valuable and historic Hermitage collections.[23]

Famous Russian women poets, Olga Berggolts, Anna Akhmatova and Vera Inber, later wrote poems encapsulating those terrible days. *Poem without a Hero* by Anna Akhmatova is dedicated to the besieged city.

Women worked in hospitals, schools, libraries, theatres; they baked bread daily for the starving people under very difficult conditions, quite often standing in water in semi-ruined, flooded buildings. They did their utmost to save the lives of their children. Many women were decorated with the Medal for the Defence of Leningrad.

Varvara and Tatiana survived the war. Varvara lived to the age of 72. Today, Tatiana is aged 80, and still lives in Novosibirsk, Siberia. Our family keeps alive their memories of the great siege of Leningrad.

Notes

1. The official name of which was the Treaty of Non-Aggression between Germany and the Soviet Union.
2. Bryan I. Fugate, *Operation Barbarossa*, London: Presidio, 1984.
3. www.worldwar-2.net.
4. Fugate, *Operation Barbarossa*, p. 87.
5. Ibid., p. 74.
6. www.nationamaster.com/encyclopedia/Siege-of-Leningrad.
7. Harrison E. Salisbury, *The 900 Days: The Siege of Leningrad*, Basingstoke: Macmillan, 1969, p. 292.
8. Michael Jones, *Leningrad: State of Siege*, London: John Murray, 2008, intro.
9. Salisbury, *900 Days*, p. 421.
10. www.infran.ru/vovenko/60years_ww2/vita_blokada.htm.
11. Jones, *Leningrad*, p. 150.
12. Salisbury, *900 Days*, p. 485.
13. All my life I heard stories from my grandmother and my mother about my mother sleeping in the windowsill, and about the *remeslenniki* who killed my great-grandmother, Ekaterina. I was young when I heard it, and I was afraid of *remeslenniki*.
14. *The Siege of Leningrad: Disclosed Archive Documents*, Moscow and St Petersburg: Institute of Military History, Polygon, 2003, p. 72.
15. Ibid., p. 680.
16. Ibid., p. 725.
17. Nikolai Tikhonov, *Heroic Leningrad*, Moscow: Foreign Languages Publishing House, 1945, p. 24.
18. *Siege of Leningrad: Documents*, p. 72.
19. Ibid., p. 703.
20. Ibid., p. 287.
21. The house was later destroyed by a bomb and no longer exists.
22. Salisbury, *900 Days*, p. 516.
23. Debra Dean, *The Madonnas of Leningrad*, London: Harper Perennial, 2007.

Select Bibliography

This chapter has been written from the recollections and records of the personal experiences of the author's mother and grandmother, who were caught up in the Siege of Leningrad.

Bernev, Stanislav Konstantinovich, and Chernov, Sergeĭ Vladimirovich, *Blokadnye dnevniki i dokumenty*, St Petersburg: Evropeiskiĭ dom, 2007.
Gouré, Leon, *The Siege of Leningrad*, Stanford, CA: Stanford University Press, 1962.
Heroic Leningrad: Documents, Sketches and Stories of its Siege and Relief, tr. J. Fineberg, Moscow: Foreign Languages Publishing House, 1945.
Inber, Vera, *Leningrad Diary*, tr. Serge M. Wolff and Rachel Grieve, intro. Edward Crankshaw, London: Hutchinson, 1971.

Chapter 15

Lotta Svärd, Nachthexen and Blitzmädel
Women in Military Service on the Eastern Front

Paul Edward Strong

The intensity of the war on the Eastern Front led the major participants to radically shift their perceptions of the role of women in warfare. Even the ideologies of fascism and communism, both containing warped fantasies about the position of women in their utopian visions of the future, were forced to make compromises in the ways in which women were permitted to serve the state. This led to women fulfilling roles that were not permitted to their sisters in the West. In a wide range of military tasks, uniformed women proved to be more than capable of operating alongside their male colleagues but it is important to note that the situations where women excelled were often those that were deemed as traditional opportunities for women, and even the exceptional individuals who proved to be efficient killers did so in specialist roles and not as conventional front line infantry.

Finland led the world in the inclusion of women in their military preparations for the impending conflict. The *Lotta Svärd Yhdistys* (the Lotta Svärd Association), named after a Napoleonic heroine, was formed during the Russian Civil War as part of the Finnish *Suojeluskunta* (protecting or civil guard), and served as auxiliaries in the Finnish Civil War that followed the collapse of Russia. Faced with the constant threat of the reabsorption by the Soviet Union, the Finns maintained both the Civil Guard and the *Lotta Svärd* in case they were needed to supplement Finland's tiny army. The latter's role was to act as nurses, fund-raisers, drivers, cooks, cleaners and as spotters for anti-aircraft batteries, thus freeing men for front-line combat.

The *Lotta Svärd* had a national headquarters and representatives at every level, including in the districts and villages. Understandably, given the opposition of those who saw the organisation as threatening to the primacy of the family, the *Lotta Svärd* prided itself on the high moral standards of its members and their opposition to communism. Naturally, as well brought up young ladies, they were not expected to actually actively oppose communism, and it is important to note that *Lotta Svärd* were also discouraged from associating with right-wing organisations, when such organisations were seen as extremist by the Central Board of the Association. To ensure that the highest quality of volunteer was recruited, every member had to come with two recommendations from respectable individuals, and the uniform was deliberately designed to ensure that the wearer did not provoke what the *Lotta Svärd* authorities deemed to be unseemly behaviour. The *Lotta Svärd's* quietly puritanical creed included the instruction 'be not ostentatious in either habits or dress; humility is a priceless virtue'.[1]

As war loomed, the organisation expanded to over 150,000 members. Training across a number of roles was uneven but progressing with a relatively high proportion of the membership attending appropriate courses. The nursing section was particularly efficient and was able to declare that they could provide eight fully equipped and staffed field hospitals with 1,250 beds by 1939. As soon as the Soviets declared war, the *Lotta Svärd* were mobilised and assigned as an auxiliary of the Finnish Armed Forces; almost immediately old disputes with the Finnish socialists were cast aside and the membership rapidly expanded. Although some of the veteran *Lotta Svärd* thought that moral standards had been allowed to slide, very few of the organisation were dismissed for inappropriate behaviour.

Providing medical aid, making and distributing provisions, working in signals units, facilitating evacuation and assisting as spotters as part of the air defences, the *Lotta Svärd* made an immediate contribution. The 100,000 women in the *Lotta Svärd*, working on the front line in the 1939–40 Winter War, served alongside less than 350,000 men, making them proportionally the largest female auxiliary organisation in history.

The *Lotta Svärd* played a vital role in the success of the Finnish Army against the Soviet Union, and Stalin paid them the ultimate compliment by including their disbandment as one of the key clauses in the peace negotiations at the end of the Second World War. With its blue swastika badge, a symbol drawn from Finnish mythology and not fascist fantasy, and their associations with the German campaign on the Eastern Front, the *Lotta Svärd* has faded into obscurity outside of Finland and the history of the organisation is yet to be given the academic analysis it deserves.

The propaganda of the *Nationalsozialistische Deutsche Arbeiterpartei* (NSDAP but more often known as the Nazi Party) included a number of sociological assumptions about the role of women. Their role was meant to focus on what nineteenth-century Germans understood as 'natural' pursuits for women – *Kinder, Küche, Kirche*, (children, the kitchen and the church).

They were not expected to play a role in the military forces whether para-military or within the traditional armed forces (the *Wehrmacht*).

In 1920, the NSDAP manifesto made clear that they disapproved of women working, and Hitler's election speeches even included the boast that he would take 800,000 women out of the workforce. To support this policy, the NSDAP introduced legislation to encourage women to stay at home, such as the 1933 Law for the Encouragement of Marriage, which introduced loans and increased child benefit to act as an inducement for women to fulfil their 'natural' roles in society; what the Nazi Women's League described as 'servicing the needs of life'. The NSDAP even introduced a medal for mothers who provided the state with healthy children – 'The Honour Cross of German Motherhood'. Hitler noted, in a speech in 1936, that 'the woman has her own battlefield. With every child she brings into the world, she fights her own battle for the nation.' These limits on the role of women were further codified in the Reich Labour Service Law of 1935, and the secret Guidelines for the Employment of Women in War in 1938. The professions were the hardest hit by these policies, with female doctors, civil servants and members of the judiciary being summarily dismissed and the number of female students dropping by 60 per cent during the NSDAP 'reforms'. Like most NSDAP propaganda, such statements were contradicted by the harsh realities of re-establishing German industry, and there were 50 per cent more women in industry in 1939, than there had been in 1933.[2]

While the NSDAP extolled the domestic role of women, the propaganda machine also gleefully focused on the rare exceptions to the rules laid down by the state. Such individuals, where they displayed remarkable talents, were cited as exemplars that showed off the potential of Nazi women, compared to their pampered and fashion obsessed sisters in France and America. The two most interesting examples were both directly linked to the *Luftwaffe*.

Hannah Reitsch's career as an aviatrix began as a glider pilot and instructor. She soon broke a number of records (several still stand), and in 1937, she was posted to the *Luftwaffe* aircraft testing centre at Rechlin-Lärz. Her enthusiasm for both the Nazi cause and for flying made her extremely popular with the propaganda ministry and she was increasingly selected for the sort of prestige projects that showed off her talents. In 1938, she was one of the few pilots authorised to fly the Focke-Achgelis Fa61 helicopter, and during the war she flew a range of combat aircraft, including the cargo gliders eventually used at Eben Emael, the Ju88, the Do17, the Me262, the Me163 'Komet' rocket-plane and, most famously, test flew a piloted version of the V-1 (an event that was immortalised in the movie *Operation Crossbow* although Hannah's test was more about ensuring pilot safety than making the weapon operational).

Hannah was badly injured flying the Me163, but returned to the base as soon as she was declared fit. She was awarded both the *Eisernes Kreuz* (EK or Iron Cross) first and second class, and the Golden Military Flying Medal with Diamonds for her work. While she was undoubtedly an extremely courageous pilot, there is little doubt that she was also a fanatical Nazi. During the war, she tested potential piloted suicide planes for the *SS*, and to the dismay of her colleagues volunteered to lead an attack. In the final days of the war she landed in the ruins of Berlin, and attempted to convince Hitler to escape the doomed city and continue the war[3]

Another *Luftwaffe* heroine came from a very different background. Melitta Schenk Gräfin von Stauffenberg was the granddaughter of a converted Jew (her maiden name was Schiller), and although she had shown considerable talents as a physicist and aeronautical engineering she was dismissed from the *Luftwaffe* in 1936, due to her ancestry. Like Hannah Reitsch, she qualified as a pilot, and after her dismissal flew as a commercial test pilot on seaplanes.

Melitta's return to military flying came when she married into the thoroughly respectable von Stauffenberg family, and was eagerly rerecruited by the *Luftwaffe* in 1939. Her main focus was on dive-bombing, and it is estimated that she made 2,500 test dives during the war using a wide range of aircraft. The main dive-bomber was the Ju88 Stuka, an unwieldy aircraft but a deadly accurate platform for delivering tactical support to German ground forces. It commonly started its 60–80 degree dive at 15,000 feet, and soon reached 350 miles per hour. The pilot initiated the bombing sequence and activated the terror-inducing sirens at 7,000 feet, enabling the pilot to then focus on dropping the bomb accurately at around 2,000 feet, before the auto-pilot levelled off the aircraft automatically, when the bomb left the cradle. Making sure that the automatic pullout sequence functioned at 6g – the point at which most pilots suffered G-force-induced loss of consciousness – in all of the aircraft Ernst Udet wanted dive-capable was one of Melitta's main roles, and the *Luftwaffe* held her skills in high regard.

Melitta was awarded the Iron Cross second class, and the Military Flying Medal in Gold with Diamonds and Rubies, after finding herself in air combat with Allied long-range escorts in 1943. In 1944, Melitta became the head of the *Versuchsstelle für Flugzeug-Sondergerät* (Experimental Centre for Aircraft Special Devices). The Centre focused on research on anti-tank weapons, bomb-aiming devices, bomb release mechanisms, night fighter and visual night landing procedures, and on aiming devices for attacking US bomber forma-tions.[4] Understandably, given her talents, the *Luftwaffe* resisted any attempt to remove her from her post, and insisted that the *SS* leave her family un-molested. As the war situation worsened, her brother-in-law, Claus Schenk

Graf von Stauffenberg, asked her to assist in the plot to kill Hitler in July 1944, and Melitta agreed to assist him even though she was already under suspicion. Luckily, she did not manage to locate an aircraft in time to fly him to the Wolf's Lair (Hitler's Eastern Front headquarters), and although she was arrested and her brothers-in-law executed, and much of the rest of the family sent to concentration camps, the *Luftwaffe* was able to rescue her once again, and did their best to help her keep in contact with the surviving members of her family.

Serving both as a test pilot and as a nurse, Melitta remained loyal to Germany to the end, although it is clear that she despised the Nazi regime. This remarkable woman was shot down by US fighters during a routine aircraft transfer flight in April 1945.[5]

The opportunities for less exceptional German women were more constrained. With the exception of nurses, women were only officially assigned to military support roles in October 1940, and were not given full combatant status until August 1944. Given the paramilitary training of young women, with 10-year-olds joining the *Jungmädel* and 14-year-olds joining the *Bund Deutscher Mädel*, the slowness of Germany's mobilisation of women seems surprising.

A substantial number of the 450,000 women who served in uniform, worked as *Helferinnen* (helpers) or auxiliaries. These operated as air warning staff, ferry pilots, clerical staff and signals specialists (*Nachrichtenhelferinnen*) in the army (*Heer*), the navy (*Kriegsmarine*), the airforce (*Luftwaffe*), and the *Waffen Schutzstaffel* or *Waffen SS*.[6] *Blitzmädel* ('lightning girls') so named because of their badges began to be deployed to signals units in October 1940, and were eventually assigned to all services. A few served in analytical or interrogation roles (of which more later), but none were accorded the respect given to the *Fräulein Doktor*, the remarkable Dr Elsbeth Schragmüller, who had been an analyst and interrogator during the First World War. One intriguing example of a woman being assigned to interrogate prisoners appears in the memoirs of a tank soldier in the 712th US Tank Battalion, who recorded being interrogated by an *SS* doctor. The lady in question employed the *unterhaltung* technique developed in the First World War, of engaging the prisoners in casual conversation, and reducing their natural wariness by removing her uniform jacket, and cooking them breakfast. The young soldiers were sure that they had told her nothing, but *unterhaltung* was designed to give this impression. The target was only encouraged to reveal information about other units, and continued to feel that he had not let down his comrades by revealing intelligence specific to his own unit.[7]

German military intelligence only gradually utilised women in analytical roles and only belatedly discovered that the women they selected were invariably extremely competent. In the last six months of the war, the *Fremde Heere Ost* (Foreign Armies East) introduced *Stabshelferinnen* (staff helpers) to their Group I (*Führungsgruppe* or staff command group) analysis teams. These women, assigned as officer assistants to the Army Group Operations Departments, reviewed and correlated the intelligence data on enemy movements in their sector (drawn from air reconnaissance, prisoner interrogation, signals intelligence and observations by German commanders in the front line) and updated the situation reports and maps used by senior commanders. Their late inclusion in this role is all the more perplexing considering the excellent work done by the women in Group III (*Dolmetschergruppe* or interpreter group) including a specialist team of thirteen women that translated captured manuals and handbooks for most of the war and the work of the sixty women in Group VI that dealt with documentation, basic administration and discipline.[8]

The *Kriegsmarine*, as the German navy was known during the Nazi regime, assigned women to a range of support and clerical roles. A number of women served in similar headquarters roles to the Women's Royal Naval Service as clerical staff, plotters and updating operational maps. Inevitably, senior officers saw the propaganda uses for these girls and the prettiest were usually selected to be photographed, offering the returning captain flowers or a gift. In the *Luftwaffe*, some women were assigned as *Flakhelferinnen* (Flak Helpers), but these were initially restricted to searchlight units, barrage balloons and fire control units. Only in the final weeks of the war were they assigned to gun-crews, although the Nazis preferred not to let them actually fire the gun, and only a few are recorded as taking part in combat in the final *götterdämmerung* (the Wagnerian 'twilight of the gods') in Berlin. A few operated as ferry pilots but the largest group were assigned to the *Luftwaffe*'s air space surveillance (*Luftwaffen- und Flugmeldedienst*) service in roles similar to those women who served in the Women's Auxiliary Air Force in the UK.

Waffen SS helpers served in similar roles to their equivalents in the combined forces of the army, navy and airforce, and *Wehrmacht* armoured military forces units (panzer units). Most were signals personnel and clerical staff as the SS hierarchy was even more dubious about giving these women non-traditional tasks than their colleagues in the *Wehrmacht*. As the *Waffen SS* expanded, the European units that enlisted to fight bolshevism in Russia deployed their own helpers, following the German model.

Nurses and signals staff were recruited to support these units, but the latter had to be fluent in German. A Norwegian nurse in the elite 5th Panzer Division (Wiking), Anne Gunhild Moxanes, one of the 400 foreign 'Front Sisters', serving on the Eastern Front, was the only non-German woman awarded the Iron Cross. In the inevitable wave of recriminations after the war, even the nurses were imprisoned for what was understandably seen as their misguided service to the occupying forces, but the highly pragmatic Danes pardoned them on the condition that they used their valuable experience in accident and emergency units. Women from the Baltic States and the *Volksdeutsche* fared rather less well both during and after the war – they were assigned as farm labourers, to trench digging, and to 'artificial fog' production units assigned to shroud key targets in clouds of noxious vapour. It is estimated that 3,000 survived the war, but the vast majority of these were murdered by the Soviet Army in 1945.

Not all uniformed female auxiliaries served with distinction. Amongst the *SS-Krieghelferinnen* (war helpers) were those who worked as part of the staff assigned to the *Konzentrationslager* (concentration camps for civilians). Twenty-one of the 5,025 individuals tried and executed by the Allies after the Second World War were women; amongst these were some of the most ruthless *SS* operatives, including camp guards who indulged in sadistic games with the inmates, nurses who assisted in experimentation on human subjects and the staff that selected those who were to die in the gas chambers.

The uniformed female personnel in the *Wehrmacht* also included 'volunteers' from the occupied territories (*Hilfswilliger* or *Hiwis*), and the *OST-Arbeiter*, which was made up of a slave workforce from Eastern Europe, and who were made to carry out forced labour in Germany. The former were ex-Soviet 'voluntary assistants' assigned menial tasks in support of the front-line units – generally assisting with food preparation and washing. In contrast, the *OST-Arbeiter* were literally conscripted slave workers. Most of these barely qualify as uniformed, and the Nazi system treated these women with an utter indifference. To give an idea of the scale of this operation, over 1,000,000 Ukrainian women were rounded up and despatched westwards to the labour camps.[9]

The Soviets are often lauded as an example of enlightenment in the provision of opportunities for women, but the reality is far more complex. Like the Nazis, the Soviets were keen to highlight the minority of exemplars and used the majority of their female volunteers in support roles but STAVKA (the Soviet supreme headquarters) soon recognised there were specialised military tasks where women excelled and as a result the USSR was the only country to deliberately assign women to front-line combat roles.

Soviet propaganda in the Civil War (1917–23) focused on the equality of women in the revolution, and Stalin delighted in showcasing this aspect of Soviet progress and the triumph of a society that fully utilised its potential. The reality of equality in Stalin's Empire was rather less impressive but the myths of the early years of the USSR created a powerful precedent. Women volunteered in large numbers during the Great Patriotic War, around 800,000 served in support roles and 200,000 served as nurses, but the proportion that served did not exceed the UK contribution, and preparation for their deployment was extremely poor.

STAVKA experimented with women pilots and assigned a few to fighter and bomber units. Approximately 1,000 women served in combat aircrews in the Second World War. Lidiya 'Lili' Litvyak was the most successful woman-fighter ace of the war – flying 168 sorties as part of the 586th Fighter Aviation Regiment, and shooting down twelve aircraft before being herself shot down. Mariya Dolina flew Pe-2 medium bombers in the 587th Dive Bomber Regiment later redesignated the 125th 'M.M. Raskova' Borisov Guards Dive Bomber Regiment – flying seventy-two missions and dropping 45,000kg of bombs. Klava Fomicheva rose to the rank of squadron leader and after the war was promoted to the rank of lieutenant colonel.

The most famous Russian female unit was the one the Germans nicknamed the *Nachthexen* (the night witches). Formed in June 1942 by Colonel Marina Raskova as the 588th Night Bomber Regiment, the unit was redesignated in February 1943 as the 46th Taman Guards Night Bomber Regiment. The night witches flew night harassment missions, often making their final approach with the engines in idle to ensure surprise. Their main task was to damage or disrupt key German installations. The Germans soon learnt to respect these women and acknowledged that they degraded the army and the *Luftwaffe*'s capability to operate by striking at bases and airfields.[10] Johannes Steinhoff, an ace credited with 101 kills during the war, noted 'we simply couldn't grasp that the Soviet airmen that caused us the greatest trouble were in fact WOMEN. These women feared nothing. They came night after night in their very slow biplanes, and for some periods they wouldn't give us any sleep at all.'[11]

The night witches flew obsolete training aircraft, the Polikarpov Po2 biplane, but used its high manoeuvrability and slow speed to frustrate German fighters trying to ambush them (the Germans had to hit them first time or risk stalling if they tried to dogfight them). Where possible they flew in pairs to ensure that at least one pilot could watch the skies for night fighters. The women of the 46th were not provided with parachutes until 1944, as these were deemed too valuable and, unfortunately for the pilots, the Po2 had an alarming habit of bursting into flames if hit. The Germans eventually assigned Me110 night-fighters to deal with the menace and casualties rapidly mounted. Twenty-three out of the ninety Heroines of the Soviet Union flew in the 46th, and one of these pilots, Mariya Smirnova, an ex-*kindergarten* teacher, flew 935 night missions, averaging ten missions a night until her health collapsed. Records suggest that the unit flew 23,672 sorties during the war, although these were necessarily short, due to the fragility of the aircraft and the tiny bomb load, and the regiment was credited with dropping almost 3,000 tons of bombs.[12]

One of the roles where women excelled was as snipers; 2,000 are recorded as being trained in this capacity during the war, and 500 survived. It is interesting to note that their training officers often remarked on their patience, endurance and devotion to duty. Usually these women operated in pairs, with one member of the team spotting while the other engaged targets. The Germans found the use of women in this role bewildering, calling them musket-women (*flintenweiber*), and occasionally using pictures of the corpses of the snipers they killed and identified as women as proof of both the desperation and barbarism of the Soviet regime. Amongst the most notable practitioners of the sniper's art was Lyudmila Pavlichenko, who killed over 300 Germans (including thirty-six enemy snipers) in the twelve months from June 1941 until she was wounded, placing her in the elite of her chosen profession. Pavlichenko was made a Heroine of the Soviet Union and promoted to major, (transferring to the Navy after the war[13]). Another ace sniper, Roza Shanina (yet another ex-kindergarten teacher), scored fifty-four kills in the forests of Northern Russia. She was part of a specialist women's sniper unit in the 18th Rifle Division, and was finally killed on 2 April 1944, after refusing to abandon her comrades during a German counter-attack.

Another area where the Soviets recognised a role for women with a penchant for stealth and patience was in special-forces units. The *Yazyk Poiski* were reconnaissance patrols assigned the task of conducting scouting missions behind enemy lines, and seizing documents and taking prisoners for interrogation. The name literately meant 'tongue hunters' as the patrols were meant to bring in sources of information – the scouts called their work *yazykovedenie* (linguistics). As the best sources were deep within the German defensive system the *Yazyk Poiski* often had to lie in wait for days for the optimum conditions, then extract their prize before the Germans realised that there was a reconnaissance unit operating behind their lines; these prisoners were a vital element in the gathering of tactical intelligence. The 'tongue hunters' were often organised into special companies and assigned to Guards Rifle Divisions. Maria Boiko commanded one of these units in the 5th Guards Rifle Corps and was awarded the Order of the Great Patriotic War (1st degree) for taking a prisoner out from under the German's noses after a brutal fire-fight where she was forced to call in artillery fire onto her own position to prevent the enemy from rescuing her prisoner.[14]

The Soviets did assign women to more conventional roles but these individuals were incredibly rare and only the most successful ones emerge out of the chaotic records gathered during the war with enough detail for us to understand how they operated. Intriguingly, the most successful operated as tank drivers. One young field medic, Irina Levchenko, lobbied to join the tank corps after treating 168 wounded soldiers under fire during the heavy fighting in 1942, and eventually served as a tank driver in the battles in the Crimea and around Smolensk in the autumn of 1943. Mariya Oktyabrskaya became a Heroine of the Soviet Union after volunteering to be a tank driver after her husband's death, and rampaged through several German positions leading assaults conducted by the elite 26th Guards Tank Brigade. She was killed in action in the winter of 1944.[15]

Inevitably, women played a proportionally greater role in partisan units. An estimated 10 per cent of partisans were women, and although most served in support roles, a few served in the front line as snipers and saboteurs. Zoya Kosmodemyanskaya was captured in 1941, and memorably informed the Germans at her execution 'There are 200 million of us; you can't hang us all!'[16]

Although some Romanian women served with distinction in the First World War, including the remarkable Ecaterina Teodoroiu, the Romanians did not mobilise their female population as extensively as their allies and opponents, though a number of Romanian women, serving as pilots in the *Escadrilla Aviatie Sanitare* (sometimes called the *Squadriglia Bianca* or White Squadron) were awarded Red Cross medals for evacuating casualties during the campaigns on the Eastern Front.[17]

The Poles deployed the *Organizacja Przysposobienia Wojskowego Kobiet* (Women's Auxiliary Army Service) in 1939 and, after the Nazi and Soviet invasions, large numbers of Polish women served as partisans in the fight against both murderous regimes. The most spectacular burst in the recruitment of women occurred after the mobilisation of the Polish *Armia Krajowa* (Home Army) in 1944, an organisation that can plausibly claim to be the largest resistance organisation of the Second World War. Women served in a range of support roles but also in specialist units, including courier units and one that was expert in sabotage and mine-laying, the *Dywersja i Sabotaż Kobiet* (Women's Diversion and Sabotage unit) commanded by Wanda Gertz 'Kazik'. The Germans were often utterly ruthless but the Polish Home Army earned their grudging respect and 2,000 women were awarded prisoner of war status after the city surrendered (twenty of these women received the Polish Cross of Valour for their role in the defence of Warsaw).[18]

The story of women on the Eastern Front is one where ideology and expediency often collided, the assumptions of the pre-war years collapsing in the face of the pressures of total war. The Soviet example is often cited as proving that women can serve in front-line combat roles, but the evidence suggests that this assumption is simplistic. Women proved superb in specialist units but only a tiny minority proved effective in traditional combat roles. The lesson of the Second World War is that those countries that gave women the opportunity to exploit their natural talents thrived and those which failed to recognise that the entire population needed to mobilise courted disaster. Mobilisation included giving a few women the chance to fight and to take risks that many of their menfolk would find daunting. It is difficult to imagine any modern solider not respecting the bravery and talents of the night witches or the musket women! While we must often be wary of the legends woven around some of these individuals and recognise that the regimes they served often manipulated the facts to suit their ideological needs, the propaganda myths should not be allowed to obscure the proven heroism of those who served on the Eastern front and the roles in which they excelled.[19]

Notes

1. Allen Chew, *The White Death*, Detroit, MI: MSUP, 1971, William R. Trotter, *The Winter War: The Russo-Finnish War of 1939–40*, London: Aurum, 2003.

2. Jill Stephenson, *Women in Nazi Germany*, London: Longman, 2001, p. 53, see also Franz W. Seidler, *Blitzmädchen: Die Geschichte der Wehrmachthelferinnen im Zweiten Weltkrieg*, Bonn: Bernard & Graefe Verlag, 1996, and Gordon Williamson, *World War II German Women's Auxiliary Services*, London: Osprey, 2003; see also R. A. Ratcliff, *Delusions of Intelligence: Enigma, Ultra, and the End of Secure Ciphers*, Cambridge: Cambridge University Press, 2006, for criticism of the low status of women in the German Intelligence service in the Second World War.

3. Hanna Reitsch, *The Sky My Kingdom: Memoirs of the Famous German World War II Test-Pilot*, London: Greenhill, 1997. This scene is memorably portrayed in the film *Downfall* with even Hitler taken aback by Reitsch's enthusiasm for the plan.

4. Evelyn, Zegenhagen, 'German Women Pilots at War: 1939 to 1945', *Air Power History*, 56 (Winter 2009). Both Hannah and Melitta were promoted to the rank of *Flugkapitän* (flight captain) for their work.

5. www.ctie.monash.edu.au/hargrave/schiller.html.

6. The latter had been formed in 1925, as a personal protection guard unit for Adolph Hitler. In the Second World War their role was that of the armed wing of the Nazi Party, with units mirroring the army's main combat arms (panzer and infantry units) and specialist police units with a remit to assist the *Allgemeine SS* (General *SS*) in carrying out the Führer's ideological objectives.

7. George Forty, *Tank Warfare in the Second World War: An Oral History*, London: Constable, 1998, pp. 211–13. Wayne Hisson was clearly impressed by his mysterious Doctor!

8. US War Dept. General Staff, *German Military Intelligence, 1939–1945*, Frederick, MD: University Publications of America, 1984, pp. 14, 30, 32, 135, 201, 224, and 236.

9. The slave force was mostly from the territory of Reichskommissariat, eastern Ukraine. Ukrainians made up the largest portion although many Belarusians, Russians, Poles and Tatars were also used. Estimates put the number of OST-Arbeiters between 3 million and 5.5 million.

10. Richard Overy, *Russia's War*, London: Allen Lane, 1997, p. 241.

11. Harold Stockton, Dariusz Tyminski and Christer Bergström, *Marina Raskova and Soviet Female Pilots*, quoted Pratt Institute, 25 March 2007, http://pratt.edu/~rsilva/witches.htm.
12. Quoted BBC website: www.bbc.co.uk/dna/h2g2/alabaster/a5849076, 'The Night Witches: Russian Combat Pilots of World War Two'.
13. Lyudmila Pavlichenko was sent to the USA as part of the propaganda unit but was furious when US journalists bombarded her with pathetic questions about her clothing!
14. Richard Armstrong, *Red Army Legacies*, Atglen, PA: Schiffer Military History, 1995, pp. 86–7. An action movie, *The Star*, showing one of these units in action and released in 2002, has the female character offering to join the team. She is told that women should not serve in reconnaissance units and instead acts as their radio contact as the mission becomes increasingly perilous.
15. Henry Sakaida, *Heroines of the Soviet Union 1941–45*, London: Osprey, 2003.
16. Lyubov Kosmodemyanskaya, *Story of Zoya and Shura*, Moscow: Foreign Languages Publishing House, 1953 (written by Zoya's mother).
17. www.crucearosie.ro/despre-noi/istoria-sncrr-2.html. These included Maria Dragescu, Nadia Russo, Virginia Thomas, Ioana Gradinescu, Virginia Dutescu. See also http://worldwartwobalkanslevant.blogspot.com/2009/02/romanian-air-service.html. Maria Bucur, 'Between the Mother of the Wounded and the Virgin of Jiu: Romanian Women and the Gender of Heroism during the Great War', *Journal of Women's History* (2000), pp. 12, 2, 30–56; Constantin Kirițescu, *Istoria războiului pentru întregirea României: 1916–1919*, Bucharest: Romania nouă, 1924. The contrast with the experience of Ecaterina Teodoroiu is intriguing. A former scout and school teacher, Ecaterina joined the Romanian Army as a nurse in October 1916. Impressed by the patriotism of the wounded and angered by the death of her brother, she subsequently decided to volunteer as a front-line soldier. Inevitably the Romanian authorities were not sure what to do with her but she soon impressed her colleagues with her intelligence and enthusiasm. On one memorable occasion she was captured by the Germans and escaped, killing several enemy soldiers in the process. In November, she was wounded and hospitalised, but returned to the front where she was decorated and promoted to command of a platoon (roughly twenty-five men). She was killed on 3 September 1917, during the Battle of Mărășești; exhorting her men to continue advancing as she herself lay dying. According to some accounts, her last words were: 'Forward, men, I'm still with you!' She was buried in the city centre of Târgu Jiu.
18. www.polishresistance-ak.org/12%20Article.htm. See also Lynne Olson, *For Your Freedom and Ours: The Kosciuszko Squadron – Forgotten Heroes of World War II*, London: William Heineman, 2004.
19. Martin van Creveld, *Men, Women and War*, London: Cassell & Co., 2001.

Select Bibliography

Reitsch, Hanna, *The Sky My Kingdom: Memoirs of the Famous German World War II Test-Pilot*, London: Greenhill, 1997.

Sakaida, Henry, *Heroines of the Soviet Union 1941–45*, London: Osprey, 2003.

Seidler, Franz W., *Blitzmädchen: Die Geschichte der Wehrmachthelferinnen im Zweiten Weltkrieg*, Bonn: Bernard & Graefe Verlag, 1996.

United States War Dept. General Staff, *German Military Intelligence, 1939–1945*, Frederick, MD: University Publications of America, 1984.

Zegenhagen, Evelyn, 'German Women Pilots at War: 1939 to 1945', *Air Power History*, 56 (Winter 2009).

Chapter 16

Women at War
Poland

Halik Kochanski

No country was changed more by the Second World War than Poland. Six million of her citizens died during the conflict, almost half of them Jewish, and, at the end of the war, the country itself was effectively moved 200 km to the west. This is the story of Nina Kochańska, the author's aunt. It is a tale of life under Soviet rule, deportation to Kazakhstan, the often desperate struggle for survival there, the evacuation of the Polish army under General Władysław Anders from the Soviet Union to Iran accompanied by civilians, the effect of that departure on those left behind, conscription into the Kościuszko Division of the Polish army formed by the communist Polish Union of Patriots, and its entry into Poland. As a result of the war, the close-knit Kochański family was permanently separated and rendered homeless by the incorporation of Eastern Galicia into the Soviet Union.

Nina Kochańska was born in 1924, the fourth of eight children of Józefa and Leon Kochański.[1] The family lived in Stanisławów, a provincial town in the southeastern province of Eastern Galicia, then in Poland. Leon was the deputy-director of administration for the Stanisławów province, a challenging role in a region where the population was split evenly between Poles, Ukrainians and Jews. His fairness towards each ethnic group would ultimately save his life during the period of the first Soviet occupation. The family had a comfortable existence in a house built for them in the leafy suburb of Dąbrowa, and summers were spent with their maternal grandmother, Emilia Tuzinkiewicz, at her house in the small town of Tłumacz, about 30 km from Stanisławów.

The outbreak of war shattered this peaceful existence. As the German army poured into Poland on 1 September 1939, Leon summoned his family back to Stanisławów from Tłumacz. They arrived just in time to bid farewell to their brother Zbigniew, a reserve officer in the 2nd Uhlan Regiment, as he departed to join his regiment. On 8 September the *Luftwaffe* launched their first bombing raid on Stanisławów and bombs fell in the garden, shattering windows and displacing roof tiles. The family withdrew to the safety of Tłumacz and as Nina later wrote: 'It never entered my mind that I was leaving our house, our dear Dąbrowa and Stanisławów for the last time.' In Tłumacz they watched as the defeated Polish army retreated towards the temporary sanctuary of Romania.[2]

On 17 September the Soviet Union invaded eastern Poland. Although the Soviets justified their invasion to the world on the grounds that they were coming to the rescue of their fraternal Ukrainians and Belorussians from the oppression of Polish rule, the partition of Poland had been settled weeks beforehand, in a secret codicil to the Molotov–Ribbentrop Pact[3] signed on 24 August. Soviet rule was characterised by terror. The secret police, the NKVD, arrived with prepared lists of prominent Poles to be arrested. These lists included anyone who had taken an active role in the administration or political life of independent Poland. Obviously Nina's father fell into this category. On 1 December he was tipped off by a friend that he was about to be arrested, bade farewell to his family and escaped through the window of the house virtually as the NKVD were entering the door. Few of his family would see him again. Throughout Soviet-occupied Poland arrests, trials and executions terrorised the population. It has been estimated that 10 per cent of the adult male population was arrested and imprisoned. Leon fled to the small village of Bolechów in the Carpathian mountains where his brother Franciszek was hiding. Franciszek was at risk because he had worked for the Polish State Railway.[4] Zbigniew returned home briefly from the defence of Lwów against the German attack, only to go into hiding himself. In this way the three most vulnerable members of the Kochański family missed being executed in April and May 1940 as a result of Stalin's order of 5 March, which condemned to death over 20,000 Polish officers, police, administrators and other personnel central to the running of the Polish state.[5]

Although no member of the family was arrested, all the members suffered from the consequences of the Soviet occupation. In the first place the Soviet soldiers bought up all the goods in the shops, goods that were not available in their Soviet 'paradise'. Few goods were imported to replace them so food was in short supply. Economic reforms included replacing the złoty with the rouble at a rate favouring the rouble, seizing savings and the contents of safety deposit boxes, confiscating industrial concerns and, ultimately, the collectivisation of land. Private property was seized and the house at Stanisławów was taken over by Soviet pilots. The family was evicted from the house in Tłumacz and eleven people, eight of them children, were now expected to squeeze into two rooms.

The educational reforms affected Nina and her siblings most directly. Schools had remained shut at the start of the school year because of the war and when they reopened in October their appearance and the curriculum was changed. Religious symbols were stripped out of the classrooms to be replaced by propaganda posters and prayers before classes were banned. The teaching of religion, history, geography and Latin was banned, and in their stead came lessons on Marxist-Leninism. Ultimately the Ukrainian and Belorussian languages began to replace Polish as the language of instruction.[6] Political reforms affected the whole family. Following fraudulent elections and plebiscites, the whole of Eastern Galicia became 'Western Ukraine' and was incorporated into the Soviet Union. At the end of November 1939, the population of eastern Poland was ordered to accept Soviet citizenship papers.[7]

The Soviet authorities realised that not all Poles would fit into the new Soviet society and so in February 1940 the first of four mass deportations to Siberia and Kazakhstan of over 1,000,000 Poles took place. This deportation included policemen, foresters, and the military settlers (mostly from the Wołyn province) who were deported with their families to forced labour camps in Siberia. This was a familiar destination to many Poles whose ancestors had been sent there after the uprisings against Russian rule in the nineteenth century. In April 1940, another wave of deportations began.[8] This time the target were the families of those men who were in hiding, or under arrest or had fled abroad. On the night of 12/13 April the NKVD came for the Kochański and Tuzinkiewicz families. The entire household was on the list for deportation: Józefa and the children because Leon was in hiding; Emilia Tuzinkiewicz for owning a house, and her daughter Janka for being her daughter. Sixteen-year-old Stanisław, the author's father, was the only male in the group. Common to all deportations was the short time given to pack, and as one deportee later wrote: 'How do you pack a whole way of life into a trunk? How do you decide in a few short moments what is important to carry to a life you do not know?'[9] The Kochański family used a large wicker basket to transport their belongings. Resistance to deportation was rare, which makes Janka's actions so extraordinary. She declared that the Soviets would only take her mother over her dead body and, to prove her point, seized a bottle of vodka and began downing its contents until she lost consciousness. The NKVD officer was so frightened by this performance that it was agreed that Emilia could remain behind. Nina's youngest sister, baby Marta, was left in her grandmother's care, saved from deportation by an allergic rash on her face which the family told the Soviets was scarlet fever. The eldest child, Nusia, was away at the time visiting Leon in his hiding place.

The family were taken by cart to the railway station, where they were joined by other women and children. A deportee described the scene: 'We could see the aged, the pregnant, the infirm, even those on stretchers, and crying babies all being forcibly herded into carriages for animal transportation.'[10] Conditions in the wagons were appalling with overcrowding and little food, and the only toilet facility was a hole in the floor. After travelling for over two weeks the Kochańskis and Tuzinkiewiczes were left at Pieszkowko station in the Kustanai province of northern Kazakhstan. There they were taken by lorry to the *kolkhoz* at Dawidówka. Nina described their arrival: 'The people ran out to meet us. I wondered where they lived, because all around us and as far as the horizon, I could not see any houses. There was only something that looked like shabby cowsheds or stables.'[11] These were in fact huts made of cow dung – *kiziak* – that were infested with woodlice and earwigs.[12] The family was split up between different houses and Nina and her brother Stanisław had to sleep on a straw mattress on the floor of one hut. Each morning their landlady would let a pig run in to sleep on the same mattress during the day.

The Polish women and children now learnt the Soviet attitude to life – *u nas kto rabotaet tot i ne kushaet*: 'here if you don't work, you don't eat'. Life in the *kolkhoz* was extremely hard. Stringent quotas were set from above and it was only after the quota was reached that any surplus could be shared among the workers according to the amount they had worked. If the quotas were not met then the *kolkhoz* starved. Nina and Stanisław worked on the *kolkhoz* ploughing fields, weeding them, harvesting the produce and gleaning the wheat. All this hard work was made all the harder by the starvation rations they received. In the summer they boiled under the relentless sun on the shadeless steppe and in the winter froze as the *burams* (blizzards) buried the village under feet of snow. Nina's sisters, Lala and Renia, were sent to school where at least they received food: one slice of bread a day. Seven-year-old Krzysia was deeply traumatised and remained in the hut all day, every day, waiting for it all to end. Józefa and Janka did various jobs in the *kolkhoz* such as minding the children of the workers. The NKVD visited frequently at night, demanding to know where Leon was hiding.[13] There were no medical facilities, and family members suffered from the symptoms of malnutrition like boils, sores and oedema. Survival depended on work and on bartering goods brought from Poland or received in parcels, for food. The deported Poles, whether in the workcamps of Siberia and northern Russia or in the steppes of Kazakhstan, died in droves.[14]

The German invasion of the Soviet Union on 22 June 1941 transformed the situation of the deportees. In London the Sikorski–Maiskii pact was signed on 30 July 1941 and, under its terms, a Polish army was to be created on Soviet soil under General Anders and an 'amnesty' was granted to all those who had been deported. Polish citizenship was restored to all ethnic Poles from the eastern provinces. Stanisław had been working on the construction of a railway when he heard the news and immediately set off to find the recruiting office for the army. Destitute Poles from all over the Soviet Union began making their way south to where they hoped to find the Polish army. This enormous flood of Poles overwhelmed the Polish civilian and army resources, and thousands of Poles died from exhaustion and starvation on reaching the army camps and from epidemics of diseases such as typhus which swept the camps.[15] Consequently the Polish authorities ordered all those Poles who were in Kazakhstan to remain there until the situation was stabilised. This showed a certain *naiveté* as to the true state of affairs. Stanisław was told to wait until the spring before reporting to the army: and yet the family barely survived the winter. All the food was taken from the *kolkhoz* to feed the army and, now that the whole of Poland was under German occupation, the food parcels stopped arriving. During the winter of 1941–2, there was no fat or milk and no salt; there were only a few potatoes and very little bread. In desperation Stanisław and some other Poles, including the head teacher of the school, stole a sheep and shared out its meat between the people in Dawidowka. Nina later wrote: 'I feel quite certain that were it not for this "injection" of food, particularly of fat, we would not have survived that winter.'[16]

In March 1942, Stanisław left to join the army and immediately joined the first evacuation of the Anders army to Pahlevi in Iran. Families with members in the armed forces also qualified for evacuation, which meant that Józefa and the four remaining children could have left the Soviet Union. There was, however, the question of reaching the embarkation port of Krasnovodsk on the Caspian Sea. Even supposing Józefa had the money to buy a ticket, which she did not, it was not just a matter of turning up at the station and buying a ticket. The Soviet railway system was on the verge of collapse as the Poles travelled southwards, the Red Army travelled westwards, and Soviet evacuees fled eastwards. Trains were few and far between and so overcrowded that they often did not even stop at stations. When they did stop, families often became separated as individuals left the train to search for food. Józefa therefore decided to stay on the *kolkhoz* and wait for Stanislaw to send her some money. Unknown to the family he became dangerously ill soon after his arrival in Iran and could offer no assistance other than having his family members listed as future evacuees. Nina could have joined the girls' section of the cadet corps, the *Junaks*, and would have been evacuated with them in August 1942, but she felt that it was her duty to stay with her mother. Nina and Janka now made their way to Kustanai, seeking better conditions under the protection of the Polish delegature established there to care for the civilians.[17] Nina attended the school attached to the delegature and Janka worked in a local orphanage for Poles to which she brought Lala and Renia. Józefa and Krzysia remained in Dawidówka where conditions on the *kolkhoz* worsened as all the food was taken for the Red Army. In August 1942, what was to be the last evacuation of Poles from the Soviet Union took place, and the orphanage was included. Józefa gave her permission for her two daughters to leave: 'Yes, let them go, maybe they will be saved. Today I have cooked the last of the potatoes, there is nothing else.' Lala and Renia were eventually sent to India, where they stayed until 1947.[18] Józefa and Krzysia now joined Nina and Janka in Kustanai, where some aid provided by the United States reached them.[19]

The departure of the Anders army proved a watershed in Polish–Soviet relations. Polish and British hopes and appeals for further evacuations were ignored by the Soviets. The Polish delegatures were closed by the Soviets and many delegates were arrested. It gradually became clear that the Poles left behind in the Soviet Union were now trapped there. In January 1943, Polish citizenship papers were withdrawn from Nina and others who had received them in 1941, and 'so we became Soviet citizens once more and again forcibly and against our will'.[20] Janka refused to accept her Soviet passport and was imprisoned in harsh conditions until she did. In March the 'Union of Polish Patriots', under the chairmanship of Wanda Wasilewska, was established in Moscow, as the future communist government of Poland with Stalin's support. In April 1943, the Germans announced the discovery of the graves of over 4,000 Polish officers in Katyń forest near Smolensk. The demand by the Polish Government-in-Exile for an investigation by the International Red Cross gave Stalin the excuse he needed to break off relations with the London Poles. Now he would only pay attention to the Union of Polish Patriots.

Wanda Wasilewska decided that the Polish communists needed an army that would fight alongside the Red Army in its advance towards the liberation of Poland. In May 1943, Stalin approved the proposal to create the 1st Kościuszko[21] Division, and one of the few Polish senior officers still alive in the Soviet Union, Colonel (later General) Zygmunt Berling was selected to command it.[22] The shortage of Polish officers meant that the vast majority of the officers were Russians seconded from the Red Army, many of whom could not even speak Polish. Polish men and women aged between 18 and 30 were conscripted into the Berling army. Nina received orders to appear before a perfunctory medical inspection in May, and in June was ordered to report for training at Sielce, near Moscow. Janka joined her soon afterwards. The women's battalion numbered just under 1,000, and they received the same infantry training as the men. The political motivation of the recruits was suspect – indeed, most were hostile to communism – so they were subjected to intense political education on the benefits of communism during their rest periods and in the evenings. Having already spent three years in the Soviet 'paradise', the Poles were immune to attempts at indoctrination and used the lecture periods as opportunities to mend kit and to catch up on sleep. The Soviets never totally trusted the new Polish division.

At the beginning of September, Wasilewska declared the division battle-ready, and it left for the front to join the Soviet thrust to recapture the east bank of the Dnieper river. Nina and the women's battalion were stationed in Smolensk.[23] There they stood under German bombardment and in the shadows of some gallows erected by the Germans for the execution of partisans, giving the division directions towards the front. The Poles were thrust into the battle of Lenino. This battle was of such little significance that it does not appear in the main histories of the war on the Eastern Front.[24] It was, however, of great political significance since Wasilewska wanted to show the world that the communist-led Polish army was ready to fight the Germans while the II Army Corps under Anders was still training in Egypt and Palestine. The battle was a disaster for the Poles, with high casualties. The division was then withdrawn from the front for reinforcement and further training. By the summer of 1944, the division had expanded into the I Polish Army Corps.

In June 1944, the Soviets launched Operation Bagration, which aimed at the destruction of the German Army Group Centre. The I Polish Army Corps was in the rear of General Rokossovskii's 2nd Belorussian Front in the advance into the Polish province of Wołyn. This province had witnessed the slaughter of approximately 35,000 Poles as the Ukrainians turned on their Polish neighbours, murdering them with a barbarity that eclipsed many German crimes.[25] Nina, now working in the quartermaster's department, was billeted in a house where the former Polish owners were lying at the bottom of the well, weighed down by heavy stones, having been murdered by their Ukrainian neighbours. In late July 1944, the Polish army crossed the river Bug, the river the Soviets claimed should form the new western frontier of the Soviet Union, and soon afterwards entered Lublin.

There the Poles heard the news that the Armia Krajowa had launched an uprising in Warsaw on 1 August. There is not sufficient space in this chapter to explain the reasons behind the launch of the uprising nor the debates over why the Soviets failed to assist the uprising.[26] The Poles were initially too far away from Warsaw to help. On 11 September, however, the Poles were thrust into the battle for Praga, Warsaw's eastern suburb. The battle was a fierce one and Nina was on duty allocating ration cards while 'shells were exploding all around me, throwing geysers of earth up into the sky', forcing her to take shelter. Praga was captured and now the Poles were forced to watch helplessly as the battle raged on the other side of the Vistula river: 'at night the sky above Warsaw was red from burning fires and in the day a thick pall of smoke rose above the city'. The Polish artillerymen were furious because they had no ammunition for their guns and could not support their kinsmen. Between 16 and 19 September, Berling did despatch a force across the Vistula but it was unable to make any significant contribution to the uprising and was withdrawn after incurring heavy casualties.[27] At this point Nina's participation in the war ended. Throughout her army career she had suffered several severe attacks of malaria and in Praga was discharged from the army. She moved to Lublin, where Janka was acting with the Polish army theatre and in spring 1945, moved to Łódź in western Poland, where they were living when the war ended.

When the war ended Nina had two priorities: to find somewhere to live and to get the family reunited. The decisions taken at the Teheran and Yalta conferences gave Stalin the eastern provinces of Poland, which he had invaded in 1939, so the Kochański and Tuzinkiewicz families were now homeless. Nina had been in correspondence with her father since her return to Poland but just before the war ended this contact ended. Leon had been arrested by the NKVD in May 1940, and tried and acquitted in June 1941. He then served with the underground government in various capacities during the German occupation. When the Soviets reoccupied eastern Poland he was arrested again by the NKVD, and received such poor treatment in prison that he died in April 1945.[28] Józefa and Krzysia were allowed to move from Kazakhstan to the Ukraine in the autumn of 1944, and in the summer of 1945, they travelled into eastern Poland, where in December, they joined the exodus of Poles from what had been eastern Poland into the newly acquired western provinces of the new Poland.[29] Nusia and Zbigniew both survived the war: Nusia worked as a courier for the Armia Krajowa in Lwow, but little is known about Zbigniew's activities other than that he was conscripted into the Berling army in 1944.[30] Stanisław fought in the Italian campaign and in 1946, travelled with the Anders army to Britain, where he settled. The end of the Second World War therefore saw the Kochański family permanently separated, and most of them struggling for existence in the war-ravaged western area of Poland.[31]

Notes

1. The full list of names and dates of birth is: Zbigniew 1919; Nusia 1921; Stanisław 1923; Nina 1924; Lala 1938; Renia 1930; Krzysia 1933; Marta 1938.
2. The Polish army and air force crossed into Romania and Hungary where they were interned. The internment was so loosely applied that many escaped to France where they formed the bulk of the new Polish army that fought in the 1940 campaign for France, were evacuated to Britain and then returned to fight in 1944 in Normandy and at Arnhem. The Polish air force, of course, made a major contribution to victory in the Battle of Britain.

3. The Treaty of Non-Aggression between Germany and the Soviet Union, signed Moscow, August 1939.
4. Franciszek was caught by the NKVD and sentenced to ten years in the Gulag. He died in February 1941. This was not discovered by the family until the 1990s.
5. A. Cienciala, ed., *Katyń: Crime without Punishment*, London: Yale University Press, 2007, pp. 118–20.
6. Before the war, Polish schools in Stanisławów taught in Polish, with the Ukrainian language as a compulsory subject: and Ukrainian and Jewish schools taught in Ukrainian or Yiddish (some in Hebrew). There was also a German school for the German population of the town. T. Olszański, *Kresy Kresów Stanisławów*, Warsaw: Wydawnictwo ISKRY, 2008, p. 37.
7. The best book on the subject of the Soviet occupation is J. Gross, *Revolution from Abroad*, Princeton: Princeton University Press, 1988.
8. There were two subsequent deportations in June 1940 and in June 1941. For details of who was taken in these deportations and their destinations see Z. Siesmaszko, 'The Mass Deportation of the Polish Population to the USSR, 1940–1941', in K. Sword, ed., *The Soviet Takeover of the Polish Eastern Provinces 1939–41*, Basingstoke: Macmillan, 1991, pp. 217–35.
9. J. Żebrowski-Bulmahn quoted in T. Piotrowski, *The Polish Deportees of World War II: Recollections of Removal to the Soviet Union and Dispersal throughout the World*, Jefferson, NC: McFarland, 2004, p. 31.
10. S. Buczak-Zarzycka quoted ibid., p. 18.
11. Nina wrote her memoirs in 1999, and any quotations without attribution either come from these memoirs or from subsequent interviews between the author and Nina.
12. *Kiziak* also formed the staple heating material and children would follow the cattle on the steppe collecting it.
13. Unknown to the family and to the NKVD in Kazakhstan, Leon was at that time in the custody of the NKVD in Lwów.
14. The Polish Government-in-Exile produced figures suggesting that about 10% of the Poles died during the first year.
15. For more details see K. Sword, *Deportation and Exile: Poles in the Soviet Union*, Basingstoke: Macmillan, 1996, pp. 42–59.
16. The management of the *kolkhoz* blamed the disappearance of a sheep on wolves.
17. It was exceptional for the Soviet Union to allow representatives of a foreign power the freedom to set up centres all over the Soviet Union to care for their nationals.
18. Polish civilians were sent to India, Lebanon, Palestine, East Africa, New Zealand and Mexico.
19. For example, Nina received a pair of US army-issue boots which were far too big but at least kept her feet warm and dry.
20. The Polish Government-in-Exile and the British Government protested formally about the Soviet action. The Soviets probably forced the Poles from eastern Poland to accept Soviet citizenship as part of their campaign to have the 1941 frontier internationally recognised.
21. Tadeusz Kościuszko was a national hero to the Poles for his leadership in the 1794 uprising against the Russians and Prussians. The Poles were offended by the adoption of his name by the communists.
22. Berling was imprisoned with other Polish officers but willingly offered his services to the Soviet authorities in 1940. Nothing came of these plans. In 1941 he was a liaison officer with the Anders army and was expected to leave the Soviet Union with them but chose to remain

behind. Z. Berling, *Wspommienia (Memoirs)*, 2 vols, Warsaw: Polski Dom Wydawniczy, 1990, vol. II, pp. 74–80. For more details on the political background and the formation of this army see C. Grzelak, H. Stańczyk and S. Zwoliński, *Bez MoŻliwości Wyboru: Wojsko Polskie Na Froncie Wschodnin 1943–1945*, Warsaw: Wydawnictwo Bellona, 1993.

23. One acquaintance of Nina's was told by a local man 'If only the trees could talk, what tales they would have'. The Soviets told the Poles about the Katyń massacres, blaming them on the Germans, but the Poles suspected the Soviets. A Polish army chaplain said Mass in the Katyń Forest.

24. Neither J. Erickson, *The Road to Berlin*, London: Cassell, 1983, nor C. Bellamy, *Absolute War*, London: Macmillan, 2007, mention the battle. See Grzelak *et al.*, *Bez Możliwości Wyboru*, for details of the battle.

25. See T. Piotrowski, *Genocide and Rescue in Wolyn*, Jefferson, NC: McFarland, 2000, for details of this slaughter.

26. See Mark Edelman, 'The Warsaw Ghetto Uprising: The Ghetto Fights Back', a pamphlet, Interpress, n.d.

27. For details of Berling's assistance to the uprising see A. Borowiec, *Destroy Warsaw! Hitler's Punishment, Stalin's Revenge*, Westport, CT: Praeger, 2001.

28. For details of Leon's career during the war see: J. Węgierski, 'Kim Byli "Hilary" i "Hugo" w Lwowskiej Armi Kajowej i w Orkrêgowej Delegaturze Rzdu ("Wino")?', *Sowiniec* (2006), 27–34.

29. Between 1944 and 1948 over 1.5 million Poles were moved from the former eastern Poland provinces into the new borders of Poland. J. Kochanowski, 'Gathering Poles into Poland: Forced Migration from Poland's Former Eastern Territories', in P. Ther and A. Siljak, eds, *Redrawing Nations: Ethnic Cleansing in East-Central Europe, 1944–1948*, Lanham, MD: Rowman & Littlefield, 2001, pp. 135–54; J. Czerniakiewicz, *Repatriacja ludności polskiej z ZSRR 1944–1948*, Warsaw: Panstwowe Wydawnictwo Naukowe, 1987.

30. The Berling army fought extensively in the campaigns for the liberation of Poland, the Pomeranian coast and most notably captured Kolberg (now Kołobrzeg) before turning south towards Berlin.

31. The house in Stanisławów is now inhabited by four families. The house in Tłumacz now serves as the children's library for the town.

Select Bibliography

The chapter was written partly with the aid of Nina Kochańska's memoirs.

Gross, J., *Revolution from Abroad*, Princeton: Princeton University Press, 1988.

Grzelak, C., Stańczyk, H., and Zwoliński, S., *Bez Możliwości Wyboru: Wojsko Polskie Na Froncie Wschodnin 1943–1945*, Warsaw: Wydawnictwo Bellona, 1993.

Kochanowski, J., 'Gathering Poles into Poland: Forced Migration from Poland's Former Eastern Territories', in P. Ther and A. Siljak, eds, *Redrawing Nations: Ethnic Cleansing in East-Central Europe, 1944–1948*, Lanham, MD: Rowman & Littlefield, 2001, pp. 135–54.

Piotrowski, T., *The Polish Deportees of World War II: Recollections of Removal to the Soviet Union and Dispersal throughout the World*, Jefferson, NC: McFarland, 2004.

Sword, K., ed., *The Soviet Takeover of the Polish Eastern Provinces 1939–41*, Basingstoke: Macmillan, 1991.

Chapter 17

Women who Thawed the Cold War

Grace Filby

Winston Churchill led the country in fighting threats to its peace, health and prosperity, only to face new threats from 1945 onwards – the dark political conflict and military tension of the Cold War with the USSR. This chapter looks first at the women closest to Churchill's heart, to the west of the Iron Curtain. The author finds a recurring theme of bacterial infections and the need to combat them. What a surprise to discover, on the other side, that there is a 'silver lining'. During the Cold War, a team of women held together a scientific programme that prevents and treats harmful bacteria.

To the West of the 'Iron Curtain'

Throughout a challenging childhood and the turbulent development of his political career, Winston Churchill came to draw on female influences and feminine strengths to support and comfort him. Archives and diaries give us plenty of evidence: it was often beyond words and in subtle gestures that he showed his appreciation for the women who nurtured him.

The words he did choose described his captivating American mother, Lady Randolph Churchill, (Jennie) as shining 'like an evening star'.[1] His nanny, Mrs Elizabeth Everest, he called 'Woom', and she was his 'dearest and most intimate friend'.[2] His first love, Pamela Plowden, was 'the most beautiful girl' he had ever seen.[3] She went on to marry an earl but always kept in fond contact. Winston Churchill himself found lifelong wedded bliss with Clementine Hozier (Clemmie) – in his own words, 'happily ever after'.[4] Clemmie bore him five children, and hugely influenced his decisions and actions. His mainly female household – just one son, and daughters Diana, Sarah, and Mary – would eventually accompany Winston on foreign trips and missions, becoming trusted officers in the WRNS, WAAF and ATS respectively.

Even though Churchill had his own experiences of dangerous scrapes and medical challenges, and we know that he appreciated being nursed through these,[5] they were hardly comparable to a tragic event in the First World War

(1914–18) that affected him severely. In 1915, he was First Lord of the Admiralty and responsible for planning the ill-fated Gallipoli campaign when nearly 500,000 Allied troops were lost through injury or illness.

Bullets, bayonets and cannon fire accounted for only some of the losses; lice, flies and poor hygiene were possibly more significant as a cause of weakness and death. Were the infections even correctly diagnosed and could they have been prevented? Did anyone raise these questions?[6] As early as November 1914, Professor Twort, a distinguished British scientist advised the Royal Army Medical College that dysentery was going to be a major problem; a scientific investigation might prove to be of highest importance.[7] Even though his offer of a year's research 'in the field' was rejected on financial grounds, by December 1915, he had specifically mentioned dysentery and a possible cure in a learned scientific paper.[8] We shall return to this point and look at it in more detail in the context of microbiology and a new discovery. If only Churchill had known about Twort's perceptive observations through a microscope, it might have saved his humiliating loss of office in the First World War, and perhaps provided crucial guidance for the future throughout the Second World War, and then the Cold War.

The disastrous event at the Dardanelles may have haunted Churchill for the rest of his life. His wife Clemmie said she thought he would die of grief.[9] How did he deal emotionally with being blamed, perhaps unjustly? It was with the love of his family that he came through. His sister-in-law Lady Gwendeline Spencer-Churchill, 'Goonie', introduced him to painting as a pastime, and he could explore his new gift as a talented artist. Intense sunlight and bright colours raised his spirits.[10]

More traumas were to shock and sadden Winston Churchill, not least from the many obituaries that he wrote for his military colleagues during the First World War. He had suffered his own huge family losses with the early death of his father from a brain tumour in 1895.[11] When his loving nanny, Mrs Everest, was dying of peritonitis, he employed a nurse, visited her and enabled her to 'die happy'.[12]

The dramatic demise of his mother, Jennie, took place after she fell downstairs in 1921, and suffered a double fracture near her left ankle, and then developed gangrene. In those days, if bacterial infections set in, there was little option for a doctor but to amputate. This is indeed what happened. The wound haemorrhaged and the result was fatal for Jennie. Both her sons, Winston and John (Jack), rushed to her bedside,[13] but she had slipped into a coma and the doctors could not save her life.

Only ten weeks later, there was more heartbreak for Winston and Clementine. Their youngest child, baby Marigold, was also struck down by an infection. The four children had been entrusted to a nursery governess when the 2-year-old, nicknamed 'Duckadilly', developed a sore throat. Untreated, it turned to septicaemia and she died.

Common enemies and recurrent nightmares in peacetime were not necessarily thousands of miles away, armed with heavy ammunition and the latest military hardware. Infectious germs could lurk invisibly – in the air and anywhere, taking unsuspecting and innocent victims from any family. A military man who had earned him medals and high status could do nothing when his mother and baby daughter both died in front of his eyes, in the space of only a few weeks.

Churchill's 'sensitivity to the problems of ordinary people and his appreciation for their achievements' has been remarked upon by an American writer.[14] Grace Hamblin, who lived near their Chartwell estate in Kent, was Churchill's 'greatly loved and ever-efficient' secretary for over forty years. Nicknamed 'Hambone' by the children, she was to realise that he rarely offered thanks, yet understood that he showed, in small, unspoken ways, his appreciation of her assistance.[15]

Nearby, there was an old widowed gipsy woman who lived in a caravan. She, too, acquired a nickname – 'Mrs Donkey Jack' and 'the Donkey Lady'[16] – and via the children Churchill furtively sent little packages to her – a gesture of generosity, to support her financially in old age and infirmity, after a broken ankle that didn't set.[17]

In 1938, a hardworking Chartwell secretary, Violet Pearman, whom he always referred to as 'Mrs P.', had a serious stroke in her mid-thirties. Divorced and raising two daughters, she was unable to work again. Churchill wrote to her affectionately, confirming his offer of financial support and advising her to relax and take a good long rest and a holiday. Sadly, Mrs P. died soon afterwards, yet Churchill made sure that her daughter Rosemary would be provided for over the next seven years, to complete her education.[18]

Personal tragedies and sensitivity could well have been triggers for Churchill's creative and constructive genius. A typical example of his creativity concerns the Cinque Port of Dover, ideally placed to defend the nation from foreign invasion. Churchill himself, on coming to power in May 1940, insisted on two huge cross-Channel guns. These guns, named 'Winnie' and 'Pooh', certainly had massive range pointing south across the English Channel but lacked precision, so it was not long before two more smaller guns were installed that had this necessary refinement. In a magnanimous tribute to femininity, the two new guns were named: 'Jane' and 'Clem'.

Who was Jane? In the popular culture of the Second World War, England, Jane was a national heroine. She was a beautiful 'blonde bombshell' of a pin-up girl whose fictional misadventures featured regularly in a strip cartoon in the *Daily Mirror* newspaper. She was considered a very wholesome influence by both men and women across the nation and the ongoing story had many fans. What a fillip for the troops and working folk to open the newspaper each morning to a gorgeous cartoon creature in army uniform. She worked undercover and frequently got into scrapes where her skimpy underwear (and more) is revealed! Morale was high on the agenda of military leaders and the newspaper men. Churchill himself described the fictitious Jane as 'Britain's secret weapon'.[19] Like a whiff of smelling salts or the tiniest drop of heart medicine, Jane had a magical power to revive the troops, for sure!

How fitting that the partner gun in Dover was named after his wife Clementine, who no doubt held highest eminence in his own private life, and could be relied upon to provide a spoonful of medicine at a crucial moment. Once, a neighbour's young son at Chartwell had watched as Mrs Churchill administered her husband a spoonful of medicine when he was pretending to be seriously injured. He said it was just like the fictional Tigger taking Roo's extract of malt – his Strengthening Medicine.[20]

It was Clementine who, between 1941 and 1947, headed up a massive fundraising effort with the Red Cross 'Aid to Russia' Fund. This enabled £7.5 million-worth of medical supplies and equipment to be sent from the West to help the Soviet Union.[21] Some of her personal letters of thanks, in her own handwriting, are still kept as treasured objects.

In the media meanwhile, cultured, sweet female voices could be heard. Churchill's favourite film of all was *That Hamilton Woman* (Emma, Lady Hamilton), made in 1941, starring Vivien Leigh, which reputedly he watched over a hundred times.[22] Elocution lessons had paid off for Jean Metcalfe, who became the first female radio announcer in the new BBC-War Office venture, the worldwide service. Her grandfather was Mr Churchill's top-class barber.[23] As a welcome relief from wartime news, Forces sweetheart Vera Lynn was lifted to singing stardom, symbolising the spirit of Great Britain, just like Winston Churchill.[24]

Mr Churchill's Russian-language interpeter, Mr Hugh Lunghi, advises us that although shrouded in deep Soviet secrecy at the time, the battle which won the war and liberated Europe was the battle of the Kursk Salient in the summer of 1943. Six thousand tanks took part; the Red Army lost more troops in that one battle than the Western Allies lost in the whole war.[25] As Churchill put it, 'The Red Army tore the guts out of the Nazi forces.'

Then with more big guns, international collaboration, intelligence, deception and the secret masterminding of Operation Overlord and D-Day, the largest amphibious invasion in history began on 6 June 1944. By that summer, the end of the Second World War was in sight.

Victory over bacterial infections was in sight too, with a huge media buzz right across the Western world feting Penicillin as a medical marvel. It was now available in large amounts to treat wounded Allied soldiers, especially in Normandy after the D-Day landings. June 1944 was also when the discoverer of this antibiotic, Alexander Fleming, now Minister of Health, advised on a BBC production called 'War Against Microbes'. It included Penicillin.

The British public received this news with joy, although one Surrey couple noticed an omission from that BBC programme.[26] They were the microbiologist team, Dr F. W. Twort FRS and his wife Nony, who had fought valiantly for years to make the point about a possible cure for bacterial infections. Let us remember the subject of the Dardanelles and the predicted deaths from dysentery, and F. W. Twort's learned paper in 1915.[27] He had found some 'ultramicroscopic' bacteria-eaters, which later became known as 'bacteriophage'. Perhaps the Allied troops and the British public were denied a form of medicine that had been discovered years earlier?

After the jubilation of VE Day in 1945, there was unfinished business between the West and the USSR. This came to be known as the Cold War, after October 1945, when British author and journalist George Orwell wrote of a 'Cold War'. He repeated this in print, in March 1946, before it was taken up internationally as a common expression.[28]

The chilling phrase, the 'Iron Curtain' was even more graphic. Churchill used it in his classic lecture of March 1946, 'The Sinews of Peace', which he delivered at Westminster College, in Fulton, Missouri, after receiving an honorary degree. By now, he was no longer Prime Minister, but Leader of the Opposition.[29] The 'Iron Curtain' symbolized a boundary, dividing Europe into two separate areas, after the ending of the Second World War. The next forty-six years were a continuing state of political conflict, military tension, and economic competition.

By the 1980s the word *Perestroika* was being used by Soviet leader Mikhail Gorbachev. Its literal translation from Russian to English is 'reconstruction'. Here again, a female influence can be acknowledged. Britain's first female Prime Minister, Margaret Thatcher, famously remarked in 1985: 'I like Mr Gorbachev, we can do business together.'[30] This was a contributory factor to the thawing of the Cold War. With some teamwork and the idea of *Perestroika* spreading like a 'good virus',[31] the Iron Curtain was to be opened wide. What revelations there would be.

In 2009, Churchill College, Cambridge, hosted a conference about the Cold War and its legacy.[32] A panel of eminent historians put forward the leading technologies of the Cold War: 'In the Shadow of the Bomb'. On the technology front, there had been hugely powerful and brilliant developments. These included nuclear weapons, the Trident missile, radar, plutonium, the transistor, carbon fibre and medical isotopes.

Then Sir John Boyd, British Ambassador in Japan, and former Master of Churchill College, put forward an aspect that the eminent historians had overlooked – cell biology and biotechnology!

Dr Graham Farmelo, historian and biographer, suggested another branch which has been seriously underestimated – molecular biology. Could this be explained by the lack of reporting in the popular press? In turn, the Honourable Franklin C. Miller KBE, former Pentagon and NSC staff official, acknowledged 'the power of the press to distort things'.

The 'Silver Lining' to the East of the 'Iron Curtain'

Now is a chance to reveal a great team of Cold War biotechnologists, mostly women, who worked for the advancement of microbiology, medicine and the reduction of the global threats of biological weapons, making a huge difference in the Former Soviet Union throughout those forty-six years of secrecy and information blackout.

A clue to where we look is identified as 'one symptom of unfinished business' after the Cold War.[33] The exotic country of Georgia is over 2,000 miles away from the United Kingdom. It is one of the places the author visited as a Winston Churchill Travelling Fellow,[34] researching the health value of bacteriophages. The Black Sea is on Georgia's western coast – the sea route towards the Mediterranean and beyond, through the historic, controversial Dardanelles strait. The great Caucasus mountains bordering old Imperial Russia, and the Former Soviet Union are to the north, and Turkey, the old great Ottoman Empire, is to the south. To the east is the Silk Route, and a gateway for the oil-rich neighbouring countries in central Asia and the Caspian. A number of unique features make Georgia significant in this story.

There is an amazing connection between this region and the Churchill family via King Edward VII and a close mutual friend – Grand Duke Michael (1861–1929), a cousin of the Romanov Russian Tsar.[35] He had spent the first twenty years of his life in the capital spa city of Tbilisi and the summer palace in Borjomi, central to the ancient mountains and rivers. He discovered that Borjomi's natural spring water has a unique taste and also curative properties, so from 1890 onwards he built a bottling factory, creating a great flow of fortune for his family. It enabled them to live luxuriously and entertain lavishly in the south of France and Great Britain, for most of the rest of their lives. Although banished from Russia for having married 'beneath his station',

Grand Duke Michael and his Prussian wife Countess Sophie mixed freely in British royal and aristocratic circles.[36] They kept a constant reminder of Georgia by naming their villa *Kasbek* after the ice-topped mountains on the great Military Highway towards Russia.

After the Russian Revolution of 1917, Georgia's mineral water continued to be exported eastwards and was known famously across the whole of the Soviet Union. Today Borjomi water is still Georgia's top export, being a natural resource for health. Another valuable resource for health is microbiology. Other Georgian priorities are academic standards, linguistic expertise and the value of women in society. A simple indicator of the importance of scientific expertise is that today there are eighty-six scientific institutes in Georgia.[37]

The George Eliava Institute of Bacteriophage, Microbiology and Virology is now named in honour of its founder. There, in the capital city of Tbilisi, amassed since 1923, is a vast library of over 500 historic books, articles and dissertations, written by scientists and physicians in Russian and Georgian. The science and medicine it contains have revolutionised the prevention and treatment of disease behind the Iron Curtain, even without access to Western antibiotics. There is also an extensive refrigerated collection of microbes – bacteria and viruses of many, many strains. The word 'bacteriophage' in the title of the institute refers to the vast subgroup of water-borne viruses that infect and destroy only bacteria, not plants, animals or humans.

The Soviet authorities, under Joseph Stalin, had given the institute their blessing. Just as Winston Churchill was concerned to avoid unnecessary deaths from infections amongst the British and allied troops, so too was Stalin concerned to maintain the strength of the Red Army. To the Soviets, it would be worthwhile investment in research and treatment programmes if advances in microbiology could prevent epidemics and heal battle wounds effectively.

The twist of fate is that the original discoveries of bacteriophage had in fact been published in the West, for example Dr Twort's paper in Britain's *The Lancet* in 1915.[38] Being wartime, there were difficulties in taking research findings forward. Trying to overcome these financial constraints, he volunteered his services to the British Army, and he was sent off to Salonika, where dysentery and malaria were rampant. Whilst there, he took the opportunity to give lectures about the potential of the ultramicroscopic virus he had observed – a 'bacteriolytic agent' – in other words, a naturally occurring 'dissolving substance', with the ability to burst, or 'lyse' bacteria.

In 1917 French-Canadian microbiologist Félix d'Herelle discovered the invisible microbe antagonistic to bacterial dysentery, which he additionally named bacteriophage, or phage (from the Greek – eat, destroy). Within two years he was curing human patients of dysentery and cholera in Paris by this method, 'phage therapy'.

Around the same time at Tbilisi, Georgia, scientist George Eliava observed the natural activity among river water bacteria himself, and he travelled to the Pasteur Institute in Paris to learn more. As a result, Félix d'Herelle was officially invited to Georgia several times in the years following to develop the research systematically.

A serious scientist, George Eliava also had a charismatic personality. His elegant lifestyle and good looks earned him a place firmly in the hearts of the growing number of researchers and other personnel. He would await them in the mornings at the entrance to the grand new institute in Tbilisi, his lips puckered with a kiss for each one, whether male or female. He brought perfumes from Paris, smuggled amongst his laboratory supplies. A 1930s archive photo shows George Eliava with an encircling array of smiling women.[39] He was to mysteriously disappear one day in 1937, never to be seen or talked of again during the Soviet regime. He had been executed. A new villa being constructed in the grounds for the Eliavas and the d'Herelles would not stand empty – the secret service moved in.[40]

From then onwards, all the way through to the 1960s, Eliava's former female assistant Elena Makashvili took up the reins. Devotedly and forcefully, Elena would play a major role in training and leadership, setting high standards in competence and scientific discipline. Whether or not she had been in love with George Eliava, as has been claimed by co-worker Nina, 'Nunu', Kilasonidze,[41] clearly Elena was inspired and driven by bacteriophage research.

It was to be 1949 before research reports of this work were made available by a mainstream publisher in English. Penguin Books published a volume of the popular *Science News*, containing articles by both Twort and d'Herelle.[42] D'Herelle reported on the successful use of phages to stop epidemics in several countries around the world in both military and civilian contexts – Soviet and non-Soviet. However, this crucial finding was not made use of by the British government, nor the press, nor the BBC. It was a different story in the East, on the other side of the Iron Curtain. In Georgia, the Eliava Institute was manufacturing its medicinal phage products, eventually on a huge scale of several tons a day between the 1950s and the 1980s and exporting them far and wide, all over the Soviet Union.[43]

Looking at a photograph of over a hundred Eliava researchers during the Cold War era, it is remarkable that the proportion of women was very high – 70 per cent or more. The numbers grew until at one stage there were over 1,200 researchers and support staff.[44] This was the twentieth-century heyday of the use of therapeutic phage.

When Russia eventually released its hold on Georgia at the end of the Cold War, free trade between these neighbours came to a sudden stop, and Georgia's economy collapsed. The last delivery of phage products from Georgia to Central Asia was in the spring of 1989.[45] Payments, too, had stopped. Russia would continue with its own institutes, and the Eliava Institute's fate would hang in the balance for some years. Production dropped drastically.

Yet again, the next generation of Georgian phage scientists was to save the day. Some of the women continued, often without pay, and in freezing conditions, knowing that their important work could still benefit millions of people in future. Senior researcher Marina Tediashvili commented with realism and fortitude for the *New York Times*: 'Of course, the men naturally move on to better things.'[46]

It wasn't until 2006 that an Eliava Head of Laboratory, Dr Zemphira Alavidze, had the first ever opportunity to talk in the United Kingdom about phage therapy since she had joined the Institute in 1968. In this personal interview she confirmed that there have been thousands of phage therapy patients in Georgia.[47] In the six months previously, ten had visited from the USA for treatment and one from Australia. In her experience, at Tbilisi's new Phage Therapy Center, they see between ten to fifteen patients per day. Her opinion is that there is big competition with the antibiotics companies. She emphasised that scientists need to work together to use phages for the good of the people, adding that 'Bureaucracy is so slow.' I asked whether this was deliberate. 'Who knows?', she smiled sweetly in a diplomatic reply. Zemphira also explained the need for genome sequencing – the genetic map of these bacteriophages. 'It needs a lot of input into genetic research worldwide.'

On visiting Georgia a year later in 2007, it was evident to me that the Eliava Institute attracts visitors and enquirers from all over the world, and has enormous potential for the power of good. Not only are bacteriophages used throughout entire hospitals but they are available without prescription in pharmacies for just 9 lari (about £3) for a box of ten vials, suitable for common skin or intestinal infections. Laboratory work enables unusual bacterial infections to be matched to their specific phage.

The imposing entrance to the Eliava Institute leads to spacious accommodation with laboratories, a lecture theatre and the library, packed with yellowing documents. It is mostly staffed by women and especially young, inspired, female postgraduates, willing to travel to laboratories and conferences in Europe, America and elsewhere. I was given a tour by Dr Mzia Kutateladze, Head of the Scientific Council. Renovations were being brought about from substantial international investment, and a year later on their completion, a major news event was the presidential opening of an international conference there.

In 2009, the practical application of bacteriophage research had a terrific boost because of a new literature review.[48] It was now published in English, rather than Georgian or Russian – the languages of the papers and books in the care of Librarian Ms Tsitsino Gvantseladze. Available from the Eliava Institute from 2010 onwards, this G8-priority report was funded by the UK Global Threat Reduction Programme and managed by the International Science and Technology Center, Moscow. It includes remarkable scientific and medical accounts, for example of Russian soldiers as far back as 1939, desperate for phage therapy to relieve their pain and suffering – although they would return to the battlefront soon enough. With less complications, the number of days in hospital was reduced; there was less bandaging and less transportation.[49]

One soldier's case history of 1940, described him as 'delirious, agitated and in a serious condition, four weeks after a mine explosion'. His wounds contained streptococcus infections and the report continues:

> 12.01. Piobacteriophage was injected into every wound and infectious pockets, in addition 2 ml of phage was administered subcutaneously.
> 13.01. The patients (*sic*) condition is joyful, slept at night.

The author, Dr Nina Chanishvili, concludes this 184-page historic literature review with a chapter about bioterrorism – how to foil attempts to spread dangerous pathogens like anthrax, cholera or brucella. Details are given of scientific work going back to the 1930s, with white mice, guinea pigs, rabbits, dogs, horses, milking cows, chickens, human adults and children. The methodology for phage manufacture on an industrial scale is included as a practical step forward.

Nina, the author of over 120 scientific publications over thirty years, dedicated this review to her uncle, Professor Teimuraz Chanishvili, who dreamt of its publication for much of his life (1924–2007). She is supported by five female Georgian contributors: Dr Marina Tediashvili PhD, Dr Marina Goderdzishvili PhD, Dr Dali Gogiashvili PhD, Dr Yana Malkhavazova PhD and Mrs Nana Khurtsia MSc.

Beneficiaries of phage therapy during and since the Cold War could amount to millions around the world. They include the grandmother of the current President of Georgia, according to his televised testimony in June 2008, and the late actress Dame Elizabeth Taylor, whose life was saved in 1961, after phage medicine, flown from the USA, was applied in London. Although this news did not make the British press or scientific papers, the events are chronicled in US newspapers and biographies.[50] They include a 9-year-old boy with autism in Oklahoma whose immune system was damaged as a baby. The number of his infections dropped significantly, almost immediately after treatment.[51] Beneficiaries include military and civilian patients throughout Georgia's Military Hospital in Gori, key focus of the war with Russia in August 2008. It took the killing of a Georgian trauma surgeon right there in the hospital courtyard, for that war to be called to an abrupt halt.

Meanwhile, the Georgian women at the Eliava Institute, universities and hospitals have devotedly pursued their scientific careers for the greater good. Winston Churchill and his wife Clementine would have found that admirable. No doubt the Georgian women's special knowledge and dedication would have provided animated discussion at the dinner table or over a game of bridge during his ninety-year lifetime, had they ever been brought to his attention.

The secret spy system of the Cold War incurred huge blocks on information. Despite the dark political conflict and military tension of the Cold War, we have revealed this silver lining behind the Iron Curtain. I have a picture in my mind of Sir Winston Churchill arriving at the Eliava Institute, warmly shaking hands with the team of Georgian women who thawed the Cold War.

Notes

1. Winston S. Churchill, *My Early Life*, London: Butterworth, 1930.
2. Ibid.
3. Letter from Winston to Lady Randolph Churchill, 4 November 1896, Churchill Archive Ref. CHAR 28/22/18–23
4. W. S. Churchill, *My Early Life*.
5. John H. Mather MD, 14th Annual International Churchill Society Conference, Toronto, 1997.
6. Antony Twort, *In Focus, Out of Step: A Biography of Frederick William Twort FRS*, Stroud: Alan Sutton Publishing, 1993, ch. 8, 'Feverish writing'.
7. Ibid., pp. 70–5.
8. F. W. Twort, 'An Investigation on the Nature of Ultra-Microscopic Viruses', *The Lancet*, 186 (1915), pp. 1241–3.
9. Martin Gilbert, *Winston S. Churchill*, London: Heinemann, 1977, vol. III, p. 431.
10. Mather (see n. 5).
11. Celia Lee and John Lee, *The Churchills: A Family Portrait*, New York: Palgrave Macmillan, 2010, p. 64.
12. Letter to Mamma, 3 July 1895, Churchill Archive Ref: CHAR 28/21/49–50.
13. *New York Times*, 30 June 1921.
14. www.johninnorthcarolina.blogspot.com.
15. *Telegraph* obituary, 18 October 2002.
16. Christopher Creighton, *OpJB: The Last Secret of WW2*, New York: Simon & Schuster, 1996, p. 12; Mary Soames, ed., *Speaking for Themselves: The Personal Letters of Winston and Clementine Churchill*, London: Doubleday, 1998, pp. 370–3.
17. Ibid. Creighton; Soames.

18. Website cited n. 14. Martin Gilbert, *In Search of Churchill: A Historian's Journey*, London: Harper Collins, 1994, pp. 156–60.
19. Norman Pett and J. H. G ('Don') Freeman, *The Misadventures of Jane*, London: Titan Books, 2009.
20. Creighton, *OpJB*, p. 11. A. A. Milne, *The House at Pooh Corner*, London: Methuen, 1928.
21. *Sydney Morning Herald*, 9 October 1942. Lee and Lee, *The Churchills*, p. 215.
22. Flora Fraser, *Beloved Emma: The Life of Emma, Lady Hamilton*, London: John Murray, 2003.
23. Colin Metcalfe, BBC *People's War*, 2003–6.
24. Eric Sykes, *If I Don't Write It, Nobody Else Will: An Autobiography*, London: Fourth Estate, 2005, pp. 450–1.
25. Hugh Lunghi, personal communication to Grace Filby, 2010.
26. Letter from Alexander Fleming to Mrs N. Twort, June 1944, Personalia 1939–45, Ref: GC/186/A6/1, Wellcome Library, London.
27. F. W. Twort, 'An Investigation'.
28. George Orwell, 'You and the Atomic Bomb', the British newspaper *Tribune*, 19 October 1945. Orwell, *Observer*, 10 March 1946.
29. Robert Rhodes James, *Winston S. Churchill: His Complete Speeches 1897–1963*, London: Chelsea House Publishers, 1974, vol. VII, 1943–1949, pp. 7285–93.
30. 'Gorbachev Becomes Soviet leader', BBC News, March 1985.
31. Adam Michnik, 'Were it not for "Perestroika virus" our [democratic movement] could not have got where it is today', July 1989: www.gorby.ru.
32. Bridget Kendall, BBC Diplomatic Correspondent, 'Cold War and its Legacy', conference, Churchill College, Cambridge, 19 November 2009.
33. Ibid.
34. The Winston Churchill Memorial Trust awards grants to British citizens, resident in the UK, and from all walks of life. This enables them to travel overseas to acquire knowledge for the benefit of their profession and community, the UK as a whole, and themselves.
35. Edward, Prince of Wales, letter from to Lady Randolph Churchill, March 1898, Churchill Archives Centre, Ref: CHAR 28/64/14-158.
36. J. M. Kolbert, *Keele Hall: A Victorian Country House*, Keele: Univ. of Keele, 1986. Polesden Lacey, Surrey, photographs and visitors book. Ernest Scears, *A History of Reigate Priory*, 1950 – author's collection.
37. Dr Mzia Kutateladze, personal communication, 2010.
38. F. W. Twort, 'An Investigation', pp. 1241–3.
39. Thomas Häusler, *Viruses vs. Superbugs*, tr. Karen Leube, Basingstoke and New York: Macmillan, 2006, p. 146.
40. Dr Hubert Mazure, personal communication.
41. Häusler, *Viruses vs. Superbugs*, pp. 127 and 149.
42. J. L. Crammer, ed., *Science News 14*, Harmondsworth: Penguin Books, December 1949.
43. Elizabeth Kutter and Alexander Sulakvelidze, *Bacteriophages: Biology and Applications*, Florida: CRC Press, 2005, p. 407.
44. Häusler, *Viruses vs. Superbugs*, p. 177.
45. Ibid.
46. Lawrence Osborne, 'A Stalinist Antibiotic Alternative', *New York Times*, 6 February 2000.
47. File note, Grace Filby, 28 April 2006.

48. Nina Chanishvili, *A Literature Review of the Practical Application of Bacteriophage Research*, Tbilisi: Eliava Institute of Bacteriophage, Microbiology and Virology, 2009.

49. Ibid., ch. 3.

50. 'County Lab Sends Vaccine to Liz' , *Delaware County Daily Times*, 7 March 1961. 'Fan's Letter may have Saved Liz Taylor's Life', *The Fresno Bee*, 9 March 1961. 'Miss Taylor got aid from New Jersey – Woman recommended drug that had helped her – Actress Improves', *New York Times*, 9 March 1961. C. David Heymann, *Liz, an Intimate Biography of Elizabeth Taylor*, London: William Heinemann, 1995, p. 222. Kitty Kelley, *Elizabeth Taylor, the Last Star*, London: Book Club Associates by arrangement with M. Joseph, 1981, p. 137.

51. Mary Ann Puckett, *Take Him Home and Love Him: A Story of Autism and How to Cope with it*, Oklahoma City: L. S. Marann, 2005, pp. 27–30.

Select Bibliography

This chapter includes direct quotations from discussions between Dr Zemphira Alavidze and the author.

Chanishvili, Nina, *A Literature Review of the Practical Application of Bacteriophage Research*, Tbilisi: Eliava Institute of Bacteriophage, Microbiology and Virology, 2009.

Crammer, J. L., ed., *Science News 14*, Harmondsworth: Penguin Books, 1949.

Gilbert, Sir Martin, Churchill, *A Photographic Portrait*, London: Pimlico, 1999.

Häusler, Thomas, *Viruses vs. Superbugs: A Solution to the Antibiotics Crisis?*, Basingstoke: Macmillan, 2006.

Soames, Mary, *Clementine Churchill*, London: Cassell Ltd, 1979.

Twort, Anthony, *In Focus, Out of Step: A Biography of F. W. Twort FRS, 1887–1950*, Stroud: Alan Sutton Publishing Ltd, 1993.

Chapter 18

War Veterans

Four Short Histories

Edited by Celia Lee

1. Mrs Georgina Ivison and her family

The memoirs of Mrs Georgina Ivison were related to the author by Georgina, and by her daughters, Stella and Josie. Georgina had lived independently in her own home until age 99 years, looked after by carers, and by her daughter Mrs Stella Collingwood, who is a nurse. After that time she entered a Royal British Legion care home, Maurice House, Broadstairs, Kent.

Georgina Ivison was born on 23 February 1906, into a family of long service in the British army. In December 2007,[1] aged 101 years, Georgina began giving Celia Lee her recollections as a wartime school mistress. This is Georgina's story:

> My father, George Raynham had served in the 9th Lancers, 17th Lancers, and the Queens Own Oxfordshire Hussars. He had worked in the City of London, and knew Major John Strange Spencer-Churchill (Jack), the younger brother of the late Sir Winston Churchill, both Churchill brothers having been officers in the Oxfordshire Hussars. Jack was a stockbroker and on the board of the stock broking company, Nelke Phillips, and my father worked with him. It was Jack who invited my father to join the Oxfordshire Hussars.
>
> During the Second World War, Jack collected food parcels for the soldiers and he called at our house. He could speak good French, and sang a French lullaby to the baby.

Georgina trained as a teacher at Furneydown Training College until June 1926, when she applied to become an army school mistress. That year, she was posted to Bordon Army Camp, in East Hampshire, and later, in 1927 to Bulford Camp, Salisbury Plain, Wiltshire. Georgina says:

I was a teacher and I became a Queen's Army School Mistress, teaching the serving soldiers' children in barracks quarters. I enjoyed this work very much.

I married a soldier, Ralph Ivison, who was a corporal in the army and later a warrant officer. Our marriage took place in St Etheldreda's Roman Catholic Church in Holborn, London, on 26 December 1928.

My husband Ralph was posted to Egypt in 1936, and we sailed on HMT *Delwara*. I taught on the ship going out to Egypt. He was serving in the Royal Corps of Signals in the Cairo suburb of Abbasia. His regiment became part of the original 'Desert Rats' of the British 7th Armoured Division, and they worked in the great Sand Sea, which stretched for 150 miles to the Sahara Desert. Major Ralph Bagnold[2] was serving in the desert, and my husband led the Signals troop assigned to him for communication. Bagnold was famous as an originator of the Long Range Desert Groups.

In Egypt, I taught the older boys at the Garrison School in Abassia, which included my son Ralph (junior), who was born in Bulford on 20 December 1930.

My second child, Josephine (Josie), was born at Tidworth in Salisbury on 4 September 1935. Today, she is married and lives in New Zealand.

Georgina recalled the outbreak of the Second World War (1939–45):

Winston Churchill was the only politician who had any get up and go about him. He was an inspiration to the country to win the war, and he was the only one who could have done it.

Stella, who is Georgina's youngest daughter, and is a nurse at Kent County Hospital, takes up the story:

In September 1940, my parents had orders to evacuate the barracks as they were needed for New Zealand and Australian troops. They sailed down the Red Sea on the RMS *Empress of Britain*. As they went past an Italian base the ship was blacked out and sailed by as quiet as possible. They thought they were going to India but instead their destination was Durban in South Africa.

Dad had his promotion and was Regimental Sergeant Major at Headquarters in Abassia but was posted to Palestine. Mum didn't think she would see him again till the end of the war. She ensured the children did not forget him, and they always said 'good night' and kissed a photograph of him until they saw him again.

The Ivison's third child, Georgina, was born in Durban on 23 June 1941. Stella continues:

At one time, mum had what was called Black Water Fever. It is a complication of malaria, which causes a kidney infection. Within a few days of the onset there are chills and a high fever, jaundice, and vomiting, and the urine turns black.

Josie, now Mrs Letton, remembers:

My mother was very ill with black pee [urine] and everyone tried to keep it from us, but we listened at the door to hear the grown-ups. It was one of the rare occasions when she had to call a doctor, as they were very expensive.

Ralph Ivison was then transferred from Egypt to Palestine, and the family had to leave at short notice. Josie recalls:

When the decision was made to evacuate families from Egypt to South Africa, Mum had two days in which to pack all our (that is mum's, Ralph junior's and my) belongings, ready for boarding the boat. It was all a very worrying time with the menfolk being away at the war and convoys being shelled and torpedoed on the way down. But when we got there we managed to thoroughly enjoy the tropical sea and white sand beaches at Durban, where we developed our swimming skills – mine particularly by being thrown into a rock pool by Ralph and the gang, who were standing-by to rescue me if I didn't surface, a method that soon teaches you to swim. The sea was not generally considered safe due to sharks.

We also loved all the tropical fruits and fresh vegetables. When mangoes were in season we had to beat off the monkeys for our share, sometimes eating so many we developed sores around the mouth, much to mum's annoyance. At one time we had a banana palm growing next door, so had loads of free bananas.

Our group of wives would look out for each other, seriously. For example, if they went to a tea dance in Durban, no one was allowed more than three dances with one fellow. And there was no question of going outside after dark.

It was lovely when the menfolk came down on leave, but that was not often. I think that was when a photograph of Dad sitting on rocks in khakis was taken.

Initially, we were housed in an evacuee hotel where mum was convinced we were being ripped-off by the owner. We were not getting
our full value of rations and things like that. This led to her decision
to move out and rent a holiday chalet in the nearby resort of
Winkelspruit, south of Durban. It was pretty basic and tight going
raising the rental payments with enough left over for food. That is
why we made as much use as possible of vegetables from the garden.

Ralph and I went to the local school along with Boer children.
Inevitably, there was the occasional punch-up. Sometimes we were
invited out to one of their farms, getting there by ox-cart – a long
and slow method of transport.

These were fairly primitive people, where home-baked bread was
placed into warm beds to rise after getting up. But generally they
were good-hearted and would look after us if anything happened,
like illness.

There were snakes, and a snake was discovered wriggling down
the outside concrete steps of our Winklespruit house, leading to the
outside loo. It appeared to be a night adder, which is poisonous.
'What to do, we all cried?!' Mum snatched an axe from the garden
boy and chopped its head off. We were all intrigued how long the
body continued wriggling after death.

There were obvious differences in cultural etiquette between the English and
the native Africans. Josie recalls a Zulu who sneaked into their house thinking
he was going to have a feather bed for the night:

We were all in the lounge, reading, in preparation for bed. Mum
brought some ironing through from the back kitchen and took it into
her bedroom, when we heard her scream, yell, and shout many swear
words in English and Afrikaans. She had been surprised by a Zulu
going through her bedding. He leaped out of the window and took
off across the garden like the clappers, clearing a six feet high gate
and disappearing into the night. Ralph junior got it in the neck when
mum said: 'Didn't you hear my screams and yelling?' 'Yes', said
Ralph, 'But we thought you had trodden on a cockroach or something like that!'

Because we did not have a phone Ralph was designated to wait by
the gate until the Night Warden came past on one of his regular
patrols. We told him what happened and he phoned the police.

Mum wouldn't get into that bed until she had changed all the
bedding as she could still smell the odour of the Zulu, and the
original bedding had to be thoroughly washed.

Stella takes up the story:

> Baby Georgina developed gastro-enteritis and died on 2 January 1944, aged just over 2½ years. The family was under orders to sail back to England as Dad had already been abroad for eight years, and this was then the limit for an overseas posting. They had to leave Georgina behind in her grave.

Josie:

> The eventual return convoy from South Africa to England on the SS *Orbita* was the worst journey, for this route took us out into the Atlantic Ocean where German U-boats and ships were joined by aircraft bombing our ships. We saw several ships sunk that we knew contained families. Along the way, we were chased by a submarine, which fired a torpedo at the ship, fortunately missing, much to the applause of the troops on board.

Stella:

> Mum continued teaching the children of soldiers on the ship on the way home. The family returned in 1944, and granddad went up to meet them at the war-torn Liverpool docks, and took them back to London. Soon after, they moved to live at Herne Bay in Kent.

Josie:

> When we returned to the UK we didn't see another banana for years – a dreadful sadness to us!

Two further children were born to Georgina and Ralph at Herne Bay; Zöe on 11 February 1945, and Stella on 15 January 1946.
  Stella continues:

> From 1956, mum held a teaching position at Reculber Church of England Primary School as infant teacher for children when they first enter school, which post she retained until she retired.

Mrs Georgina Ivison did not live to see her 102nd birthday, but died peacefully and with dignity on 16 January 2008. In her last days, she sat up in her bed with a tray on her lap, writing out her recollections.[3]

2. Sister Theresa Jordan, No. 10 Casualty Clearing Station, Queen Alexandra's Imperial Military Nursing Service, Second World War

Dermott Hynes,[4] a retired barrister, related to Celia Lee the story of his wife Theresa's service as a nurse and as a nursing sister, in No. 10 Casualty Clearing Station in North Africa and France during the Second World War.

Theresa Jordan was born on 6 November 1916, into a farming family at Cortoon, Ballaghadereen, County Roscommon in the west of Ireland. She trained as a nurse in London, and joined Queen Alexander's Imperial Military Nursing Service (QAIMNS) in December 1941. Theresa remembered that suddenly she was elevated to the position of Sister, an important rank in a hospital, as previously she had been just 'nurse Jordan'. She even remembered a senior nursing sister referring to her as 'little' nurse Jordan, as she was somewhat small in stature in the sister's eyes.

Then, as now, hard work and a willingness to do whatever was required of her was an essential part of every nurse's life. Following preliminary training in her new role, and kitting out at Harrods store in London, Theresa joined No. 10 Casualty Clearing Station (CCS) in March 1942. As the Mediterranean was closed, she travelled by the next troopship, via South Africa. Despite war conditions the ship called at Cape Town for a day or two, and she remembered the kindness of local families who invited them into their homes.

A Casualty Clearing Station was the Army's front medical unit, consisting of about a dozen or so medical officers, the same kind of number of nursing sisters, and a much larger number of nurses and medical orderlies, possibly 100. All were equally necessary in their different ways, and all working as a whole to deal with the wounded, serious or otherwise, and the dead or dying, and in conditions of battle.

No. 10 CCS was of course only one of many. Theresa remembered the desert sand which, when the wind whipped it up, got into everything, including the tinned peaches in syrup which somehow the army could still manage to provide.

The nursing staff lived in tents and were situated close to the front line. They were therefore the 'first port of call' for the evacuated wounded and the dead of all combatants, and as well as British, they took in German and Italian wounded.

At that time the famous British 8th Army had retreated to El Alamein, a point on the North African coastline, some sixty miles west of Cairo. The battle had swayed backwards and forwards for some two years, and the renowned Field Marshal Rommel's German Afrika Korps, along with the Italians, now faced a critical, deciding encounter with the British and Empire forces, under their new Commander, Field Marshal Bernard Montgomery (Monty), who was looked upon affectionately by his men because, amongst other things, he gave them generous supplies of cigarettes.

Theresa remembered the gunfire at Alamein, which went on for hours before the British advanced, and of course the thousands of casualties afterwards, as Alamein was a major battle, the most decisive, perhaps, of Britain's war.

After North Africa, No. 10 CCS moved to France, some eight or nine days after D-Day, in June 1944. Theresa descended into a landing craft by climbing down a scrambling net from the ship to reach the shore. Some of the girls were nervous but they all persevered and made it. A piece of shrapnel once whizzed past Theresa's face, and on another day she had been talking to a despatch rider and an hour later he was brought in dead. Nursing at the front was not for the faint hearted.

No. 10 CCS advanced with the army into Germany, and ended up at one of the minor Concentration Camps, Sandbostel. Initially, in 1939, it was a prisoner of war camp named *Stalag X-B*, and then it became a camp of internment for civilian enemy aliens, until 1945, when about 1,000,000 inmates had passed through it, of whom about 46,000 perished. When Theresa arrived the camp was full of dying prisoners, existing in dreadful conditions of squalor and misery, and heaps of dead bodies. A couple of the original camp buildings still exist today, in the commercial estate of Immenheim. A cemetery exists in which several thousand former prisoners are buried in mass graves, just outside the town. There is today a memorial to their memory.

Recently, by chance, Dermott Hynes found on the internet the details of Freda Laycock, the daughter of a member of the QAIMNS, who had been at the Sandbostel camp at the same time as Theresa.[5] 'To my amazement there was my Theresa in a group photograph we had never seen, seventh from the right'!

Theresa's Service Record, dated 3 October 1945, and signed by Lieutenant Colonel F. S. Fiddes RAMC, Commanding 10 Brigade CCS, reads:

> Miss T. Jordan has served as nursing Sister with No.10 Casualty Clearing Station since March 1942, throughout the North African and N.W. European campaigns, with an intervening period of duty in the United Kingdom.
>
> During these years she has consistently rendered the most splendid service, and has proved her adaptability in a great variety of circumstances. Her professional skill is of the highest order, and she has successfully maintained her high standards in spite of the

difficulties encountered in the nursing of serious battle casualties in the forward areas. During the campaigns, her service was spent almost entirely in such areas, where her skill and resourcefulness were unsurpassed, and her organising abilities a great asset to the unit.

Of cheerful disposition, she has been a very popular member of the unit, and I willingly testify to her excellent qualities with sincerity and the utmost confidence.

Theresa Jordan married Dermott Hynes in 1952, and they lived happily together for fifty-three years, and had two sons, who have done well in life.

When Theresa left the service, she trained as a schoolteacher, and taught for several years at a Convent School in London. Dermott managed to 'scrape through' his Bar examination finals and became a Barrister. Of his beloved wife Dermott says:

Theresa passed away peacefully, on 12 September 2005, to the grief of all who knew her. She left behind a legacy of cheerfulness and courage, having been Mentioned in Despatches for distinguished service as follows:

By the KING'S Order the name of Sister (Miss) T. Jordan, Queen Alexandra's Imperial Military Nursing Service, was published in the *London Gazette* on 18th October 1945, as mentioned in a Despatch for distinguished service. I am charged to record His Majesty's high appreciation.

[signed] J.J. Lawson – Secretary of State for War

3. Beryl: The Story of a Wren, Second World War (recorded 2009)

Beryl was born in Cornwall in June 1920. Her father, Arthur, worked as coastguard for the Board of Fisheries, and then joined the Home Guard at the outbreak of the Second World War. Her mother, Elizabeth, was a seamstress. Beryl is rather a private person, and does not wish her surname or the names of her family to be disclosed, hence the use of first names only.

At the outbreak of the Second World War, Beryl, who was an only daughter, was aged 19, and was happily employed as a 'shop girl' (shop assistant) in an idyllic Cornish village shop. Beryl says:

It was my father's idea that I should become a Wren. I was called up and joined the WRNS in 1940, and was obliged to move from Cornwall to Mayfield College, North London, to undergo training.

Our uniform was a navy jacket and skirt, tie, sailor's hat, black woollen tights, and black shoes, and it was provided by the government.

Beryl was trained along with about thirty other girls in waiting at tables on officers of the navy, army, and air force, who numbered several hundred. The girls worked together in the commodore's mess, which was a large dining room, where they served breakfast, lunch, and dinner.

We girls slept in dormitories on hard beds. We got up at 6 o'clock in the morning to begin work. We were in training for six weeks, which included attending lectures on the war at the college.

When Beryl's training was sufficient, she was given a special assignment:

I was one of four bat women (valets) for Princess Marina, the Duchess of Kent, who was Commandant of the WRNS, and who when in London stayed nearby. I washed and ironed the Duchess's clothes and laid them out for her, and performed other little tasks, but I never met her.

Beryl says she also sewed on buttons and did other sewing or mending of Marina's clothes and such like tasks. The clothes when ironed, were always taken by someone else to Marina at her living quarters, thus avoiding any contact with Beryl and the other three valets.

There was and still is a degree of secrecy surrounding the Duchess's time in London, and as far as the author can make out, she actually used a house nearby as a London base for her work, which was possibly next door to Mayfield College, and presumably due to security the address could not be divulged.

London was something of a culture shock to Beryl, and rather frightening for a girl from a beautiful Cornish village with its milkmaids and treats for tourists of clotted cream and fudge. Beryl says: 'It was dreadful in London, there were bombs falling all around us the whole time.' Beryl did not like the work. She was not happy in London and was permanently homesick. Because of the bombing, movement was restricted and she and the other girls did not get out very much in the evenings after their day's work as it was not safe.

Beryl described a set of living conditions, which are something akin to what one might read about in a Dickensian novel. They were billeted in the attic, the beds were hard and uncomfortable, and there were no toilets or bathrooms for the Wrens indoors. Beryl complained: 'Washing, showering, and toilet facilities were outside of the main building, it was freezing cold in the mornings when we went out there especially in winter.'

Given the Duchess's position as Commandant of the WRNS, and her exhaustive tour of visits to the workplaces and living quarters of other Wrens, as described in Chapter 8, it is most surprising that she never met her four valets who lived in the garret of Mayfield College in primitive conditions without running water. Presumably her office ensured that she did not see Wrens who were living in discomfort and dissatisfied with their job, and in this case, four of whom were actually looking after her wardrobe.

After six weeks, Beryl and some of the other Wrens were posted to Billy Butlin's holiday camp at Pwllheli, Caernarfonshire, North Wales, which had been requisitioned by the government for war work, and was known as HMS *Glendower*. Beryl remembers: 'Philip Mountbatten was there, but it was before he met and married Princess Elizabeth.'

Work at Pwllheli involved 'assisting the military nurses in the sick bay for officers', which meant that Beryl's job had changed to an assistant nurse or orderly. An Act was later passed in 1943 to recognise these nursing assistants, who were given the qualification of State-enrolled Assistant Nurse (SEAN). The qualification was lower in status to the State Registered Nurse (SRN), and the SEANs worked as assistants to the SRNs.

When Beryl travelled home to Cornwall on leave the distance from both London and Pwllheli was 200 miles, and when she returned to visit her parents she travelled on a steam train 'which took twenty-two hours' to reach her destination. Beryl had two brothers, and she faced personal tragedy:

> Both of them died during the war. Edwin was in the army and was killed by a bomb in India. Freddy had been a farmer in Cardiff, and joined the army at home but died of a cerebral haemorrhage.

Beryl was not much happier at Pwllheli than she had been in London, but: 'there was more freedom and we attended dances'. At one of the dances, Beryl met her future husband, George, who was in the Royal Air Force, having joined up at age 17. Marriage, however, seemed out of the question until the war ended. 'George was from Lewisham, south east London. I didn't want to get married in the registry office so we were married in St Margaret's Church of England, in Blackheath,[6] south east London, in 1946. After the war, George became an engineer: he died 10 years ago, we have one daughter, Susan.'

Beryl's is not a happy story. She was from a comfortable, lower-middle-class background of respectability. She hated being relegated to service as a waitress, which was the same as being in domestic service, only worse in terms of living conditions, and Beryl had never worked in domestic service. Having been a shop assistant since she left school she was good at arithmetic and she should, therefore, have been given a job in keeping with her educational skills.

Presumably, at the time she joined the Wrens the government needed waitresses to wait on the male officers living in the residential part of Mayfield College and surrounding areas.

Beryl also did not like working in a hospital; she said there were 'all kinds of dreadful injuries and illnesses'. It was distressing being so far away from home, and having to take a long, arduous journey back to Cornwall when she got a few days leave. Beryl was glad when the war ended, and she married a good man and lived happily ever after in Lewisham, which for her was the only good thing that came out of her experiences.

'However, we won the war', Beryl told me proudly. Her eyes lit up and she drew herself up to her full height of about five feet eight inches. Her sense of pride that her sacrifice was worth it and she was part of the war effort was the one really cheerful moment of the interview. Like so many Wrens, Beryl received no medal or any kind of recognition of her work. There may be a number of other 'Beryls' out there, if they have lived into their eighties or nineties, and who have never told their stories but who fulfilled their duty to their country in time of war.

4. Mrs Mary (Minnie) S. Churchill

Mrs Mary (Minnie) S. Churchill was invited to give the address at the Air Transport Auxiliary Association's Annual Dinner in 2002, in the Officers Mess, RAF Lyneham, Wiltshire. The ATA was staffed by men and women pilots, who, during the Second World War, ferried aircraft, delivering them to where they were required for male RAF pilots, who went in action over the skies of Britain, fighting the German *Luftwaffe*.

Minnie dedicated her talk to her late father, Sir Gerard d'Erlanger, Commodore of the Air Transport Auxiliary service, and to the ATA, and all those wonderful and very brave pilots who were pathfinders in those dark and dangerous days of the Second World War. Minnie's talk brings the story of the progress made by women in war up to the present day. It is a fitting finale to this collection of studies, and a most optimistic note on which to conclude our book.

Air Marshal Sir Christopher Coville and Lady Coville, Group Captain and Mrs Lock, Diana [Barnato-Walker], Ladies and Gentlemen . . .

> On behalf of all the Ladies here this evening, I would like to thank Eric and Mary Viles for arranging this special evening, and Group Captain Lock for allowing us once again to have our Reunion dinner here in the Officers Mess at RAF Lyneham. It is a huge treat to visit Lyneham, and dine in this wonderful room.

My father, Gerard d'Erlanger, would be so proud to know that in 2002, sixty-two years after the outbreak of the Second World War, ATA were still holding these reunions, with many people coming, who served in ATA, and also family members to show their respect for ATA and all that it stood for.

This year we are also celebrating sixty years since the Americans came into the war, with many joining ATA, including twenty-nine women pilots. This was a time when Britain stood alone. What a great contribution was made by all these people who crossed the Atlantic to help Britain in its hour of need. I would like to quote the words of Winston Churchill in those bleak and lonely years.

Sunday evening – December 7, 1941, Winston hears of the attack on Pearl Harbour; within moments, he talks to President Roosevelt, who confirms the attack. Winston immediately, and within the hour, declares war on Japan. His feelings are expressed so well in his words: 'No American will think it wrong of me if I proclaim that to have the United States at our side was to me the greatest joy. Up to the neck and into the death. So we had won after all.' That night in Winston's own words, he went to bed and 'slept the sleep of the saved and thankful.'

Although the majority of those serving in the ATA were men, I am responding this evening on behalf of the women, and therefore I will concentrate on the role they played. I like to think that the role played by the ladies in ATA in those dark war days, helped to pioneer the way for women of today. They showed the leaders that women were capable of fulfilling so many demanding and different roles. As Hal Ewing said in his speech they served not only as pilots but also as mechanics, cooks, operations officers, telephone operators, secretaries, and motor transport drivers – all vital links in the work of ATA.

In her book, *Spreading My Wings*, our Commodore Diana Barnato-Walker[7] gives us some very interesting facts which I would like to quote for those who are not familiar with them:

> By the end of the war ATA had ferried 309,011 planes, and flown some 414,984 hours. In 1944, there had been 659 ATA pilots of whom 108 were women. No fewer than 174 people gave their lives, of whom 16 were women.

The ATA pilots came not only from the United Kingdom but were of all nationalities: Americans, Canadians, South Africans,

Australians, New Zealanders, Indians, Poles, French, Dutch, Danish, Czechoslovak, Spanish, Irish, Argentinean, Norwegian, Swedish; there were even pilots from Siam, Chile, China, Ceylon, Estonia and Ethiopia.

To start with, the opportunities for the women who flew were limited. The authorities held some strange and interesting views about women and aeroplanes. I quote just a few. The Air Ministry: 'Aviation was an unsuitable profession for a woman. Women pilots would be taking flying jobs away from men.' Other comments of the time were:

> There are Millions of women in the country who could do useful jobs in war. But the trouble is that so many of them insist on wanting to do jobs, which they are quite incapable of doing. The menace is the woman who thinks that she ought to be flying in a high speed bomber when she really has not the intelligence to scrub the floor of a hospital properly, or who wants to nose around as an Air Raid Warden and yet can't cook her husband's dinner.

Such was the feeling at the time. It soon changed! From being allowed to fly only Tiger Moths, the reason being, that (1) nobody else wanted the job and (2) light trainers would be the cheapest to replace if broken by a woman.

Pauline Gower, the first commander of the ATA women pilots, assumed that this meant that: 'The hand that rocked the cradle wrecked the crate'. She joked that in their case ATA stood for 'Always Terrified Airwomen'. These 'Terrified Airwomen' soon showed what they were made of.

Lettice Curtis, who unfortunately is not here with us this evening, was the first woman to fly a four-engine bomber. In a single day, she flew two Class 1 aircraft, a Spitfire Class 2, a Mitchell, and a Mosquito Class 4, and a Stirling Class 5. By 1943, women were flying all classes of aircraft, with the exception of Class 6 flying boats. They also, in 1943, received equal pay with the men! You have only to look at the vital role played by women in the Royal Air Force, and, here at RAF Lyneham today.

I did some research for this speech and discovered that in 1990, it was decided to allow women to train as pilots in the Royal Air Force. Those first pilots, Sally Cox and Jo Slater, soon qualified. Today, women fly every type of aircraft in all roles. Squadron Leader Nicky Smith is currently Squadron Commander of 78 Squadron in Cyprus.

Look around the officer's mess, here at Lyneham – women are the norm. It is not only in the Royal Air Force. I was interested to hear, that one young lady named Ashley, known by her fellow pilots as 'Mumbles' because of her English accent, flew bombing missions in Afghanistan earlier this year for the US Air Force. I was interested to discover that she was educated in England and went to the same school that two of my granddaughters are attending today!

Women have achieved so much in the world of aviation. They perform in every role in the Royal Air Force; they are commercial pilots, air traffic controllers, engineers, and even commanded the Space Shuttle into space. Sixty-two years on, we still have so much to thank all the women for who joined and worked for the ATA.

We are living in worrying times, nobody knows yet what will be happening this winter[8] and what role our forces will play. All I do know is, thanks to those great pathfinders, the Women of ATA, there will be women playing important roles in the battles ahead, and also in the peacekeeping work that our forces perform so admirably. I know that my father was so proud of all the people who served in ATA.

Notes

1. Mrs Georgina Ivison read an article in the *Daily Express* about the book, *Winston and Jack: The Churchill Brothers* written by Celia and John Lee, publ. privately 2007. Mrs Ivison's father, George Raynham, had worked with Major John (Jack) Spencer-Churchill in a stock-broking company in the City of London. Jack had invited George to join the Queen's Own Oxfordshire Hussars regiment. They were still working together when the First World War broke out. Mrs Ivison contacted Celia Lee to record her memories.
2. Major Ralph Bagnold founded the Long Range Desert Group, that with the Special Air Service, played such an important part in the war in Africa, during the Second World War.
3. After Mrs Georgina Ivision's death, her daughter, Mrs Stella Collingwood, pursued the story with her sister Josie, who lives in New Zealand, and gave the remainder of her mother's writings and Josie's story to Celia Lee.
4. Dermott Hynes saw a piece about Celia Lee in a newspaper and contacted her with his wife's Theresa's story as a nurse during the Second World War.
5. Freda Laycock's website: www.fredalaycock.org.uk.
6. This church is known affectionately today as 'Terry Waite's church'.
7. In 2004, Diana Barnato-Walker was 86 years of age. In 1963, she was the first British woman to break the sound barrier, flying one of the RAF's new supersonic Lightnings.
8. The war in Afghanistan began on 7 October 2001.

Index